ODYSSEUS TO COLUMBUS: A SYNOPSIS OF CLASSICAL AND MEDIEVAL HISTORY

Pg 158
167-7
24

ODYSSEUS TO COLUMBUS: A SYNOPSIS OF CLASSICAL AND MEDIEVAL HISTORY

C. Warren Hollister

JOHN WILEY & SONS, INC.
NEW YORK LONDON SYDNEY TORONTO

Library of Congress Cataloging in Publication Data:

Hollister, Charles Warren.
  Odysseus to Columbus: a synopsis of classical and medieval history.

  "A slightly revised version of the first fifteen chapters of The Western experience, C. W. Hollister . . . [and others] (Wiley, 1974)"
    Bibliography: p.
    1. Civilization—History. 2. Civilization, Ancient. 3. Civilization, Medieval. 4. Civilization, Occidental. I. The Western experience. II. Title.
CB59.H58   901.92   74-2428
ISBN 0-471-40687-2
ISBN 0-471-40689-9 (pbk.)

Printed in the United States of America

10 9 8 7 6 5 4 3 2 1

For Larry

PREFACE

This brief history of Greece, Rome, and medieval Europe is a slightly revised version of the first fifteen chapters of *River Through Time* by C. W. Hollister, John New, James Hardy, and Roger Williams (Wiley, 1974). It follows more or less the format of my *Roots of the Western Tradition: A Short History of the Ancient World* (Second edition, Wiley, 1972) and *Medieval Europe: A Short History* (third edition, Wiley, 1974) but in drastically condensed form. It is thus a highly abbreviated sketch of Western Civilization (and its Greco-Roman and Judeo-Christian antecedents) up to about the year 1500. I hope that it will be useful in several ways: as a core book around which to build a program of collateral readings for the first portions of courses in Western Civilization; as background reading for courses in Europe since 1500; as a guide for students who enroll without much previous historical training in more advanced undergraduate courses in ancient or medieval history; and as an alternative for teachers who regard the various existing "short histories" of the ancient or medieval worlds as not being short enough. Some inquisitive individuals might want to read this book simply out of an interest in the human past.

I am grateful to Mrs. Sally Vaughn (my graduate research assistant) and to Lawrence Hollister (my son, a Stanford undergraduate) for reading the manuscripts and offering valuable suggestions for its improvement.

C. Warren Hollister
Santa Barbara, California, 1974

CONTENTS

PROLOGUE: THE LEGACY OF THE ANCIENT NEAR EAST

PART I GREECE

1 The Rise and Decline of Classical Greece 15
2 The Thought and Culture of Classical Greece 45
3 The Hellenistic Age 67

PART II ROME

4 The Rise of Rome: Kingdom, Republic, Empire 85
5 Rome and Jerusalem 117
6 The Waning of the Western Empire 143

PART III
THE EARLY MIDDLE AGES: THE GENESIS OF WESTERN CIVILIZATION

7 Byzantium, Islam, and Western Christendom 157
8 Carolingian Europe and the New Invasions 177
9 Europe Survives the Siege 191

PART IV
THE HIGH MIDDLE AGES: THE FIRST FLOWERING OF EUROPEAN CULTURE

10 Economic Revolution and New Frontiers 209
11 The Politics of High-Medieval Europe 223
12 New Dimensions in Medieval Christianity 239
13 Thought, Letters, and the Arts 253

PART V
THE LATE MIDDLE AGES: THE ORDEAL OF TRANSITION

14 Church and State in the Fourteenth Century 283
15 Economic and Cultural Change 307

SUGGESTIONS FOR FURTHER READING

Subject Index 337

PROLOGUE:

THE LEGACY OF THE ANCIENT NEAR EAST

There are those who believe that history is obsolete. The present is said to be so radically different from the past that we have nothing to learn from former generations or previous ages. This view, which finds its most ardent supporters among those most ignorant of the past, cuts us off from the flow of history and prevents our seeing human society in its proper perspective: as a river through time.

The ideas, experiments, blunders, and labors of many generations underlie the modern technological marvels that have revolutionized our standard of living and our means of polluting and killing. Our political and economic institutions—parliamentary, capitalist, communist, socialist, fascist—are products of long historical processes. The same is true of our ways of thinking about religion, social justice, urban planning, and astrophysics; our achievements in medicine with their byproduct of overpopulation; and our sense of what is moral and what is obscene. These are not matters unique to us but aspects of our own moment in the evolution of an age-old civilization. Only the most indifferent will fail to wonder about the roots of the culture that surrounds us, shapes our assumptions, defines our options, and governs the very categories in which we judge and perceive. Once we grasp that we are products of a transitory moment in the flow of human culture, we can raise our vision from the features of the passing shoreline to the whole course of the river. We begin to see past the blinders of our own generation, class, and nation, and view our lives—and the lives of our contemporaries—in historical dimension. Stretching our minds and imaginations across an immense panorama of diverse, interconnected human experiences, we deepen our understanding of our own society and of ourselves.

The Formation of Ancient Near Eastern Civilizations

The Western cultural tradition reaches back some 1200 years into the European past. It rose from the debris of a still older civilization—the Greco-Roman—from which is derived much of its political, artistic, and philosophical orientation. Western Civilization drew also from the Judeo-Christian tradition of the Ancient Near East which was inspired in turn by the more ancient religious thought of Mesopotamia, Egypt, and the lands between. Greco-Roman civilization was itself a child of former cultures: Minoan, Etruscan, and, behind them, Egyptian and Mesopotamian. This connected sequence of civilizations extends, like an immense chain, backwards some six thousand years to Mesopotamia's emergence from the Stone Age, and forward into an unknown future.

What do we mean by civilization? Various simple definitions have been suggested at one time or another, but none is entirely satisfactory. Civilization is usually associated with the town or city (the Latin *civitas*), yet the people of ancient Egypt were more or less evenly spread through the Nile valley. The population of the valley was dense, but there were few cities. Do we associate civilization with writing? This art was unknown among some of the ancient civilizations of the Americas.

Civilization can only be regarded as a configuration of several elements, all of which are products of a fairly high degree of social organization. It is best understood not in the abstract but in the concrete, as a convenient label for a whole series of related developments such as were occurring in the Nile and Tigris-Euphrates valleys between about 4000 and 3000 B.C. As the fourth millennium opened, the Near East was a mosaic of Neolithic farming communities,* nomadic herdsmen, and peoples whose livelihood still depended on hunting and fishing. By 3000 B.C. in Mesopotamia the village was giving way to the city-state, a political unit that was far larger and more complex than the Neolithic community. This momentous process was accompanied by a remarkable series of fundamental discoveries and inventions: writing; mathematics; the widespread use of copper and, shortly afterward, bronze; monumental architecture; a calendar; large-scale irrigation systems; and administrative beaureaucracies. Collectively, these developments mark the transformation from primitive society to civilization.

These same processes were occurring in the Nile basin. Although the city was far less prominent in Egypt than in Mesopotamia, the Egyptians were centuries ahead of the Mesopotamians in achieving political unity. By 3000 B.C. the entire Nile valley had been organized into a single state. The fourth millennium, which witnessed the birth of civilization in Mesopotamia and Egypt, was in some respects the most fundamentally creative era in human history.

The early civilizations of Egypt and Mesopotamia evolved the basic social structures that came to characterize all subsequent civilizations up to the industrial revolution of the late eighteenth century. They were built on a broad human base of agricultural slaves (or serfs), living more or less at the subsistence level, whose economic productivity made possible the emergence of a small commercial and manufacturing class—usually of low social status—and of a tiny elite group of landed nobles and priests. At the top of the social pyramid was a prince—a king, pharaoh, or emperor, usually absolute in his political power and claiming kinship or association with the gods. It has become commonplace in recent times to condemn these civilizations as "exploitative," "repressive," or "superstitious." And in a quite evident sense, they were. Yet this was the pattern that all large-scale ancient civilizations followed, in the East as in the West, in the New World as in the Old. To condemn them all is a childish indulgence and one that blocks any serious effort at a deeper understanding. Civilizations have doubtless imposed a tragic burden on humanity. Freud argued that they are the sources of some of our basic neuroses. But they also became

*The Neolithic Age, or "New Stone Age," was itself the product of a revolutionary change in the Near East, thousands of years earlier, from the traditional hunting economy to a new agrarian and pastoral economy.

avenues of creative human expression to a degree unknown before. And they provided the large-scale political and economic organizations whereby food production could be significantly increased and, with it, the security of human lives. If the preindustrial civilizations were a kind of bondage, the profound insecurity of the previous hunting, gathering, and primitive pastoral and agrarian societies amounted to a bondage far greater—a bondage to the whims of wilderness nature. It is only from the perspective of a secure, developed civilization that the wilderness can be viewed with romance and nostalgia. Only an advanced industrial society is inclined to produce national parks. To precivilized peoples— lacking camp stoves, forest rangers, grocery stores, and comfortable homes to return to after vacation—the wilderness would have been a world of desperate insecurity and dark terror.

It was industrialization that made possible our present-day dream of economic abundance, justly shared by all. Preindustrial civilizations, lacking the necessary productivity, would have found a welfare state like modern Sweden to be beyond conception. Judging from the universality of vast socioeconomic cleavages in ancient civilizations, it would seem to have been, in reality, a choice between slave societies and the shared starvation of primitive cultures.* If there were other options, they were never taken—at least not until the High and Late Middle Ages, when slavery and, afterward, serfdom gradually disappeared from large portions of Western Europe. And deep social inequalities continued long thereafter. Indeed, they persist today, even in the most advanced and affluent societies of our world—and with far less excuse.

The pattern of agrarian slavery-serfdom and privileged elites molded the social orders of Egypt's and Mesopotamia's successor civilizations, down to the Greek, Roman, Islamic, Byzantine, and medieval European. Each had its own characteristic variations, but these were variations on a single theme: a wealthy minority and an impoverished, economically productive, politically voiceless majority.† Understanding this reality we will perhaps have the

---

*Postmedieval slavery, and the slavery of one race to another, are of course a radically different matter. Antebellum Southern slavery merely enriched the planter class and the New England slave traders; it was hardly necessary for social survival.

†The pattern was altered only in a few small societies devoted chiefly to commerce, such as some of the cities of ancient Phoenicia and Greece, where merchant classes predominated and agricultural slavery was less widespread.

wisdom not to single out and castigate the ancient Athenians for having slaves, or the medieval nobility for living off the toil of peasants. The system was thousands of years old, deeply ingrained, and omnipresent. It is perhaps the ancient Near East's most fundamental legacy to Greece, Rome, and the civilization of Western Europe.

But there are other legacies as well, far too numerous to discuss. There was the invention of writing, the subsequent development of methods of working iron, the study of the stars by Babylonian astrologers, discoveries in practical chemistry by Egyptians as they mummified their pharaohs, advances in engineering, dike building, temple construction, road building, and administrative organization. The ancient Persians developed a remarkably efficient postal system. The ancient Canaanites invented the alphabet, reducing the hundreds of syllabic signs of earlier scripts to 29 symbols representing the consonants, and thus opened the way to a vast expansion of literacy.

Religion

Beyond all these contributions, the ancient Near East shaped the religious concepts of Western Europe, Byzantium, and Islam. Whatever one's personal attitude toward religion might be, no sensitive student would ignore religion's tremendous role in human history. The civilizations of Egypt and Mesopotamia, no less than the primitive societies that preceded them, were god-ridden. Early peoples tended to regard all inanimate objects as personalities with wills of their own. Mountains, trees, rivers, even sticks and stones, were alive and had volition. The more spectacular aspects of nature —the wind, the sky, the sun, and the earth—were commonly regarded as gods. Thus, whereas modern peoples regard the world around them as inanimate—as an "it"—primitive and early civilized peoples regarded the world as animate—as a "thou." To them, human beings were linked to nature in an "I-Thou" relationship.

The various ancient civilizations, each in its distinctive way, gave expression to these attitudes and, in a few cases, went beyond them. The Mesopotamians, awed and terrorized by nature, and by the incessant threat of barbarian invasion, saw themselves as playthings of the gods—as tragic figures subject to the whims of nature. "Mere man—," the Mesopotamians observed, "his days are numbered. Whatever he may do, he is but wind." The Egyptians on the other hand, protected by the deserts that surrounded their Nile Valley, regarded the gods more optimistically, believing that nature had blessed them and would continue to do so. Much later, the Persians made a sharp break with the Near Eastern religious tradition, replacing it with a doctrine of ethical monotheism known as Zoroastrianism. The Persian Zoroastrians viewed the world as an arena of combat between a god of goodness, light, and spirit, and a god of evil and darkness who created the physical universe. The great Zoroastrian goat was to liberate the soul from the physical body and thus escape from the realm of evil and matter into the world of spirit. This Zoroastrian dualism between good and evil exerted a powerful influence on various important religions of the Greco-Roman world—including Christianity itself. But far greater was the influence of the Israelites, whose contribution to religious thought is altogether unique in the history of the ancient world.

The Israelites

No other ancient Near Eastern people are as familiar to us as the Israelites. Their Bible has been studied by scholars and men of faith throughout the centuries of Western Civilization. It is the fountainhead of Judaism, Islam, and Christianity, and a crucial element in the heritage of modern man. As a historical source it enables us to endow the dry bones of ancient Israel with flesh and life. But it also raises serious problems of historical criticism. The Biblical critics of the nineteenth century rejected the traditional belief in divine inspiration and subjected the Bible to painstaking scrutiny of the sort that historians normally apply to their documents. These critics doubted the historical existence of Abraham, Jacob—even Moses—and concluded that the Bible was not especially good history. More recently, however, certain Biblical episodes that were previously rejected as mere myth have been corroborated by new archaeological discoveries and by comparisons with non-Biblical sources. Scholars are now inclined to regard the Bible as a relatively reliable body of ancient historical documents.

According to the Bible, the history of the Jews begins when the patriarch Abraham entered into an agreement or *Covenant* with a specific deity, "the God of Abraham." Abraham promised not to recognize or worship any other god, and, in return, he and his family were taken under the special protection of the God of Abraham. The Covenant was renewed by all succeeding generations of Abraham's clan, and became a basic ingredient of Jewish religious thought. It seems unlikely that Abraham viewed his God as the only god. Had he been asked, he would probably have conceded the existence of other deities, yet from the *practical* standpoint even Abraham was a monotheist. The existence of other gods was irrelevant to him, for it was his God alone that Abraham honored.

Under Jacob, Abraham's grandson, the clan is said to have been driven by famine from Palestine to Egypt. This migration, sometime around 1600 B.C., was probably not limited to Jacob and his immediate family, but included kindred folk who would be known henceforth as Hebrews. The Hebrews seem to have prospered in Egypt for a time, but around 1570 the Egyptians enslaved all foreigners, forcing them to labor for the state. During this prolonged period of bondage, the Covenant of Abraham was extended to include more and more of the Hebrews.

At length, perhaps sometime in the fourteenth century B.C., a Hebrew, trained in the Egyptian bureaucracy and bearing the Egyptian name of Moses, led a band of his own and other enslaved peoples to freedom. For a long generation they wandered in the wilderness of the Sinai Desert. Under Moses' superb leadership they were forged into a unified people and the personal Covenant was transformed into a Covenant between God and the whole Hebrew nation. The God of Abraham was given the name "Yahweh" (traditionally translated as Jehovah). It is to this Sinai period that the Bible ascribes the divine dictation of the Ten Commandments.

Moses had promised to lead his people to the "promised land" of Palestine or Canaan, but when the Hebrews emerged at last from the wilderness, Moses was dead, and a new generation had arisen. Under the leadership of Joshua, the Hebrews entered the land of the Canaanites, perhaps around the beginning of the thirteenth century, and won a series of important victories. The best known of Joshua's battles was fought at the ancient city of Jericho whose walls, we are told, came tumbling down. But the struggle with the Canaanites did not end with these initial battles. It continued with many ups and downs for another two centuries during which the Hebrews were deeply influenced by Canaanite civilization. They adopted a Canaanite dialect and used the Canaanite alphabet. Some even began to worship Canaanite gods, much to the chagrin of the orthodox. During these centuries the Hebrews were loosely organized into tribes under local military leaders known inappropriately as "judges." The epoch of the judges gave way at length to a unified monarchy which was made necessary by the increasing military pressure of an aggressive tribe of invaders: the Philistines.

The United Israelite Kingdom and Its Aftermath

In 1020, the priest Samuel anointed Saul, Israel's first king. Saul waged war against the Philistines with some success but was far outshone by his able successor, David (1005–965), who is said to have demonstrated his prowess even as a child by slaying the great Philistine, Goliath, with a slingshot. Under David and his son Solomon (965–925), Israel reached its political zenith. Their kingdom was the most powerful in the ancient history of Syria-Palestine, dominating the entire area and extending far inland toward the Euphrates River. This was the golden age that etched itself on Israel's imagination for all time to come—the age that for endless generations the Jews never despaired of recovering.

It was David's great hope to build a permanent, central temple for Yahweh in Jerusalem, a city that he had recently conquered, and under Solomon the temple was completed. Jerusalem itself became the cosmopolitan capital of a wealthy empire. Solomon surrounded himself with all the trappings of Near Eastern monarchy from bureaucrats to concubines. But Solomon's subjects were obliged to pay for all this imperial glory with heavy taxes and forced labor, and many of them concluded that the price was too high. Upon Solomon's death (925 B.C.) Israelite particularism reasserted itself, and the kingdom split into two halves: a large state to the north known thenceforth as Israel, and a much smaller but more coherent state to the south, centering on Jerusalem, that was called Judah.

This political schism brought an early end to Hebrew imperialism. Around 900 B.C., the Near East entered a new age of great empires. The first of these, the Assyrian Empire, exerted increasing military pressure against both Israel and Judah. Israel fell to the Assyrians in 722, and her people were scattered across the Near East where they faded into the local populations and vanished from history. Judah survived the Assyrian attacks only to fall to Assyria's imperial successor, the Babylonian Empire, in 586. Judah's political and intellectual leaders were banished to Babylon where they and their children endured that tragic epoch in Biblical history, the

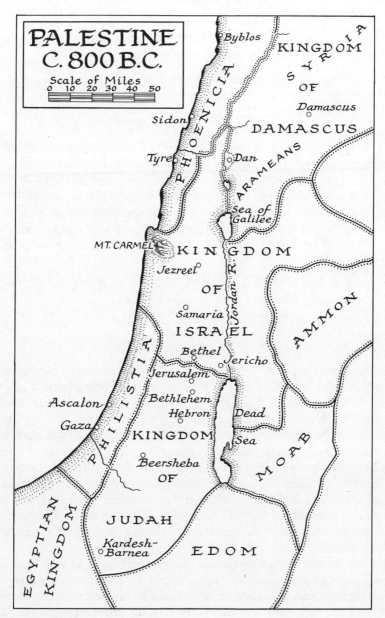

PALESTINE
C. 800 B.C.

Scale of Miles
0 10 20 30 40 50

Byblos

KINGDOM

SYRIA

OF

Damascus

DAMASCUS

PHOENICIA

Sidon

Tyre

Dan

ARAMEANS

Sea of
Galilee

MT. CARMEL

KINGDOM

Jezreel

OF

Jordan R.

Samaria

ISRAEL

AMMON

Bethel

Jericho

Jerusalem

Bethlehem

Hebron

Dead

Ascalon

Gaza

PHILISTIA

KINGDOM

Sea

MOAB

Beersheba

OF

EGYPTIAN KINGDOM

JUDAH

Kardesh-
Barnea

EDOM

Palestine, 800 B.C. [from C. W. Hollister, Roots of the Western Tradition *(2nd ed., Wiley), p. 44].*

The Legacy of the Ancient Near East **9**

Babylonian Captivity (586–539 B.C.). The bitterness of exile is captured in the opening lines of the 137th Psalm:

> *By the rivers of Babylon,*
> *There we sat down, yea, we wept,*
> *When we remembered Zion.*

The Prophets

The devastating experience of divided kingdom and Babylonian Captivity evoked a profound religious response. The moral initiative now passed from kings and priests to inspired individuals known as prophets whose boldly original spiritual insights—arising out of an age of agony and despair—deepened and ennobled the Hebrew religion immeasurably. To the prophets, law and ritual were insufficient without sincerity of purpose and righteousness of life. The prophet Micah expressed this insight with striking brevity:

> *It has been shown to you, O man, what is good*
> *and what the Lord requires of you:*
> *Only to do justice*
> *and live loyally*
> *and walk humbly with your God [6:8].*

The teachings of the prophets were based on two fundamental concepts: (1) the covenant between God and his Hebrew people, and (2) the consequent obligation of Israelites to treat one another justly. Their vision of justice and righteousness was not applied to mankind at large but only to the Israelite community; yet even with that important qualification it was a profound affirmation of human dignity. The prophetic teachings became a fundamental component of Hebrew thought. More than that, they underlie the tradition of social justice that has developed in Western Civilization. The prophets' insistence that all Israelites were equal in the sight of God would ultimately be expanded into the doctrine of universal human equality.

In the hands of the prophets, the concept of Yahweh was universalized. They explained the collapse of Solomon's empire and the Assyrian and Babylonian conquests by asserting that Yahweh had used the Hebrews' enemies to punish his chosen people for their transgressions and to prepare them for a triumphant future. But if this was so, then Yahweh's power was evidently not limited to the Hebrews, but embraced all peoples. Whereas Yahweh had formerly been the only God that *mattered*, he was now proclaimed as the only God that *existed*. The prophet Amos quotes the Lord as saying,

> *Did I not bring up Israel*
> *from the land of Egypt*
> *and the Philistines from Caphtor*
> *and the Syrians from Kir? [9:7].*

Yahweh was the Lord of nations, yet the Hebrews remained His chosen people. History itself could be understood only in terms of Israel's encounter with God. The Hebrews were unique among the peoples of the Ancient Near East in their sensitivity toward history, for to them, God's relations with man occurred in a historical dimension, and history itself was directed by God toward certain predetermined goals. Thus, it was Yahweh, not the Babylonians, who sent the Hebrews into exile, and in the fullness of time, so the prophets said, Yahweh would build their kingdom anew. A divinely appointed leader of the house of David—a Messiah—would one day be sent to consummate the divine plan by reestablishing the political glory of Israel. This assurance sustained the Hebrew exiles in Babylon, and they preserved their integrity and their faith against the lures of a powerful alien culture. A few succumbed to the temptations of Babylon, but the majority held fast in the conviction that history was on their side.

Later Jewish History

In 539 B.C. the Babylonian Empire gave way to the Persian Empire, and the Hebrews were permitted to return to their homeland and rebuild the temple of Jerusalem. They could now practice their faith without interference, but they remained under Persian political control. Two centuries thereafter Persian rule gave way to Greek rule, and in time the Greeks were replaced by the Romans. During these post-exilic centuries, the Hebrew sacred writings were collected, sifted, and expanded, and the Old Testament acquired its final form. As always, the Israelites were torn between the desire to preserve the purity of their heritage and the impulse to accommodate themselves to outside cultural influences. From time to time they rebelled against their political masters but never with lasting success. Their final rebellion, in A.D. 70, prompted the

Romans to destroy their temple and scatter them throughout the Empire. There followed an exile far more prolonged than their earlier ones in Egypt and Babylonia, lasting until the present century. But the Jews had demonstrated long before that they could survive as a people and a faith without political unity.

The impact of the ancient Hebrews on future civilizations has been immense. The Old Testament, a tremendous literary monument in itself, has been of incalcuable importance in the development of European culture. The Hebrews' sense of history—as a dynamic, purposive, morally-significant process of human-divine interaction —went far beyond the historical concepts of other Near Eastern peoples and became a fundamental element in the historical vision of Western Civilization. But at the core of everything is their ethical monotheism—their vision of a single God of incredible power who is also a God of righteousness and mercy. The Hebrew confronted his universe in a new way. The world was no longer pregnant with spirits; nature was no longer a "Thou," but rather the handiwork of a far greater "Thou." The myriad spooks and demons of tree, rock and mountain dissolved before the unutterable holiness of the God of Israel.

Chronology of the Ancient Hebrews (All Dates Except the Last Are B.C.)

?1600–1350:	Migration to Egypt and bondage there
?1350–1310:	Moses and the Sinai Period
?1300–1020:	Era of the Judges
1020–925:	United Kingdom of Israel
925–722:	Political split: Israel and Judah
722:	Israel falls to the Assyrians
586–539:	Judah falls: Babylonian captivity
539:	Establishment of Persian Empire; Babylonian captives return to Palestine
330:	Greek domination replaces Persian
c.189:	Roman domination replaces Greek
A.D. 70:	Last Hebrew rebellion; Romans destroy Temple of Jerusalem and scatter the Jews throughout the Empire

PART ONE
GREECE

ONE

THE RISE AND DECLINE OF CLASSICAL GREECE

The World of the Ancient Aegean

One of the supreme Greek epic poems, Homer's *Odyssey*, tells of the perils and adventures of the ancient Greek chieftain Odysseus as he returned home by sea after the fall of Troy. As a tale of a hero's conquest of the terrors of the ocean, the *Odyssey* symbolizes a central quality of the Greek experience. For the Greeks were, above all, a seafaring people. Sailing out from their barren, mountainous homeland, they planted colonies far and wide and eventually came to dominate the commerce of the eastern Mediterranean. In the end, they, like their mythical hero Odysseus, conquered the sea and gained fame and sorrow in the process.

The two great Homeric epics, the *Odyssey* and the *Iliad*, originated in the eighth century B.C. Both epics tell of the conclusion and aftermath of a half-legendary, long-ago war between the Greeks and the Trojans—a struggle that ended with the Greek conquest of Troy. The *Iliad* and the *Odyssey* mark the dawn of written Greek literature; yet both hark back to a culture far older than that of classical Greece. Archaeologists have found independent evidence of such a culture centering on the island of Crete and extending to the Greek mainland. This early Aegean civilization is known as the Minoan (after Minos, a legendary king of Crete) or Mycenaean (after an ancient fortress-town on the Greek mainland). Its memory endured in later Greek literature like a half-remembered dream.

The archaeologists have concluded that Minoan civilization arose in the third millennium B.C. on the island of Crete. The Minoans derived their technological and artistic skills from the still earlier civilizations of Mesopotamia, Egypt, and Asia Minor, but developed them in novel and vitally creative directions. Excavations on Crete have unearthed ruins of great, rambling palaces, their walls decorated with vivacious paintings, their rooms containing exquisite statuettes and delicate polychromatic pottery fashioned with consummate skill and taste. Minoan art is light and flowing: plants, animals, marine life, and youths playing games—all are portrayed with stylistic flair and stunning naturalism. Like the later Greeks, the Minoans were a commercial, seafaring people. The absence of fortifications in the Cretan ruins suggests that the island was politically unified under the Minoan "sea kings" of Greek legend, and that its navy was regarded as an adequate defense. Its agriculture was devoted chiefly to the production of grain, wine, and olive oil—the so-called "Mediterranean triad"—which were also to be the major agricultural commodities of classical Greece.

The Mycenean Greeks

The Minoans of Crete were not a Greek-speaking people at all. Not until sometime after about 2000 B.C. did the first Greeks begin settling the peninsula that would later bear their name. Bringing little or no civilization with them, they gradually passed under the influence of Minoan culture, although retaining their political independence. After about 1580 B.C., great fortress cities began to arise in the district of southwestern Greece known as the Peloponnesus—cities such as Mycenae, Tiryns, and Pylos. With time, the political power of these cities spread, until at length all the princes of southern Greece may have come to recognize the supremacy of the warrior-kings of Mycenae.

These early Greeks were divided into tribes, which themselves were subdivided into clans. Each clan consisted of a number of related families, which had their own distinctive religious cult and held their lands and wealth in common. The Mycenaean Greeks learned much from the Minoans. Their culture differed from that of Crete in its emphasis on weapons and fortifications. They adapted the Minoan script to their own, very different language. Their art, architecture, and customs were all strongly influenced by the Minoans; and Greek women began adopting Minoan dress, hairdos, and cosmetics. (The painted face is traditionally a mark of primitivism in men; of sophistication in women.)

Before long, Mycenaean sailors were challenging the Cretan supremacy in the Aegean. During the 1400s, Minoan civilization was devastated by invasions that left the Cretan towns, villas, and palaces in ruins. The great palaces were never rebuilt on their former scale, and the Minoan state seems to have disintegrated. The Mycenaean Greeks fell heir to the Minoan mastery of the Aegean.

Between about 1400 and 1200 the Greeks grew rich on their commerce and flourished exceedingly. At the end of this period, perhaps around 1200, King Agamemnon of Mycenae led the Greeks against Troy. But even at the time of the Trojan War, the political stability of Mycenaean Greece was being disturbed by the initial attacks and migrations of the Dorian Greeks and other tribes that were largely untouched by the civilizing effects of Minoan-Mycenaean culture. About 1120 B.C., the Dorian invasion of the Peloponnesus began in earnest. The writing inscribed on tablets found in Mycenaean cities of this era disclosures frantic but vain preparations for defense. One after another, the cities of Greece were sacked and burned, and the civilization that had begun in Crete, and later spread to the mainland, came to an end at last.

The Greek Dark Age (c. 1120–800 B.C.)

Between Mycenaean and classical Greece lies a gap of several centuries known as the "dark age" of Hellenic history.* The Greeks lapsed into illiteracy, and when they began to write once again it was not in the old Minoan syllabary but in an alphabet derived from

*Hellenic = Greek; Hellas = Greece.

that of the Canaanites. The Mycenaean Greeks were violently displaced by the invasions. Most of the Peloponnesus became Dorian, and in time the leadership of that area, once exercised by Mycenae, passed to the new Dorian city of Sparta. Athens, as yet an unimportant town, held out against the invaders and became a haven for refugees. A group of mainland Greeks known as Ionians fled across the Aegean and settled along the western coast of Anatolia (Asia Minor) and on the islands offshore. Thenceforth, that region was known as Ionia and became an integral part of Greek civilization (see the map on p. 25). Throughout most of dark-age Greece, political conditions were chaotic, and sovereignty descended to the level of the village and the clan.

Homer

With the appearance of the Homeric epics in eighth-century Ionia the darkness began to lift. Both the *Iliad* and the *Odyssey* are the products of a long oral tradition carried on by the minstrels of Mycenean and post-Mycenean times who recited their songs of heroic deeds at the banquets of the nobility. Whether the epics in their final form were the work of one man or several is in dispute. Someone has facetiously suggested that the epics should not be associated with Homer at all, but with an entirely different person of the same name.

Both epics are filled with vivid accounts of battle and adventure, but at heart both are concerned with ultimate problems of human life. The *Iliad* depicts the tragic consequences of the quarrel between two sensitive and passionate Greek leaders, Agamemnon and Achilles, toward the end of the Trojan War:

Divine Muse, sing of the ruinous wrath of Achilles, Peleus' son, which brought ten thousand sorrows to the Greeks, sent the souls of many brave heroes down to the world of the dead, and left their bodies to be eaten by dogs and birds: and the will of Zeus was fulfilled. Begin where they first quarrelled, Agamemnon the King of Men, and great Achilles.*

Despite Homer's allusion to the will of Zeus, his characters are by no means puppets of the gods, even though divine intervention

*Translated by H. D. F. Kitto in *The Greeks* (rev. ed., Penguin, 1957), p. 45.

occurs repeatedly in his narrative. Rather they are intensely—sometimes violently—human, and they are doomed to suffer the consequences of their own deeds. In this respect, as in many others, Homer foreshadows the great Greek tragic dramatists of the fifth century.

Achilles' dazzling career no less than that of the seafaring Odysseus, prefigures the career of Greece itself. The gods were said to have offered Achilles the alternatives of a long but mediocre life or glory and an early death. His choice symbolizes the tragic, meteoric course of Hellenic history.

Homer was the first European poet known to us and he has never been surpassed. The *Iliad* and the *Odyssey* were the Old and New Testament of ancient Greece, studied by every Greek schoolboy and cherished by Greek writers and artists as an inexhaustible source of inspiration. The epics were typically Greek in their rigorous and economical organization around a single great theme, their lucidity, and their moments of tenderness that never slip into sentimentality—in short, their brilliantly successful synthesis of intellectualism and humanity.

The Homeric Gods

The gods of Mt. Olympus, who play such a significant role in the Homeric poems, had a great variety of individual backgrounds. Poseidon, the sea god, was Minoan; Zeus, the hurler of thunderbolts and ruler of Olympus, was a Dorian god; Aphrodite, the goddess of love, was an astral deity from Babylonia; Apollo was from Asia Minor; and a number of other gods were local deities long before they entered the divine assemblage of Olympus. By Homer's time these diverse gods had been arranged into a coherent hierarchy of related deities common to all Greeks. The Olympic gods were anthropomorphic; that is, they were human in form and personality, capable of rage, lust, jealousy, and all the other traits of the warrior-hero. But they also possessed immortality and various other superhuman attributes. The universality of the Olympic cult served as an important unifying force that compensated in part for the localism that always characterized Greek politics. Yet each clan and each district also honored its own special gods, many of whom, like Athena the patron goddess of Athens, were represented in the Olympic pantheon. The worship of these local gods was associated with feelings of family devotion or regional and civic pride. The gods were concerned chiefly with the well-being of social groups rather than the prosperity or salvation of the individual, and their worship was therefore almost indistinguishable from patriotism.

Among the lower classes ancient fertility deities remained immensely popular. Demeter, the goddess of grain, and Dionysus, the god of wine, were almost ignored in the Homeric epics but seem to have been far more important to the Greek peasantry than were the proud, aristocratic deities of Olympus. Eleusis, a small town near Athens, became the chief religious center for the worship of Demeter, and the rites celebrated there, the Eleusinian Mysteries, dramatized the ancient myth of death and resurrection. The worship of Dionysus was characterized by wild orgies during which female worshipers would dance and scream through the night. (In time these rites became more sedate and respectable.) Both Demeter and Dionysus offered their followers the hope of personal salvation and immortality that was lacking in the Olympic religion. At the bottom of the social order animism persisted in all its bewildering and exotic forms: the world of the Greek peasant, like that of his Near-Eastern contemporaries, was literally crawling with gods.

The Polis

By Homer's time, Greek culture was developing throughout the area surrounding the Aegean Sea—in Ionia along the coast of Anatolia, on the Aegean islands, in Athens and its surrounding district of Attica, in the Peloponnesus, and in other regions of mainland Greece. (See the map on p. 25). The roughness of the Ionian Coast, the obvious insularity of the islands, and the mountains and inlets that divided Greece itself into a number of semi-isolated districts discouraged the development of a unified pan-Hellenic state, but the existence of the myriad city-states of classical Greece cannot be explained entirely by the environment. There are numerous examples of small independent states separated by no geographical barriers whatever—of several autonomous districts, for example, on a single island. Perhaps the Greeks lived in city-states simply as a matter of choice. Whatever the reason, classical Greek culture without the independent city-state is inconceivable.

We have used the term "city-state" to describe what the Greeks knew as the "polis." Actually, "polis" is untranslatable, and "city-state" fails to convey its full meaning. In classical times the word was packed with emotional and intellectual content. Each polis had its own distinctive customs and its own gods and was an object of intense religious-patriotic devotion. More than a mere region, it was a community of citizens—the inhabitants of both town and surrounding district who enjoyed political rights and played a role in government. Words such as "political," "politics," and "polity" come from the Greek "polis"; to the Greeks, politics without the polis would be impossible. Aristotle is often quoted as saying that man is a political animal; what he really said was that man was a creature who belonged in a polis. In a vast empire like that of Persia, so the Greeks believed, slaves could live—barbarians could live—but not free and civilized men. The polis was the Greeks' answer to the perennial conflict between man and the state, and perhaps no other human institution has succeeded in reconciling these two concepts so satisfactorily. The Greek expressed his intense individualism *through* the polis, not in spite of it. The polis was sufficiently small that its members could behave as individuals rather than mass men. The chief political virtue was participation, not obedience. Accordingly, the polis became the vessel of Greek creativity and the matrix of the Greek spirit. A unified pan-Hellenic state might perhaps have eliminated the intercity warfare that was endemic in classical Greece. It might have brought peace, stability, and power, but at the sacrifice of the very institution that made classical Greece what it was.

Still, the system of independent warring "city-states" was a remarkably inefficient basis for Greek political organization. The Greeks were able to evolve and flourish only because they developed in a political vacuum. The Minoans were only a memory, and Macedonian and Roman imperialism lay in the future. During the formative period of the polis system in the ninth, eighth, and seventh centuries the Assyrians were concerned primarily with maintaining their land empire, and the seafaring Phoenicians* were not a dangerous military power. The chief threat to the Greek of the dark age was the violence of his own people. As a matter of security

---

*Settled on a narrow coastal strip along the eastern Mediterranean, the Phoenicians were a commercial people descended from the ancient Canaanites. They introduced the Canaanite alphabet to dark-age Greece.

the inhabitants of a small district would often erect a citadel on some central hill which they called an acropolis (high town). The acropolis was the natural assembly place of the district in time of war and its chief religious center. As local commerce developed, an agora or market place usually arose at the foot of the acropolis, and many of the farmers whose fields were nearby built houses around the market, for reasons of socialibility and defense.

The Social Orders

At about the time that the polis was emerging, descendants of the original tribal elders were evolving into a hereditary aristocracy. An occasional polis might be ruled by a king (*basileus*) but, generally speaking, monarchy died out with Mycenae or was reduced to a ceremonial office. By about 700 B.C., or shortly thereafter, virtually every Greek king had been overthrown or shorn of all but his religious functions, leaving the aristocracy in full control. The aristocrats had meanwhile appropriated to themselves the lion's share of the lands that the clan members had formerly held in common. Slowly the polis was replacing the clan as the object of primary allegiance and the focus of political activity, but the aristocracy rode out the waves of change, growing in wealth and power.

Below the aristocracy was a class of small farmers who had managed to acquire fragments of the old clan common lands or who had developed new farms on virgin soil. These Greek farmers had no genuine voice in political affairs, and their economic situation was always hazardous. The Greek soil is the most barren in Europe, and while the large scale cultivation of vine and olive usually brought a profit to the aristocrat, the small farmer tended to sink gradually into debt. His deplorable condition was portrayed vividly by the eighth-century poet Hesiod, a peasant himself, who wrote in a powerful, down-to-earth style. In his *Works and Days* Hesiod describes a world that had declined from a primitive golden age to the present "age of iron," characterized by a corrupt nobility and a downtrodden peasantry. For the common farmer, life was "bad in winter, cruel in summer—never good." Yet Hesiod insists that righteousness will triumph in the end. In the meantime the peasant must work all the harder: "In the sweat of your face shall you eat bread." Out of an age in which the peasant's lot seemed hopeless indeed, Hesiod proclaimed his faith in the ultimate victory of social justice and the dignity of toil.

Colonization (750–550 B.C.)

Even as Hesiod was writing his *Works and Days,* a movement was beginning that would bring a degree of relief to the small farmer and the still lower classes of the landless and dispossessed. By 750 B.C. the Greeks had once again taken to the sea—as pirates in search of booty or as merchants in search of copper and iron (rare in Greece) and the profits of trade. In this adventurous age a single crew of Greek seamen might raid and plunder one port and sell the loot as peaceful merchants in the next. During the course of their voyaging they found many fertile districts ripe for colonization, and during the two centuries between about 750 and 550 B.C., a vast movement of colonial expansion occurred that was to transform not only Greece itself but the whole Mediterranean world. Most of the more important Greek city-states sent bands of colonists across the seas to found new communities on distant shores, and in time some of these colonies sent out colonies of their own to establish still more settlements. The typical colonial polis, although bound to its mother city by ties of kinship, sentiment, and commerce and a common patriotic cult, was politically independent. We cannot speak of colonial empires in this period; even the word "colony" is a little misleading.

The motives behind the colonial movement are to be found in the economic and social troubles afflicting the Greek homeland. Colonization meant new opportunities for the landless freeman and the struggling peasant. It provided the aristocracy with a useful safety valve against the revolutionary pressures of rising population and accumulating discontent. And there were always a few disaffected aristocrats to lead the enterprise. In the rigorous environment of the pioneer colony, hard work was much more likely to bring its reward than in the Greece of Hesiod. Here were all the opportunities for rapid social and economic advancement commonly associated with a frontier society.

Accordingly, in the course of two centuries or so the Greek polis spread from the Aegean region far and wide along the coasts of the Mediterranean and the Black Sea. The great Ionian polis of Miletus alone founded some 80 colonies. So many Greek settlements were established in southern Italy and Sicily that the whole area became known as *Magna Graecia*—Great Greece. The small colonial polis of Byzantium, dominating the trade route between the Black Sea and the Mediterranean, became, a millennium later, the capital of the East Roman Empire (under the name of Constantinople) and remained throughout the Middle Ages one of the greatest cities in the world. The Greek colony of Neopolis (New Polis) in southern Italy became the modern Napoli or Naples; Nikaia on the Riviera became the modern Nice; Massilia became Marseilles; Syracuse in Sicily remains to this day one of the island's chief cities. Through the city-states of *Magna Graecia,* Greek culture and the Greek alphabet were transmitted to the Romans, but this was merely one important episode in a process that saw the diffusion of Greek civilization all along the shores of Southern Europe, North Africa, and Western Asia.

The colonial experience was profoundly significant in the evolution of the Greek way of life. The flourishing commerce that developed between the far-flung Hellenic settlements brought renewed prosperity to Greece itself. The homeland became an important source of wine, olive oil, and manufactured goods for the colonies. The needs of the new settlements stimulated the growth of industrial and commercial classes: smiths and potters, stevedores and sailors, transformed many Greek city-states from quiet agrarian communities into bustling mercantile centers. A new elite of merchants and manufacturers began to rival the old landed aristocrats in wealth and to challenge their traditional monopoly of political power. During the seventh and sixth centuries many of these wealthy upstarts forced their way into the councils of government alongside the old noble families.

The Tyrants

The century from about 650 to 550 was an age of fundamental economic and political change: the introduction of coinage from Lydia (in Aisa Minor) was a boon to the mercantile elite, but tended to sharpen and amplify differences in wealth. It was in this age that the Ionian poet Pythermus wrote the golden line that alone of all his works has survived: "There's nothing else that matters— only money." The ever-increasing abundance of metal brought the heavy armor necessary in the warfare of the day within the financial reach of the middle class, and the mounted aristocratic army of earlier times began to give way in the early seventh century to a citizens' army of well-drilled, mailed infantrymen called hoplites. It was not long before the classes who fought for the polis began to demand a voice in its affairs.

At length, the colonial movement began to wane. The best colonial sites were gradually preempted, and the rise of new powers like

CLASSICAL
GREECE

Scale of Miles
0   25   50   75   100

Carthage in the west and Lydia and Persia in the east prevented further expansion. As the safety valve slowly closed, the old pressures of economic and social discontent asserted themselves with renewed fury. One after another the city-states of Greece and Ionia were torn by bloody civil strife as the middle and lower classes rose against the wealthy and privileged. In many instances these conflicts resulted in the overthrow of aristocratic control by "tyrants" who, like many of their modern counterparts, claimed to govern in the interests of the common people.

To the Greeks a tyrant was not necessarily an evil man but simply a ruler who rose to power without hereditary or legal claim. Typically, the tyrants did not smash the machinery of government but merely controlled it. They were new men, attuned to the currents of their age, who used the new coined money to hire armies of mercenaries and manipulated social discontent to their own advantage. Since they owed their power to the masses, they sought to retain their support by canceling or scaling down debts, sponsoring impressive public works projects, redistributing the lands of aristocrats, and reforming taxation. But in most Greek communities tyranny did not last long. Some tyrants were overthrown by the older privileged classes, others by the middle and lower classes who, as they became increasingly self-confident, sought to assume direct control of political affairs. By the opening of the fifth century the Greek political structure displayed every imaginable configuration of upper, lower, and middle class rule.

Sparta

Sparta and Athens, the two dominant city-states of fifth century Greece, stood at opposite ends of the Greek political spectrum. Neither played an important role in the colonization movement, for both adopted the alternative course of territorial expansion in their own districts. But while Athens evolved through the traditional stages of monarchy, aristocracy, tyranny, and democracy, Sparta acquired a peculiar mixed political system that discouraged commerce, cultural inventiveness and the amenities of life for the sake of iron discipline and military efficiency.

During the eighth and seventh centuries Sparta underwent the same political and social processes as other Greek states and played a vigorous role in the development of Greek culture. Yet from the beginning the Spartan spirit was singularly sober and masculine, and military concerns were always central to Spartan life. The stern severity of its art and its Dorian architecture contrasted sharply with the charming elegance of Ionia and the cultural dynamism of Attica. Politically, Sparta had always been conservative. When the aristocracy rose to power, the monarchy was not abolished but merely weakened. With the rise of the commoners certain democratic features were incorporated into the Spartan constitution yet the monarchy and aristocracy endured. Sparta could adapt cautiously to new conditions but found it terribly difficult to abandon anything from its past.

Toward the end of the eighth century, when other Greek states were beginning to relieve their social unrest and land hunger by colonization, Sparta conquered the fertile neighboring district of Messenia, appropriating large portions of the conquered land for its own citizens and reducing many Messenians to slavery. These unfortunate people, described by a Spartan poet as "asses worn by loads intolerable," were Greeks themselves and were too proud to accept their enslavement with resignation. In the late seventh century the Spartans crushed a Messenian revolt only after a desperate struggle. It became clear that the Messenians could be held down only by strong military force and constant watchfulness. It was at this point that Sparta transformed herself into a garrison state whose citizens became a standing army. Culture declined to the level of the barracks; the good life became the life of basic training.

Sparta became a tense, humorless society dedicated to the perpetuation, by force, of the status quo. Fear of Messenian rebellion grew into a collective paranoia as some 8000 Spartan citizens assumed the task of keeping 200,000 restless slaves in a state of permanent repression. Between the citizens and the slaves was a group of freemen without political rights who engaged in commercial activities (forbidden to the citizens themselves). The state slaves themselves—the helots—included not only Messenians but other Greek families as well, some of whom had been enslaved during the original Dorian conquests. The Spartan state divided its lands into numerous lots, one for each citizen, and the helots who worked these lots relieved the citizens of all economic responsibility, freeing them for a life of military training and service to the state.

The Constitution of "Lycurgus"

The writers of antiquity ascribed the Spartan constitution to a legendary lawgiver named Lycurgus, and, despite its evolutionary elements, the constitution operated with such rigorous logical consistency as to suggest the hand of a single author. Sparta had two kings whose powers had been greatly reduced by the sixth century. One or the other of them served as supreme commander on every military campaign, but at home their authority was overshadowed by that of three other bodies: (1) an aristocratic council of elders, (2) an executive board of five *ephors* elected from the whole citizenry, and (3) an assembly that included every Spartan citizen over thirty. Thus, if one counts only her handful of citizens, Sparta was a democracy, although a limited one. The assembly had the function of approving or disapproving all important questions of state, but it did so by acclamation rather than ballot, and its members were not permitted to debate the issues. Accordingly, this democratic assembly was by no means an arena of rough and tumble political conflict. It was characterized rather by the same dreary conformity that overhung all Spartan life.

The lives of Sparta's citizens were tended and guided by the state from cradle to grave, always for the purpose of producing strong, courageous, highly disciplined soldiers. The introduction of styles, luxuries, and ideas from without was rigorously controlled. At a time when coinage was stimulating economic life elsewhere Sparta used simple iron bars as her medium of exchange. Spartan citizens seldom left their homeland except on campaigns, and outsiders were discouraged from visiting Sparta. Spartan infants were abandoned to die of exposure if they were puny or malformed. At the age of seven the Spartan boy was turned over to the state and spent his next thirteeen years in a program of education in military skills, physical training, the endurance of hardships, and unquestioning devotion to the polis. The typical product of this system was patriotic, strong, and courageous, but incurious. At twenty he entered the citizen army and lived his next ten years in a barracks. He might marry, but he could visit his wife only if he was sufficiently resourceful to elude the barracks guards (this seems to have been regarded as a test of skill). At thirty he became a full-fledged citizen. He could now live at home, but he ate his meals at a public mess to which he was obliged to contribute the products of his assigned fields. The fare at these public messes was Spartan in the extreme. One visitor, after eating a typical meal, remarked, "Now I understand why the Spartans do not fear death."

The Spartan citizen had almost no individual existence; his life was dedicated to the state. If the helot's life was hard, so was the citizen's. Life in Sparta would seem to be a violent negation of Greek individualism, yet many Greeks were unashamed admirers of the Spartan regime. To them, Sparta represented the ultimate in self-denial and commitment to a logical idea. The Greeks admired the ordered life, and nowhere was life more ordered than in Sparta. To the Greek, there was a crucial difference between the helot and the Spartan citizen: the helot endured hardships because he had to; the citizen, because he *chose* to. And the Spartans always remembered that the object of their heroic efforts was the maintenance of the status quo—not aggressive imperialism. They were the best warriors in Greece, yet they employed their military advantage with restraint. To the accusation of artistic sterility a Spartan might reply that his state was artistic in the most basic sense of the word —that Sparta, with all its institutions directed uncompromisingly toward a single ideal, was itself a work of art.

Athens

Athens dates from the Mycenaean Age, but not until much later did it become prominent in Greek politics and culture. By about 700 B.C. the earlier monarchy had been deprived of political power by the aristocracy, and the entire district of Attica had been united into a single state whose political and commercial center was Athens itself. But the free inhabitants of Attica became Athenian citizens, not Athenian slaves, and the district was held together by bonds of mutual allegiance rather than military might. To be an Attican was to be an Athenian.

The unification of Attica meant that the polis of Athens comprised a singularly extensive area, and consequently the Athenians suffered less severely from land hunger than many of their neighbors. Athens therefore sent out no colonists, yet as a town only four miles from the coast it was influenced by the revival of Greek commerce. Very slowly, new mercantile classes were developing. Athenian political institutions were gradually modified, first to extend political power to the lesser landed gentry, next to include the merchants and manufacturers, and finally to accommodate the increasing demands of the common citizens.

Solon and Pisistratus

In the 590s a wise and moderate aristocratic poet-statesman named Solon was given extraordinary powers to reform the laws of Athens. His reforms left the preponderance of political power in the hands of the wealthy but nevertheless moved significantly in the direction of democracy. Solon's laws abolished enslavement for default of debts and freed all debtors who had previously been enslaved. More important, the lowest classes of free Athenians were now admitted into the popular assembly (whose powers were yet distinctly limited), and a system of popular courts was established, whose judges were chosen by lot from the entire citizenry without regard to wealth. For the Athenian, selection by lot was simply a means of putting the choice into the hands of the gods. Its consequence was to raise to important offices men who were their own masters and owed nothing to wealthy and influential political backers. Of course the system also produced a predictable quota of asses and nincompoops, but recent history attests that the elective principle is by no means immune to that fault. Of the whole, selection by lot worked well in Athens and gradually became a characteristic feature of Athenian democracy.

Solon's laws were seen by many among the privileged classes as dangerously radical, but the lower classes demanded still more reforms. The consequence of this continued popular unrest was the rise of tyranny in Athens. Between 561 and 527 a colorful tyrant named Pisistratus dominated the Athenian government. Twice he was expelled by angry aristocrats; twice he returned with the support of the commoners. At length he achieved the elusive goal of all despots: he died in power and in bed. Pisistratus was the best of all possible tyrants: he sponsored a magnificent building program, patronized the arts, revolutionized agriculture by confiscating vast estates of recalcitrant noblemen and redistributing them among the small farmers, and established Athenian commercial outposts in the Dardenelles, thereby taking the first crucial steps along the road to empire. He gave Athens peace, prosperity, and a degree of social and economic harmony that it had long needed.

The Constitution of Cleisthenes

Pisistratus' two sons and successors proved incompetent and oppressive. One was assassinated; the other was driven from power by exiled nobles who returned with Spartan military support. But many of the aristocrats had grown wise in exile and were willing to accept popular rule. Under the leadership of a statesmanlike aristocrat named Cleisthenes, a new and thoroughly democratic constitution was established in the closing decade of the sixth century, which became the political basis of Athens' most glorious age. Cleisthenes administered the final blow to the aristocratic leaders of the old tribes and clans. Until the time of his reforms, loyalty to clan and tribe had remained strong. Now, Cleisthenes abolished these ancient groups, replacing them with ten new "tribes" whose membership was no longer based on kinship. Each of the ten tribes was made up of numerous small territorial districts scattered throughout Attica. Consequently, members of every class—commercial, industrial, rural, and aristocratic—were about evenly divided among the ten tribes.

Cleisthenes may also have been responsible for introducing the principle of ostracism, which provided a further safeguard against the evils of violent factionalism. In any case, its first recorded use was in 488. Each year thereafter the Athenians decided by vote whether or not they would ostracize one of their number. If they decided affirmatively, then any citizen might propose the name of a person whom he considered a threat to the well-being of the polis. Whichever candidate received the most votes in the Assembly was banished from Athens for ten years. He kept his citizenship and his property but was no longer in a position to interfere with the operation of the polis.

All matters of public policy were decided by the Assembly whose membership included all Athenian citizens from landless laborers to great aristocrats. Citizenship was given to every Athenian freeman of eighteen years or over, and in the mid-fifth century the total citizenry has been estimated at about 50,000 men. There were also, exclusive of women and children, about 25,000 resident aliens called "metics" who were free but without political rights, and perhaps some 55,000 adult male slaves. When we speak of Athenian democracy we must always remember that a considerable group of Athens' inhabitants were enslaved and had no voice in politics whatever, while another large group, including every non-enslaved Attican woman, was "free," but without the rights and status of a citizen. The philosopher Aristotle was expressing a deep Hellenic (and Near Eastern) bias when he "proved" the natural inferiority of women and slaves. Nevertheless, citizenship was far less exclusive in Athens than in Sparta, and with respect to the citizenry itself, Athens was more thoroughly democratic than any modern state. The citizens did not elect the legislators; they *were* the legislators.

For the transaction of day-to-day business, Cleisthenes provided a smaller body—a Council of Five Hundred—for which every Athenian citizen over thirty was eligible. The Council was made up of 50 men from each tribe chosen annually by lot from a list of tribal nominees. Each of these 50-man tribal groups served for one-tenth of the year. Their order of rotation was determined by a crude machine that archaeologists have recently discovered. It worked much like our modern bubble gum machines: a stone for each of the ten tribes was put in the machine, and each month one stone was released, thus preventing any tribe except the last from knowing in advance when its term would begin.

Random selection pervaded the Athenian constitution. Every day a different chairman for the 50-man panel was chosen by lot. Most of the various magistrates and civil servants also came to be selected by lot for limited terms and were strictly responsible to the Council of Five Hundred and the Assembly. This was a citizens' government in every sense of the word—a government of amateurs rather than professional bureaucrats.

But neither Council nor Assembly could provide the long range personal leadership essential to the well-being of the state. The Assembly was too unwieldy, the Council too circumscribed by rotation and lot. Consequently, the chief executive power in Athens came to be exercised by a group of ten generals (*strategoi*), one from each tribe, who were elected annually by the Assembly and were eligible for indefinite reelection. Even the most zealous democrat could scarcely wish to see his generals chosen by lot or rotated every year. These were offices for which special talent was essential, and the Athenians wisely tended to choose as their *strategoi* men from the aristocracy who had behind them a long tradition of military and political experience. The greatest Athenian *strategos* of the fifth century, Pericles, was precisely such a man, and his extended tenure in office illustrates the remarkable equilibrium achieved in the golden age between aristocratic leadership and popular sovereignty. Even Pericles was subject to the Assembly on which he depended for support and reelection. He could exercise his authority only by persuasion or political manipulation—never by force.

Sixth-Century Ionia and the Expansion of Persia

During the sixth century, while Solon, Pisistratus, and Cleisthenes were transforming Athens into a prosperous democracy, the cultural center of the Hellenic world was Ionia. Here on the shores of Anatolia the Greeks came into direct contact with the ancient Near East. The results of this contact were fruitful indeed, for the Ionian Greeks adapted Near Eastern art, architecture, literature, and learning to their own, different outlook, creating a brilliant, elegant culture, far more gracious and luxurious than any that existed in Greece itself. It was in this setting that Greek philosophy, science, and lyric poetry were born. Ionian polises underwent much the same political and economic developments as those of Greece, and by the sixth century the lower classes were attempting to overthrow the control of the aristocrats. In Miletus, the aristocrats and commoners went to the extreme of burning one another alive.

These internal social struggles were affected drastically by the intervention of outside powers. During the 560s and 550s the coastal cities of Ionia fell one by one under the control of the Lydians, and when Lydia was conquered by the Persian Empire in 546, they passed under Persian control. In 499 there occurred a general Ionian rebellion against Persian rule during which the Athenians were persuaded to send 20 ships to aid their desperate kinsmen. But the Athenian aid proved insufficient, and by 494 the Persians had crushed the insurrection, punctuating their victory by sacking Miletus. Ionia's gamble for independence had failed and, even more important, Darius the Great, King of Persia, was now bent on revenge against Athens. The Persian Wars, the Greek historian Herodotus observes, were precipitated by the sending of 20 ships.

The Persian Wars (490–479 B.C.)

In 490 Darius led an army across the Aegean to teach the Greeks a lesson in respect. As was so often the case, the Greeks, even in the face of this calamity, found it impossible to unite. The Spartans held aloof in the Peloponnesus, claiming that they could not send their army until the moon's phase was auspicious, and other states preferred to await further developments. Consequently Athens was obliged to face the Persians almost alone. At Marathon in Attica the two armies met, and the Athenian hoplites, fighting shoulder to shoulder for the preservation of their homes and their polis, won a brilliant victory that not only postponed the Persian threat but also stirred a powerful sense of pride and self-confidence in Athens. The sovereign of the world's greatest empire had been defeated by a small army of free Athenian citizens. For such men as these, so it seemed, nothing was impossible.

The buoyant optimism that filled Athens in the wake of Marathon was tempered by the sobering thought that the Persians were likely to return in far greater numbers. Darius the Great spent his last years planning a devastating attack against Greece, but when the new invasion came in 480, it was led by Darius' successor, Xerxes. A Persian army of about 180,000 fighting men, stupendous by the standards of the age, moved by land around the northern Aegean shore accompanied by a powerful armada. Xerxes had paved his way into Greece by alliances with a number of opportunistic Greek cities such as Argos and Thebes. In the meantime, Athens had been preparing for the onslaught under the enterprising leadership of Themistocles, a statesman of great strategic imagination, who saw clearly that Athens' one hope was to build a strong fleet and seize control of the Aegean from the Persian Empire. By the time Xerxes led his forces into Greece, Themistocles' fleet was ready.

Sparta had by now awakened to the danger of a Persian conquest and was equally alarmed at the possibility of Athens winning additional prestige from another miraculous, single-handed victory. As Xerxes moved southward through northern Greece, a small army of Spartans and other Greeks placed itself across the Persian path at Thermopylae, a narrow pass between sea and mountains through which Xerxes' host had to move before breaking into the south. When the two armies met, the Persians found that their immense numerical superiority was of little use on so restricted a battlefield and that man for man they were no match for the Greeks. But at length a Greek turncoat led a contingent of the Persian army along a poorly defended path through the mountains to the rear of the Greek position. Now completely surrounded, the Greeks continued to fight and died to the last man in defense of the field. Although the battle of Thermopylae was a defeat for the Spartans, it was also a symbol of their dedication. The inscription that was later placed over their graves is a model of Spartan brevity and understatement:

> Tell them the news in Sparta, passer by,
> That here, obedient to their words, we lie.

Much delayed, Xerxes' army now moved against Athens. The Athenians, at Themistocles' bidding, evacuated Attica and took refuge elsewhere; some in the Peloponnesus, others on the island of Salamis just off the Attican coast. The refugees on the island had to look on helplessly as the Persians plundered Athens and burned the temples on the Acropolis. But Themistocles' strategy was vindicated when the Greek and Persian fleets fought a decisive naval engagement in the Bay of Salamis. The bay provided insufficient room for the huge Persian armada to maneuver, and the lighter, faster Greek fleet, with the new Athenian navy as its core, won an overwhelming victory. Persia's navy was decimated before the eyes of Xerxes, who witnessed the disaster from a rocky headland. Commanding his army to withdraw to northern Greece for the winter, Xerxes himself departed for Asia, never to return.

In the following spring (479) the Persian army was routed at Plataea on the northern frontier of Attica by a Pan-Hellenic army under Spartan command, and the Greeks won a final victory over the tattered remnants of the Persian army and fleet at Cape Mycale in Ionia. Now, one after another, the Ionian cities were able to break loose from Persian control. Hellas had preserved its independence and was free to work out its own destiny. As an ironic postscript to the momentous struggle, Themistocles, the key figure in Athens' triumph at Salamis, fell from power shortly thereafter, was exiled, and ended his days in the service of the king of Persia.

The Athenian Empire

To some historians, the moment of truth for classical Greece was not Marathon, Salamis, or Plataea but rather, the brief period immediately afterward when the possibility of establishing the Spartan-led Pan-Hellenic League on a permanent basis was allowed to slip by. Yet as more recent history attests, it is much easier to unite against a common foe than to hold together a wartime confederation in the absence of military necessity. Common fear is a stronger cement than common hope, and the creation of a Pan-Hellenic state from the Greek alliance of 480 to 479 was of the same order of difficulty as the creation of a viable world state from the United Nations of World War II. Considering the intense involvement of the typical Greek in his polis, it seems doubtful that Greek federalism was ever a genuine option.

Nevertheless, the Greek world in 479 could not be certain that the Persian invasions were truly over. Sparta, always fearful of a helot revolt at home, withdrew from the league to concentrate on its own affairs, and Sparta's Peloponnesian confederates withdrew also. Athens, however, was unwilling to lower its guard. A large fleet had to be kept in readiness, and such a fleet could not be maintained by Athens alone. Consequently a new alliance was formed under Athenian leadership which included most of the maritime cities on the coasts and islands of the Aegean from Attica to Ionia. The alliance was known as the Delian League because its headquarters and treasury were on the island of Delos, an ancient Ionian religious center. Athens and a few other cities contributed ships to the Delian fleet; the remaining members contributed money. All were entitled to a voice in the affairs of the Delian League, but Athens, with its superior wealth and power, gradually assumed a dominant position.

Slowly the Delian League evolved into an Athenian Empire. In 454 the league treasury was transferred from Delos to Athens, where its funds were diverted to the welfare and adornment of Athens itself. The Athenians justified this extraordinary policy of financial juggling by the argument that their fleet remained always vigilant and ready to protect league members from Persian aggression. But their explanation was received unsympathetically in some quarters. An Ionian visiting Athens might well admire the magnificent new temples being erected on the Acropolis. But his admiration would be chilled by the reflection that his own polis was contributing financially toward their construction. Certain members decided to withdraw from the league only to find that Athens regarded secession as illegal and was ready to enforce the continued membership of disillusioned cities by military action. With the development of this policy in the 460s the transformation from Delian League to Athenian Empire was complete.

The half century (480 to 431) between Salamis and the beginning of the showdown with Sparta was the Athenian Golden Age. The empire rose and flourished, bringing Athens unimagined wealth, not merely from imperial assessments but also from the splendid commercial opportunities offered by Athenian domination of the Aegean. Athens was now the commercial capital of the Mediterranean world and the great power in Greece. Sparta and her Peloponnesian allies held aloof, yet Athenian statesmen such as Pericles hoped that one day they too would be brought by force under Athens' sway.

The Golden Age

The economic and imperialistic foundations of Athens' Golden Age are interesting to us chiefly as a backdrop for the momentous cultural explosion that has echoed through the centuries of Mediterranean and European civilizations. Through a rare and elusive conjunction of circumstances, a group of some 50,000 politically conscious Athenian citizens created in the decades after Salamis a unique, many-sided culture of superb taste and unsurpassed excellence. The culture of the Golden Age was anticipated in the sixth and even earlier centuries, and the period of creativity continued, especially in the intellectual sphere, into the fourth. But the zenith of Greek culture was reached in imperial Athens during the administration of Pericles in the middle decades of the fifth century. We will examine this achievement more closely later. For now, suffice it to say that fifth century Athens showed what the human spirit at its best is capable of attaining.

The Athenian achievement is so glittering that one is in danger of viewing the Golden Age as a utopia. In reality, the architecture and sculpture of the Acropolis, the tragic dramas, and the probing philosophical speculation, were produced against a background of large-scale slavery, petty politics, commercial greed, and growing imperial arrogance. Pericles, who remained in power almost continuously from shortly after 460 to his death in 429, provided much-needed direction to democratic Athens, but he maintained the support of the commercial classes by advocating an ever-expanding empire. His policy of extending Athenian imperialism to dominate the entire Greek world aroused the fear and hostility of Sparta and its Peloponnesian League. Corinth, the second greatest city in the league and Athens' chief commercial rival, was especially apprehensive of Pericles' imperialism. In 431 these accumulating tensions resulted in a war between the Peloponnesian League and the Athenian Empire—a protracted, agonizing struggle that ultimately destroyed the Athenian Empire and shook the Greek political structure to its foundations. The fifth century saw the polis system at its best and at its worst: on the one hand, the culture of Periclean Athens; on the other, the Peloponnesian War.

The Peloponnesian War

The war ran from 431 to 404. Athens dreamed of bringing all Hellas under its sway, and Sparta and its allies were determined to end the threat of Athenian imperialism. Athens was coming to be regarded as a tyrant among the states of its own empire, but so long as Athenian ships patrolled the Aegean, rebellion was minimized. Ironically, the mother of democracies was driven to ever more despotic expedients to hold its empire together.

In 430 and 429 Athens, crowded with refugees, was struck by a plague that carried off perhaps a quarter of its population, including Pericles himself. The loss of this far-sighted statesman, combined with the terrible shock of the plague, led to a rapid deterioration in the quality of Athenian government. Leadership passed into the hands of extremists, and the democracy acquired many of the worst characteristics of mob rule. A general who, through no fault of his own, failed to win some battle might be sent into exile. (Such was the experience of Thucydides, Athens' greatest historian.) When the Athenians captured the island of Melos, an innocent neutral in the struggle, all its men were slaughtered and its women and children sold as slaves.

Pericles had observed on the eve of the war that he was more afraid of Athens' mistakes than of Sparta's designs. His fear was

Pericles the Athenian statesman.

well founded, for as the war progressed along its dreary course Athenian strategy became increasingly reckless. The better part of the Athenian fleet was lost when two ill-planned expeditions against distant Syracuse ended in complete disaster. As Athens' grip on the

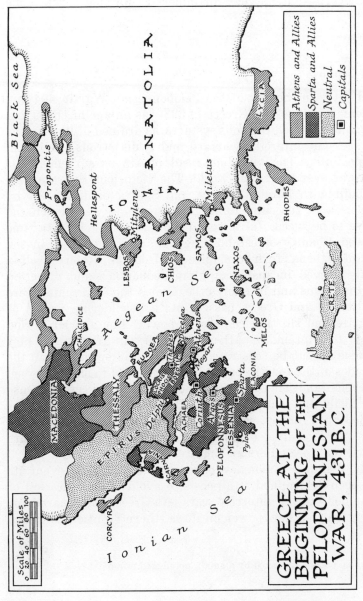

GREECE AT THE BEGINNING OF THE PELOPONNESIAN WAR, 431 B.C.

Aegean loosened, its subject cities began to rebel, and at length a Peloponnesian fleet, financed in part by Persian gold, destroyed what was left of Athens' navy. In 404 Athens surrendered—its wealth lost, its spirit broken, and its empire in ruins. Long thereafter it remained the intellectual and cultural center of the Greek world—it was even able to make something of an economic and political recovery—but its years of imperial supremacy were gone forever.

The Fourth Century

The period between the end of the Peloponnesian War in 404 and the Macedonian conquest of Greece in 338 was an age of chaos and anticlimax during which the polis system was drained of its creative force by incessant intercity warfare and a disastrous decline in social responsibility. The immediate result of Athens' surrender was Spartan power over the Greek world. The victorious Spartan fleet had been built with Persian money, and Sparta paid its debt by allowing Persia to reoccupy Ionia. The Spartans were much too conservative to be successful imperialists, and although for a time they followed a policy of establishing oligarchic regimes* in the city-states of Athens' former empire—indeed, in Athens itself— they quickly proved incapable of giving coherence and direction to Hellas. In Athens and in many other states the oligarchies were soon overthrown, and Greece passed into a bewildering period of military strife and shifting centers of power. For a brief period Thebes rose to supremacy. Athens itself began to form a new Aegean league only to be frustrated by Persian intervention. In the middle decades of the fourth century, power tended to shift between Sparta, Athens, and Thebes, while the Greek colony of Syracuse dominated Sicily and southern Italy. Envoys from Persia, always well supplied with money, saw to it that no one state became too powerful. A Greece divided and decimated by incessant warfare could be no threat to the Persian Empire.

Ironically, Persia's diplomacy paved the way for an event its rulers had been determined at all costs to avoid: the unification of Greece. The debilitating intercity wars left Greece unprepared for the intervention of a new power on its northern frontier. Macedon

---

*An *oligarchy* is a state governed by a small, privileged minority.

was a backward mountain kingdom whose inhabitants, although distantly related to the Greeks, knew little of Hellenic culture. In 359 a talented opportunist named Philip became king of Macedon. He tamed and unified the wild Macedonian tribes, secured his northern frontiers, and then began a patient and artful campaign to bring Greece under his control. Having spent three years of his boyhood as a hostage in Thebes, he had acquired a full appreciation of both Greek culture and Greek political instability. He hired the philosopher Aristotle as tutor for his son Alexander, and he exploited the ever-increasing Greek distaste for war by bluffing and cajoling his way into the south. His conquests of Greek towns were accompanied by declarations of his peaceful intentions, and when at last Athens and Thebes resolved their ancient rivalry and joined forces against him it was much too late. In 338 Philip won the decisive battle and Greece lay at his feet.

Philip allowed the Greek states to run their own internal affairs but he organized them into a league whose policies he controlled. With the subordination of Greek freedom to the will of King Philip the classical age of Greek history came to an end. With the accession of Philip's illustrious son, Alexander the Great, two years later, a new age began which would see the spread of Greek culture throughout the Near East and the transformation of Greek life into something drastically different from what it had been before.

The Decline of the Polis

Classical Greece was a product of the polis, and when the polis lost its meaning classical Greece came to an end. The essence of the polis was participation in the political and cultural life of the community. The citizen was expected to take care of his private business and at the same time attend the assembly, participate in decisions of state, serve in the administration, and fight in the army or navy whenever necessary. Statesmen such as Pericles were at once administrators, orators, and generals. The polis at its best was a community of well-rounded men—men who had many interests and capabilities—in short, amateurs. In the sixth and early fifth centuries, when Greek life had been comparatively simple, it was possible for one man to play many roles. But as the fifth century progressed the advantages of specialization grew. Military tactics became more complex. Administrative procedures became increasingly refined. Oratory became the subject of specialized study. As the various intellectual disciplines progressed it became more and more difficult to master them. The age of the amateur gradually gave way to the age of the professional. The polis of the fourth century was filled with professional administrators, orators, scholars, bankers, sailors, and businessmen whose demanding careers left them time for little else. Citizens were becoming absorbed in their private affairs, and political life, once the very embodiment of the Greek spirit, was losing its fascination. Citizen-soldiers gave way increasingly to mercenaries, partly because civic patriotism was running dry but also because fighting was now a full-time career. The precarious equilibrium achieved in the Golden Age between competence and versatility—between individual and community—could only be momentary, for the intense creativity of the fifth century led inevitably to the specialization of the fourth: It has been said that "Progress broke the Polis,"* yet progress was a fundamental ingredient of the way of life that the polis created.

*Kitto, *The Greeks*, p. 161.

TWO

THE THOUGHT AND CULTURE OF CLASSICAL GREECE

The Hellenic Mind

The civilizations of the ancient Near East did significant pioneer work in mathematics, engineering, and practical science; the Hebrews developed a profound ethical system based on divine revelation; but it was the Greeks who first took the step of examining man and his universe from a rational standpoint. It was they who transcended the mythical and poetic approach to cosmology and began to look at the universe as a natural rather than a supernatural phenomenon, based on discoverable principles of cause and effect rather than on the divine will. It was they who first attempted to base morality and the good life on reason rather than revelation. Accordingly, the Greeks were the first philosophers—the first logicians—the first theoretical scientists. The Babylonians had studied the stars to prophesy; the Egyptians had mastered geometry to build tombs, and chemistry to create mummies. The Greeks had much to learn from their predecessors, but they turned their knowledge and their investigation toward a new end: a rational understanding of man and the universe. Their achievement has been described as "the discovery of the mind."

This is not to say that the Greeks were irreligious. Their dramas, their civic festivals, their Olympic Games were all religious celebrations; their art and architecture were devoted largely to honoring the gods; their generals sometimes altered their strategy on the basis of some divine portent. But the Greek philosophers succeeded by and large in holding their gods at bay and untangling the natural from the supernatural. Like the Jews, they rejected the "I-thou" relationship of man and nature, but unlike the Jews they were not intensely involved in the worship of a single, omnipotent deity. The Greeks had no powerful official priesthood to enforce correct doctrine. To them as to other ancient peoples the cosmos was awesome, but they possessed the open-mindedness and the audacity to probe it with their intellects.

Ionia: the Lyric Poets

Open-mindedness and audacity—so alien to the despotisms of the Middle East—were nourished by the free turbulent atmosphere of the polis. Greek rationalism was a product of Greek individualism, and among the first manifestations of this new spirit of self-awareness and irreverence for tradition was the development of lyric poetry in seventh and sixth century Ionia. Greek lyric poetry was a notable literary achievement, but its importance transcends the realm of letters. The works of lyric poets such as Archilochus in the seventh century and Sappho of Lesbos in the sixth disclose self-consciousness and intensity of experience far exceeding anything known before. At a time when Spartan mothers were sending their sons to war with the stern admonition, "Return with your shield— or on it," the Ionian Archilochus was expressing a far more individualistic viewpoint:

> *Some lucky Thracian has my shield,*
> *For, being somewhat flurried,*
> *I dropped it by a wayside bush,*
> *As from the field I hurried;*
> *Thank God, I made it clear away,*
> *To blazes with the shield!*
> *I'll get another just as good*
> *When next I take the field.*

With such lines as these Archilochus ceases to be a mere name and emerges as a vivid, engaging personality. He is history's first articulate coward.

The most intensely personal of the lyric poets was Sappho, an aristocratic lady of sixth-century Lesbos, who became the directress of a school for young girls—apparently a combination finishing school and religious guild dedicated to Aphrodite, the goddess of Love. Her passionate love lyrics to her students used to raise eyebrows and have given enduring meaning to the word "lesbian," but the people of antiquity saw Sappho as the equal of Homer. Never before had human feelings been expressed with such perception and sensitivity:

> *Love has unbound my limbs and set me shaking*
> *A monster bitter-sweet and my unmaking.**

The Ionian Philosophers

The same surge of individualism that produced lyric poetry gave rise to mankind's first effort to understand rationally the physical universe. So far as we know the first philosopher and theoretical scientist in human history was the sixth-century Ionian, Thales of Miletus, who set forth the proposition that water was the primal element of the universe. This hypothesis, although crude by present standards, constitutes a significant effort to impose a principle of intellectual unity on the diversity of experience. The world was to be understood as a single physical substance. Presumably, solid objects were made of compressed water and air of rarefied water. Empty space was perhaps composed of dehydrated water. Thales' hypothesis did not commend itself to his successors, but the crucial point is that Thales had successors—that other men, following his example, would continue the effort to explain the physical universe through natural rather than supernatural principles. Intellectual history had taken a bold new turn and was headed into a fruitful, uncharted land.

The Ionian philosophers after Thales continued to speculate about the primal substance of the universe. One suggested that air was the basic element, another, fire. The Ionian Anaximander set forth a primitive theory of evolution and declared that men were de-

*Greek Literature in Translation, ed. Oates and Murphy, p. 972.

scended from fish. But these intellectual pioneers, their originality notwithstanding, disclose a basic weakness that characterized Greek thought throughout the classical age: an all-too-human tendency to rush into sweeping generalizations on the basis of a grossly inadequate factual foundation. Beguiled by the potentialities of rational inquiry they failed to appreciate how painfully difficult it is to arrive at sound conclusions. Consequently, the hypotheses of the Ionians are of the nature of inspired guesses. Anaximander's theory of evolution, for example, was quickly forgotten because, unlike Darwin's, it had no significant supporting data.

The Pythagorean School

Pythagoras (c. 582–507 B.C.) represents a different intellectual trend. A native of Ionia, he migrated to southern Italy where he founded a strange brotherhood, half scientific, half mystical. He drew heavily from the mystery cults of Dionysus and Demeter and was influenced especially by Orphism, a salvation cult that was becoming popular in the sixth century. The cult of Orpheus stressed guilt and atonement, a variety of ascetic practices, and an afterlife of suffering or bliss depending on the purity of one's soul. This and similar cults appealed to those who found inadequate solace in the heroic but worldly gods of Olympus. Following the basic structure of Orphic dogma, Pythagoras and his followers advocated the doctrine of transmigration of souls and the concept of a quasi-monastic communal life. Entangled in this was their profoundly significant notion that the basic element in nature was neither water, air, nor fire, but *number*. The Pythagoreans studied the intervals between musical tones and worked out basic laws of harmony. Having demonstrated the relationship between music and mathematics, they next applied these principles to the whole universe, asserting that the cosmos obeyed the laws of harmony and, indeed, that the planets in their courses produced musical tones that combined into a cosmic rhapsody: the music of the spheres. Implicit in this bewildering mixture of insight and fancy is the pregnant concept that nature is best understood mathematically.

The mathematical thought of the Pythagoreans included a mystical reverence for the number 10, which they saw as magical. But despite their number mysticism, which modern science rejects, they played a crucial role in the development of mathematics and mathematical science. They produced the Pythagorean theorem and the multiplication table, and their notions contributed to the development of modern science in the sixteenth and seventeenth centuries. The Greeks were at their best in mathematics, for here they could reason deductively—from self-evident concepts—and their distaste for the slow, patient accumulation of data was no hindrance.

The Fifth Century

In the course of the fifth century a great many of the central problems that have occupied philosophers ever since were raised and explored: whether the universe is in a state of constant flux or eternally changeless; whether it is composed of one substance or many; whether or not the nature of the universe can be grasped by the reasoning mind. Democritus set forth a doctrine of materialism that anticipated several of the views of modern science. He maintained that the universe consists of countless atoms in random configurations—that it has no center and no periphery but is much the same one place as another. In short, the universe is infinite and the earth is in no way unique. Like Anaximander's theory of evolution, Democritus' atomism was essentially a philosophical assertion rather than a scientific hypothesis based on empirical evidence. And since infinity was not a concept congenial to the Greek mind, atomism long remained a minority view. But in early modern times Democritus' notion of an infinite universe contributed to the development of a new philosophical outlook and to the rise of modern astronomy.

It was in medicine and history rather than in cosmology that the Greeks of the fifth century were able to resist the lure of the spectacular generalization and concentrate on the humble but essential task of accumulating verified facts. In the field of medicine, Hippocrates and his followers recorded case histories with scrupulous care and avoided the facile and hasty conclusion. Their painstaking clinical studies and their rejection of supernatural causation started medicine upon its modern career.

A similar reverence for the verifiable fact was demonstrated by the Greek historians of the period. History, in the modern sense, begins with Herodotus, a man of boundless curiosity who, in the course of his extensive travels, gathered a vast accumulation of data for his brilliant and entertaining history of the Persian Wars. Herodotus made a serious effort to separate fact from fable, but he was far surpassed in this regard by Thucydides, a disgraced Athenian general who wrote his masterly account of the Peloponnesian War with unprecedented objectivity and an acute sense of historical criticism. "Of the events of the war," writes Thucydides, ". . . I have described nothing but what I either saw myself or learned from others whom I questioned most carefully and specifically. The task was laborious, because eyewitnesses of the same events gave different accounts of them, as they remembered or were interested in the actions of one side or the other." To Thucydides, the polis was a fascinating arena where diverse political views contended, and since he was inclined to view political issues as the central problems of existence, he ascribed to the polis a dominant role in the dynamics of history.

The Sophists

In philosophy, history, and science, reason was winning its victories at the expense of the supernatural. The anthropomorphic gods of Olympus were especially susceptible to rational criticism, for few people who were acquainted with Ionian philosophy or the new traditions of scientific history and medicine could seriously believe that Zeus hurled thunderbolts or that Poseidon caused earthquakes. Some philosophical spirits came to see Zeus as a transcendent god of the universe; others rejected him altogether. But if one doubts that Zeus tosses thunderbolts one is also likely to doubt that Athena protects Athens, and the rejection of Athena and other civic deities was bound to be subversive to the traditional spirit of the polis. Religious skepticism was gradually undermining civic patriotism, and as skepticism advanced, patriotism receded. Once again we are brought face to face with the dynamic and paradoxical nature of the Greek experience: the polis produced the inquiring mind, but in time the inquiring mind eroded the most fundamental traditions of the polis.

The arch skeptics of fifth-century Athens were the Sophists, a heterogeneous group of professional teachers drawn from every corner of the Greek world by the wealth of the great city. Much of our information about the Sophists comes from the writings of Plato, who disliked them heartily and portrayed them as intellectual prostitutes and tricksters. In reality most of them were dedicated to the life of reason and the sound argument. Unlike the Ionian philosophers, they were chiefly interested in man rather than the cosmos. They investigated ethics, politics, history, and psychology and have been called the first social scientists. In applying reason to these areas and teaching their students to do the same, they aroused the wrath of the conservatives and doubtless encouraged an irreverent attitude toward tradition. Of course, the Greeks were not nearly so tradition-bound as their predecessors and contemporaries, but there is a limit to the amount of skepticism and change that any social system can absorb. Many of the Sophists taught their pupils techniques of debating and getting ahead, while questioning the traditional doctrines of religion, patriotism, and dedication to the welfare of the community. One of them is described by Plato as advocating the maxim that might makes right. In other words, the Sophists as a whole stimulated an attitude of iconoclasm, relativism, and ambitious individualism, thereby contributing to the dissolution of the polis spirit.

A Greek classroom.

Socrates (469–399 B.C.)

Socrates, the "patron saint" of intellectuals, was at once a part of this movement and an opponent of it. During the troubled years of the Peloponnesian war he wandered the streets of Athens teaching his followers to test their beliefs and preconceptions with the tool of reason. "An uncriticized life," he observed, "is scarcely worth living." Like the Sophists Socrates was interested in human rather than cosmic matters, but unlike many of them he was dissatisfied merely with tearing down traditional beliefs. He cleared the ground by posing seemingly innocent questions to his listeners which invariably entangled them in a hopeless maze of contradictions. But having devastated their opinions, he substituted closely-reasoned conclusions of his own on the subject of ethics and the good life. Knowledge, he taught, was synonymous with virtue, for a person who knew the truth would act righteously. Impelled by this optimistic conviction he continued to attack cherished beliefs—to play the role of "gadfly" as he put it.

Gadflies have seldom been popular. The Athenians, put on edge by their defeat at Sparta's hands (which was hastened by the treachery of one of Socrates' pupils) could at last bear him no longer. In 399 he was brought to trial for denying the gods and corrupting youth and was condemned by a close vote. In accordance with Athenian law, he was given the opportunity to propose his own punishment. He suggested that the Athenians punish him by giving him free meals at public expense for the rest of his life. By refusing to take his trial seriously he was in effect condemning himself to death. Declining an opportunity to escape into exile, he was executed by poison and expired with the cheerful observation that at last he had the opportunity of discovering for himself the truth about the afterlife.

Plato (427–347 B.C.)

Socrates would not have made good on an American university faculty, for although he was a splendid teacher, he did not publish.* We know of his teachings largely through the works of his student Plato, one of history's towering intellects and a prolific and graceful writer. In his *Republic*, Plato outlined the perfect polis—the first utopia in literary history. Here, ironically, the philosopher rejected the democracy that he knew and described an ideal state far more Spartan than Athenian. The farmers, workers, and merchants were

---

*Jesus would not have qualified for tenure either.

without political rights; a warrior class was trained with Spartan rigor to defend the state; and an intellectual elite, schooled in mathematics and philosophy, constituted a ruling class. At the top of the political pyramid was a philosopher-king, the wisest and most virtuous product of a state-training program that consumed the better part of his life. Culture was not encouraged in the Republic; dangerous and novel ideas were banned, poets were banished, all music was prohibited except the martial, patriotic type.

What are we to make of a utopia that would encourage Sousa but ban Brahms—a polis that could never have produced a Plato? We must remember that democratic Athens was in decline when Plato wrote. He could not love the polis that had executed his master, nor was he blind to the selfish individualism and civic irresponsibility that characterized fourth-century Greece. Plato had the wit to recognize that through the intensity of its cultural creativity and the freedom and breadth of its intellectual curiosity the polis was burning itself out. Achilles had chosen a short but glorious life; Plato preferred long-lived mediocrity, and stability was therefore the keynote of his Republic. There would be no Sophists to erode civic virtue, no poets to exalt the individual over the community (or abandon their shields as they fled from battle). Plato's cavalier treatment of the mercantile classes represents a deliberate rejection of the lures of empire. Like a figure on a Grecian urn his ideal polis would be frozen and rigid—and enduring.

There remains the paradox that this intellectually static commonwealth was to be ruled by philosophers. We tend to think of philosophy as a singularly disputatious subject, but Plato viewed truth as absolute and unchanging and assumed that all true philosophers would be in essential agreement—that future thinkers would simply affirm Plato's own doctrines. This assumption has proven to be resoundingly false, yet Plato's conception of reality has nevertheless exerted enormous influence on the development of thought. His purpose was to reconcile his belief in a perfect, unchanging universe with the kaleidoscopic diversity and impermanence of the visible world. He stated that the objects we perceive through our senses are merely pale, imperfect reflections of ideal models or archetypes that exist in a world invisible to man. For example, we observe numerous individual cats, some black, some yellow, some fat, some skinny. All are imperfect particularizations of an ideal cat existing in the Platonic heaven. Again, we find in the world of the senses many examples of duality: twins, lovers, pairs of jackasses, and so forth, but they merely exemplify more or less inadequately the idea of "two" which, in its pure state, is invisible and intangible. We cannot see "two." We can only see two *things*. But—and this is all important—we can *conceive* of "twoness" or abstract duality. Likewise, with sufficient effort, we can conceive of "catness," "dogness" and "rabbitness"—of the archetypal cat, dog or rabbit. If we could not, so Plato believes, we would have no basis for grouping individual cats into a single category. In short, the world of phenomena is not the *real* world. The phenomenal world is variegated and dynamic; the real world—the world of archetypes —is clear-cut and static. We can discover this real world through introspection, for knowledge of the archetypes is present in our minds from birth, dimly remembered from a previous existence. (Plato believed in a beforelife as well as an afterlife.) So the philosopher studies reality not by *observing* but by *thinking*.

Plato illustrates this doctrine with a vivid metaphor. Imagine, he says, a cave whose inhabitants are chained in such a position that they can never turn toward the sunlit opening but can only see shadows projected against an interior wall. Imagine further that one of the inhabitants (the philosopher) breaks his chains, emerges from the cave, and sees the real world for the first time. He will have no wish to return to his former shadow world, but he will do so nevertheless out of a sense of obligation to enlighten the others. Similarly, the philosopher-king rules the Republic unwillingly through a sense of duty. He would prefer to contemplate reality undisturbed. Yet he alone can rule wisely, for he alone has seen the truth.

Plato's doctrine of ideas has always been alluring to people who seek order and unity, stability and virtue, in a universe that appears fickle and chaotic. Plato declared that the greatest of the archetypes is the idea of the Good, and this notion has had great appeal to men of religious temperament ever since. His theory of knowledge, emphasizing contemplation over observation, is obviously hostile to the method of experimental science, yet his archetypal world is perfectly compatible with the world of the mathematician—the world of pure numbers. Plato drew heavily from the Pythagorean tradition—"God is a geometer," he once observed—and Platonic thought, like Pythagorean thought, has contributed profoundly to the development of mathematical science. As for philosophy, it developed for almost the next two thousand years in the shadow of two giants. One of them is Plato; the other, Aristotle, Plato's greatest pupil.

Aristotle (384–322 B.C.)

Plato founded a school in Athens called the Academy (from which arises our word, *academic*). To this school came the young Aristotle, the son of a Thracian physician in the service of the king of Macedon. Aristotle remained at the Academy for nearly two decades. Then, after serving at the Macedonian court as tutor to Alexander the Great, he returned to Athens, founded a school of his own (the Lyceum), and wrote most of his books. At length he was condemned by the Athenians for impiety, fled into exile, and died shortly thereafter in 322, one year after the death of Alexander. Thus Aristotle's life is concurrent with the final phase of Classical Greece.

Aristotle was nearly a universal scholar. He wrote definitively on a great variety of topics including biology, politics, literature, ethics, logic, physics, and metaphysics. He brought Plato's theory of ideas down to earth by asserting that the archetype exists in the particular—that one can best study the archetypal cat by observing and classifying individual cats. Thus observation of things in this world takes its place alongside contemplation as a valid avenue to knowledge. Like Hippocrates and Thucydides, but on a much broader scale, Aristotle advocated the painstaking collection and analysis of data, thereby placing himself at odds with the main body of Greek thought. Although his political studies included the designing of an ideal commonwealth, he also investigated and classified the political systems of many existing city-states and demonstrated that several different types were conducive to the good life. His splendid biological studies followed the same method of observation and classification, and he set forth the concepts of genus and species which, with modifications, are still used. His work on physics has been less durable since it was based on an erroneous concept of motion, a fundamental belief in *purpose* as the organizing factor in the material universe, and an emphasis on qualitative rather than quantitative differences (for example, that the heavenly bodies were more perfect than objects on the earth). Mathematics had no genuine role in his system; in general, early modern science was to draw its experimental method from the Aristotelian tradition and its mathematical analysis from the Pythagorean-Platonic tradition.

Aristotle's physics and metaphysics were based on the concept of a single God who was the motive power behind the universe—the unmoved mover and the uncaused cause to which all motion and all causation must ultimately be referred. Hence, Aristotelian thought was able to serve as a philosophical framework for the later religious thought of Islam and Christianity. Aristotle's immense significance in intellectual history arises from his having done some of the best thinking up to his time in so many significant realms of thought. It was he who first set forth a systematic logic, who first (so far as we know) produced a rigorous, detailed physics, who literally founded biology. A pioneer in observational method, he has been criticized for basing conclusions on insufficient evidence. Even Aristotle was not immune to the tendency toward premature conclusions, yet he collected data as no Greek before him had done. His achievement, considered in its totality, is without parallel in the history of thought.

Plato and Aristotle represent the apex of Greek philosophy. Both were religious men—both, in fact, were monotheists at heart. But both were dedicated also to the life of reason, and, building on a rational heritage that had only begun in the sixth century, both produced philosophical systems of unprecedented sophistication and depth. Their thought climaxed and completed the intellectual revolution that brought such glory and such turmoil to Greece.

Periclean Culture and Life

History has never seen anything like the intense cultural creativity of fifth-century Athens. It has been said that the Athenians of the Golden Age were incapable of producing anything ugly or vulgar. Everything from the greatest temple to the simplest ornament was created with unerring taste and assurance. Emotions ran strong and deep, but they were controlled by a sure sense of form that never permitted ostentation yet never degenerated into formalism. The art of the period was an incarnation of the Greek maxim: "nothing in excess"—a perfect embodiment of the taut balance and controlled excitement that we call "the classical spirit."

It is not difficult to understand how Greek citizens, whose freedom far exceeded that of any previous civilized people, produced such a dynamic culture. It is less easy to explain the harmony and restraint of Greek classicism, for no people had ever before lived with such intensity and fervor. Herodotus tells us that even the barbaric Scythians lamented the Greek impulse toward frenzy, and a speaker in Thucydides observes that the Athenians "were born into the world to take no rest themselves and to give none to others." The Greek ideal was moderation and restraint precisely because these were the qualities most needed by an immoderate and unrestrained people. A degree of cooperation and self-control was essential to the communal life of the polis, and civic devotion acted as a brake on rampant individualism. During its greatest years the polis stimulated individual creativity but directed it toward the welfare of the community. Individualism and civic responsibility achieved a momentary and precarious balance.

The achievement of this equilibrium in the fifth century was a precious but fleeting episode in the evolution of the polis from the aristocratic conservatism of the previous age to the irresponsible individualism of the fourth century and thereafter, hastened by the growth of religious doubt and the tendency toward specialization. This process is illustrated clearly in the evolution of Greek art from the delicate, static elegance of the "archaic style" through the serious, balanced classical style of the fifth century to the increasing individualism, naturalism and particularism of the late-classical fourth century. In sculpture, for example, one observes a development from aristocratic stiffness to a harmonious serenity that gradually displays signs of increasing tension and individualization. The works of the fifth-century sculptors were idealized human beings—we might almost say Platonic archetypes. The fourth-century sculptors tended to abandon the archetype for the specific and the concrete. In short, as Greek life was evolving from civic allegiance to individualism, from traditionalism to originality and self-expression, from aristocracy to democracy, there was a moment when these opposites were balanced—and the moment was frozen and immortalized in some of the most superb works of architecture, sculpture, and dramatic literature the world has known.

In Periclean Athens individualism was still strongly oriented toward the polis. One of the most basic differences between the daily life of the fifth-century Athenian citizen and that of the modern American is the Athenian's emphasis on public over private affairs. The private life of even the most affluent Athenian was simple: his clothing was plain, his home was humble, his furniture was rudimentary. With the intensification of individualism in the fourth century, private homes became much more elaborate, but during the Golden Age the Athenian's private life was, by our standards, almost as Spartan as the Spartan's. The plainness of private life was counterbalanced, however, by the brilliant diversity of public life. Under Pericles, imperial Athens lavished its wealth and its genius on its own adornment. The great works of art and architecture were dedicated to the polis and its gods. Life was enriched by the pageantry of civic religious festivals, by spirited conversation in the marketplace (the agora), by exercise in elaborate civic gymnasiums complete with baths and dressing rooms, and of course by participation in political affairs. The Greeks socialized the amenities of life. The pursuit of excellence in body and mind, so typical of Greek culture, was carried on in a communal atmosphere. The good life was not the life of the individual but the life of the citizen.

Only a minority of the inhabitants of Athens were actually citizens. As we have seen, slaves, metics (resident aliens), women, and children were all excluded from the privileges of citizenship. Although many metics prospered in business, many slaves were well-treated and many women had loving husbands, only the citizens could participate fully in the life of the polis. The citizen's wife in Periclean Athens remained in the home. She had heavy domestic duties but few social responsibilities, and was legally under her husband's control. Since her education was confined to the level of "home economics," her husband was not likely to find her especially interesting. At the parties and festive gatherings of the citizens the only ladies present were foreigners, often Ionians, who were more notable for their charm and wit than for their virtue. Typical of these ladies was Pericles' mistress, Aspasia, a sophisticated, well-educated Ionian whose name, appropriately enough, means "welcome." The wives of Athens were denied the rich public life of the Golden Age, and their lot is expressed eloquently in one of the tragedies of Euripides: "For a man may go, when home life palls, to join with friends and raise his spirits in companionship. But for us poor wives it is solitary communion with the one same soul forever."

Drama

The civic culture of the Golden Age achieved its most notable triumphs in drama, architecture, and sculpture. All three illustrate the public orientation of Greek cultural life. Greek tragedy arose out of the worship of Dionysus, as the songs and dances of the worshipers gradually evolved into a formalized drama with actors and a chorus. The sixth-century Athenian tyrant Pisistratus gave vigorous support to the Dionysian drama, and by the fifth century it had become a great civic institution. Wealthy citizens were expected to finance the productions, and each year a body of civic judges would award prizes to the three best tragedies. By modern standards the performances were far from elaborate. The most important of them took place in an outdoor "Theater of Dionysus" on the southern slope of the Acropolis. The chorus sang and danced to a simple musical accompaniment and commented at intervals on the action of the drama. Behind the chorus were low, broad steps on which the actors performed. There were never more than three actors on the stage at one time, and the sets behind them were simple in the extreme. The dramas themselves were based on mythological or historical themes, often dealing with semilegendary royal families of early Greece, but the playwrights went beyond the realm of historical narrative to probe deeply some of the fundamental problems of morality and religion. The immense popularity of these stark, profound, and uncompromising productions testifies to the remarkable cultural elevation of fifth-century Athens. The citizens who flocked to the Theater of Dionysus constituted a critical and sophisticated audience. Many had themselves participated in the numerous dramas that were constantly being performed both in the city and in the surrounding Attican countryside. It has been estimated that each year some 3000 citizens had the experience of performing in a dramatic chorus, and thousands more had been trained, as a part of the normal Athenian curriculum, in singing, dancing, declamation, and acting. The drama was a central and meaningful element in the life of the polis and serves as an added illustration of the many-sidedness of human experience in the Golden Age.

The three great tragedians of fifth-century Athens were Aeschylus, who wrote during the first half of the century; Sophocles, whose productive period covered the middle and later decades of the century; and Euripides, a younger contemporary of Sophocles. All three exemplify the seriousness, the order, and the controlled tension that we identify as "classical," yet they also illustrate the changes the classical spirit was undergoing. Aeschylus, the first of the three, tended to emphasize traditional values. Deeply devoted to the polis and the Greek religious heritage, he probed with majestic dignity the fundamental relationship of man and his gods, the problem of injustice in a righteous universe, and the terrible consequences of overweening pride. Sophocles was less intellectually rigorous, less traditional than Aeschylus, but he was a supreme dramatic artist with an unerring sense of plot structure and characterization. His plays treat the most violent and agonizing emotional situations with restraint and sobriety. In Sophocles the perfect classical equilibrium is fully achieved. Never have passions been so intense yet under such masterly control. The younger dramatist Euripides displays the logic, the skepticism, and the hard-headed rationalism of the Sophists who were then the rage of Athens. One of his characters makes the audacious statement, "There are no gods in heaven; no, not one!" And Euripides, far more than his predecessors, demonstrated a deep, sympathetic understanding for the hopes and fears, the unpredictability and irrationality, the *individuality* of human nature. Aeschylus' characters were chiefly types rather than individuals; in Sophocles the individual emerges with much greater clarity; but Euripides portrays his characters with profound insight and psychological realism. With the tragedies of Euripides the new age of skepticism and acute individualism has dawned.

The depth and power of fifth-century tragedy is exemplified in Sophocles' *Antigone* which deals with the perennial problem of individual conscience and state authority. Antigone's brother has betrayed his country and has been killed. Her uncle, the king of Thebes, refuses to permit her brother's burial even though burial was regarded as mandatory in the Greek religious tradition. Torn by the conflict between the royal decree and her sense of religious obligation, Antigone defies the king, buries her brother, and is condemned to death. She addresses the king in these words:

I did not think that thy decrees were of such force as to override the unwritten unfailing laws of heaven. For their duration is not of today or yesterday, but from eternity, and no man knows when they were first put forth. And though men rage I must obey those laws. Die I must, for death must come to all. But if I am to die before my time, I'll do it gladly; for when one lives as I do, surrounded by evils, death can only be a gain. So death for me is but a trifling grief, far better than to let my mother's son lie an unburied corpse.

The lighter side of the fifth-century theater is represented by the great comic playwright Aristophanes who, taking advantage of the freedom of the Athenian theater, subjected his fellow citizens great and small to merciless ridicule as he exposed the pretensions and follies of imperial Athens during the Peloponnesian War. A product of the age of Socrates and the Sophists, Aristophanes expressed his deep-rooted conservatism by lampooning them. Socrates appears in a comedy called *The Clouds* hanging from a basket suspended in the air so that he could contemplate the heavens at closer range, while his students below studied geology, their noses in the earth and their posteriors upraised toward the sky. Aristophanes was an ardent pacifist who condemned Athenian participation in the Peloponnesian War and mocked the war leaders with a frankness that would seldom be tolerated by a modern democracy during wartime. The audacity of his criticism illustrates the degree of intellectual freedom that existed in fifth-century Athens, yet his plays betrayed a yearning for the dignity and traditionalism of former years and a disturbing conviction that all was not well.

Architecture and Sculpture

Every aspect of fifth-century culture displays the classical spirit of restrained excitement. We find it in Athenian drama where the most violent deeds and passions are presented in an ordered and unified framework. We find it in the history of Thucydides, who treats with penetrating and dispassionate analysis the impetuous and often childish excesses of the Peloponnesian War. And we find it in the architecture and the art of fifth-century Anthens: deeply moving yet perfectly balanced and controlled. When Xerxes burned the Acropolis he left the next generation of Athenians with a challenge and an opportunity to rebuild the temples in the new, classical

The Parthenon, the Temple of Athena at Athens.

The Charioteer of Delphi.

style—to crown the polis with structures of such majesty and perfection as the world had never seen. Athenian imperialism provided the money with which to rebuild, and Pericles, against the opposition of a conservative minority, pursued a lavish policy of civic beautification as a part of his effort to make Athens the cultural center of Hellas. The age of Pericles was therefore a period of feverish public buildings. Its supreme architectural monument was the central temple on the reconstructed Acropolis—the Parthenon. This superb structure, dedicated to the patron goddess Athena, is the ultimate expression of the classical ideal. It creates its effect not from a sense of fluidity and upward-reaching as in the much

The god Zeus or Poseidon.

Hermes with infant Dionysus; a masterpiece by Praxiteles.

later Gothic cathedral, but from an almost godlike harmony of proportions. Here indeed was "nothing in excess."

The genius of the architects was matched by that of the sculptors who decorated the temples and created the great statues that were placed inside them. The most distinguished of the fifth-century sculptors was Phidias, the master sculptor of the Parthenon, who was responsible either directly or through his helpers for its splendid reliefs. Phidias made a majestic statue of Athena in ivory and gold for the interior of the Parthenon and a still larger statue of the same goddess which was placed in the open and could be seen by ships several miles at sea. The work of Phidias and his contemporaries comes at the great moment of classical balance. Their works portray man as a type, without individual problems or cares, vigorous yet serene, ideally proportioned, and often in a state of controlled tension.

The architecture and sculpture of the Parthenon and its surrounding temples exemplify perfectly the synthesis of religious feeling, patriotic dedication, artistic genius, and intellectual freedom that characterized the age of Pericles. It would be pleasant to think of the Athenians of this period enjoying the beauty of these temples that so wonderfully express the mood of the age. But such was not the case. The Parthenon, the first of the Acropolis structures to be completed, was not finished until 432, a scant year before the outbreak of the Peloponnesian War that ultimately brought Athens to her knees. By 432 the old civic-religious enthusiasm was already waning. For centuries after, Greek art would be a living, creative thing; indeed, some of its most illustrious masterpieces were products of these later centuries. But the balanced, confident spirit of Periclean Athens—the spirit that informed the works of Sophocles and Phidias and inspired the Parthenon—could never quite be recovered.

THREE

THE HELLENISTIC AGE

Alexander The Great (336–323 B.C.)

The decline of the polis in the fourth
century culminated, as we have seen, in
the triumphs of King Philip and the
subordination of Greece to the power of
Macedon. In 336 B.C., barely two years
after his climactic victory over Athens
and Thebes, Philip of Macedon was murdered as a consequence of a petty palace
intrigue and was succeeded by his son,
Alexander, later to be called "the Great."
In his final months Philip had been
preparing a large-scale attack against
the Persian Empire, hoping to transform the grudging obedience of the
Greek city-states into enthusiastic support by leading a great Pan-Hellenic
crusade against the traditional enemy
of Hellas. Alexander, during a dazzling
reign of thirteen years, exceeded his
father's most fantastic dreams, leading
his all-conquering armies from Greece
to India and redirecting the course of
the ancient world.

Although he was only twenty when he inherited the throne, Alexander possessed in the fullest measure that combination of physical attractiveness, athletic prowess, and intellectual distinction which had always been the Greek ideal. He had a godly countenance, the physique of an Olympic athlete, and a penetrating, imaginative mind. He was a magnetic leader who inspired intense loyalty and admiration among his followers, a brilliant general who adapted his tactics and strategy to the most varied circumstances and won for himself a reputation of invincibility, and an ardent champion of Hellenic culture and the Greek way of life. He was the product of two master teachers: Aristotle, celebrated philosopher and universal intellect, and King Philip himself, the greatest general and most adroit political opportunist of the age. Alexander's turn of mind is symbolized by the two objects that he always kept beneath his pillow: the *Iliad* and a dagger.

At first the Greek city-states were restive under Alexander's rule. He quelled their revolts with merciless efficiency, destroying rebellious Thebes and frightening the rest into submission. But there was real enthusiasm for his campaign against the Persian Empire, and in time, as one victory followed another, Alexander came to be regarded as a national hero—the champion of Greece against the barbarian. In the spring of 334 B.C., he led a Greco-Macedonian army of some 40,000 men across the Dardanelles into Asia Minor. During the next three and one-half years he won a series of stunning victories over the aged and ramshackle Persian Empire, freeing the Ionian cities from Persian control and conquering the Persian provinces of Syria and Egypt. Then, striking deep into the heart of the empire, Alexander won a decisive victory over the unwieldy Persian army near Arbela on the Tigris in 331. The triumph at Arbela enabled Alexander to seize the vast imperial treasure, ascend the imperial throne, and bring an end to the dynasty of ancient Persia.

This was a glorious moment for the Greeks. The foe that had so long troubled Hellas was conquered. More than that, the ancient Near East was now under Greek control, open to the bracing influence of Greek enterprise, Greek culture, and Greek rationalism. Alexander's conquest of Persia set the stage for a new epoch—a period known as the *Hellenistic Age* as distinct from the previous *Classical Age*. The Greeks were now the masters of the ancient world, and under their rule a great cosmopolitan culture developed, distinctly Greek in tradition yet transmuted by the influence of the

Alexander the Great.

subject oriental civilizations and by the spacious new environment in which the Greeks now lived.

The Hellenization of the Near East was stimulated by Alexander's policy of founding cities in the wake of his conquests and filling them with Greek settlers. These communities, although intended chiefly as military and commercial bases, became islands of Greek culture which were often able to exert a powerful influence on the surrounding area. Most of them were named, immodestly, after their founder. The greatest of them by far was Alexandria in Egypt which Alexander founded near the mouth of the Nile. Alexandria quickly outstripped the cities of Greece itself to become the great commercial center of the Hellenistic world, and before long it had developed a cultural and intellectual life that put contemporary Athens to shame.

No sooner had he ascended the throne of Persia than Alexander began preparations for further campaigns. The final seven years of his life were occupied in conquering the easternmost provinces of Persia and pushing on into India, impelled by an insatiable thirst for conquest and by the lure of undiscovered lands. His spirit and ingenuity were taxed to the utmost by the variety of difficulties that he encountered: the rugged mountains of Afghanistan, the hostile stretches of the Indus Valley, fierce armies equipped with hundreds of elephants. At length his own army, its endurance exhausted, refused to go further. Alexander returned to central Persia in 323 where, in the midst of organizing his immense empire, he fell ill and died, perhaps of malaria, at the age of thirty-two.

The empire of Alexander was the greatest that the world had ever seen—more extensive even than the Persian Empire. Wherever he went Alexander adapted himself to the customs of the land. He ruled Egypt as a divine pharaoh and Persia as an oriental despot, demanding that his subjects prostrate themselves in his presence. (His Greek followers objected vigorously to this.) He married the daughter of the last Persian emperor and urged his countrymen to follow his example by taking wives from among the Persian aristocracy. His goal was nothing less than a homogeneous Greco-Oriental empire—a fusion of east and west. To what extent this policy was the product of deliberate calculation, to what extent a consequence of his intoxication with the splendors of the ancient Orient will never be known. But the project was scarcely underway when Alexander died, leaving behind him an overwhelming sense of loss and bewilderment and a vast state that nobody but a second Alexander could have held together.

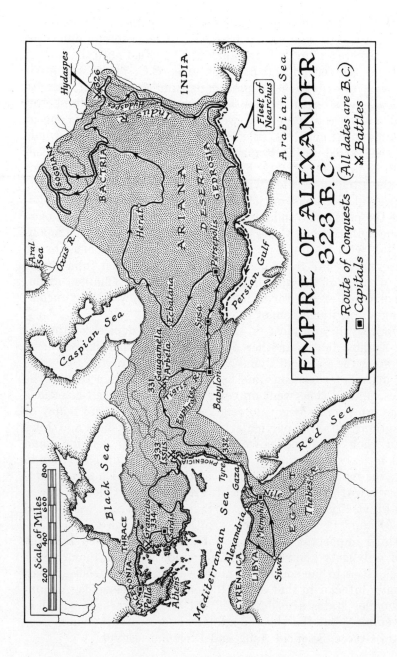

EMPIRE OF ALEXANDER
323 B.C.

Route of Conquests (All dates are B.C.)
■ Capitals
✕ Battles

Fleet of
Nearchus

Hydaspes

INDIA

Indus R.

Hydaspes ✕326

SOGDIANA

BACTRIA

Herat

ARIANA

GEDROSIA

DESERT

Persepolis ■

Ecbatana

Susa ■

Arbela
Gaugamela
331 ✕

Tigris R.

Euphrates R.

Babylon ■

Arabian Sea

Persian Gulf

Aral Sea

Oxus R.

Caspian Sea

Black Sea

THRACE

MACEDONIA

Pella ■

Athens

Granicus
334 ✕

Sardis

Issus
333 ✕

PHOENICIA

Tyre

Gaza 332 ✕

Mediterranean Sea

Alexandria

Red Sea

Nile

Memphis

EGYPT

Thebes

Siwa

LIBYA

CYRENAICA

Scale of Miles
0 200 400 600 800

The Successor States

The empire was divided among the able and ambitious generals of Alexander's staff who founded a series of Macedonian dynasties that ruled Greece and most of the ancient Near East until the Roman conquests of the second and first centuries B.C. There was great conflict over the division of the spoils, and for several decades after Alexander's death the political situation remained fluid. But in broad outline the succession went as follows: Ptolemy, one of Alexander's ablest generals, ruled Egypt, establishing the Ptolemaic dynasty that lasted until a Roman army deposed Cleopatra, the last of the Ptolemies, in 30 B.C. From Alexandria, their magnificent capital, the Ptolemies ruled with all the pomp and severity of the most powerful pharaohs, enriching themselves by merciless exploitation of the peasantry and suppressing all political activities, even among the multitudes of Greeks in Alexandria. The great metropolitan capital, with its imposing public buildings, its superb library and museum, its far flung commerce, and its million inhabitants was the wonder of the age, but elsewhere Egypt remained essentially unchanged except for a growing hostility toward the uncompromising authoritarianism of the Greek regime.

Northern Syria and most of the remaining provinces of the old Persian Empire fell to another of Alexander's generals, Seleucus, who founded the Seleucid dynasty. The kingdom of the Seleucids was far more heterogeneous and loosely organized than that of the Ptolemies, and as time went on certain of the more self-conscious Near Eastern peoples began to rebel against the Seleucid policy of Hellenization. This was particularly true of the Persians and Jews who had each produced powerful transcendental religions and resented bitterly the influx of Greek religious thought. Farther to the east, the more remote provinces of the Persian Empire gradually fell away from Seleucid control. The center of Seleucid power was the great city of Antioch in northern Syria which was second only to Alexandria in population, wealth, and opulence.

The third important successor state, Macedon, passed into the hands of a dynasty known as the Antigonids whose authority over the Greek cities to the south was never very firm and whose power was usually inferior to that of the Ptolemies and Seleucids. A number of smaller states also developed out of the wreckage of Alexander's empire, but the three dominant successor kingdoms were Antigonid Greece, Seleucid Asia, and Ptolemaic Egypt.

An old market woman, an example of Hellenistic realism.

The Change in Mood

These huge political agglomerations now replaced the small city-states as the typical units of the Greek world. The new environment provided vast opportunities and encouraged a sense of cosmopolitanism that contrasts with the provincialism of the polis. This was a prosperous age, an age of vigorous and profitable business activity and successful careers in commerce and banking. The good life was reserved, however, to the fortunate few. Slavery continued, even increased, and the peasants and urban commoners were kept at an economic level of bare subsistence. The typical agrarian unit was no longer the small or middle-sized farm but the large plantation worked by slaves.

The city-states in Greece itself retained throughout the new age a portion of their earlier autonomy. Old civic institutions continued to function, and citizens still had a voice in domestic politics. But the Greek peninsula was now an economic backwater, and cities like Athens and Thebes were overshadowed by the new superstates. Ambitious Greeks were lured by opportunity far from their homeland, as they had once been lured to imperial Athens. No longer involved in political affairs or in the intense life of a free community, the overseas Greek found himself adrift in a wide and bewildering world over which he had no control. The cosmopolitanism of the Hellenistic age was accompanied by a sense of estrangement and alienation, of uncertainty, loneliness, and impotence. The trend toward extreme individualism, professionalism, and specialization which we have already observed in the fourth century was enormously accelerated. The impulse toward greater realism and individualism in sculpture was pushed to its limits, and many Hellenistic sculptors turned to portraying the bizarre and the grotesque—ugliness, deformity, agony, and old age—sometimes with exceedingly effective results. The civic consciousness of the comic playwright Aristophanes in the fifth century gave way to the highly individualized and superficial realism of the Hellenistic drawing-room comedy and bedroom farce. The Hellenistic Age produced superb works of art, but they lacked the serenity and balance of the earlier period. Whether this fact detracts from their artistic merit or adds to it is a matter of taste, but they are obviously products of a radically different society—still brilliant, still intensely creative, but anchorless.

Religion and Ethics

Hellenic religion with its traditional civic orientation was all but transformed in this new, kaleidoscope age. Old bonds and old loyalties were broken as many adventurous Greeks were uprooted from their home cities and thrown on their own. The result was a mood of intense individualism which found expression in a variety of religious and ethical ideas stressing personal fulfillment or personal salvation rather than involvement in the community. Individualism and cosmopolitanism went hand in hand, for as the Greek abdicated spiritually from the polis and retired into himself, he came to regard all humanity as a multitude of individuals—a universal brotherhood in which intelligent Persians, Egyptians, and Jews were no worse than intelligent Greeks. The traditional contrast between Greek and barbarian faded, for it had been the free spirit of the polis that had set the Greek apart, and the polis, in its traditional sense, was now becoming an anachronism. Yet the concept of cosmopolis, the idea of human brotherhood, was too abstract to provide the sense of involvement and orientation that the polis had formerly given. The rootless Greek tended to turn away from his old Olympic gods and seek solace in more personal and potent religious concepts. Hellenistic religion is characterized by a withdrawal from active social participation—a search for sanctuary in a restless, uncertain world.

The Hellenistic age saw a vigorous revival of mystery and salvation cults such as Orphism and the worship of Dionysus and Demeter which had always lurked behind the Olympic foreground. And various Near Eastern mystery religions now became popular among the Greeks. Almost all of these were centered on the death and resurrection of a god and the promise of personal salvation. From Egypt came the cult of Osiris who died, was reborn, and now sat in judgment of the dead. From Asia Minor came a version of the ancient and widespread fertility cult of the Great Mother. From Persia, somewhat later, came the cult of Mithras, a variation of Zoroastrianism, which added to the traditional concept of a cosmic moral struggle between good and evil the idea of a savior-hero who redeemed mankind. Alongside these and other oriental cults came a revival of Babylonian astrology, of magic, witchcraft, and sorcery. Many ambitious men of the upper class were devoted to the goddess of Fortune who rewarded talent and ambition and brought her worshipers material well-being. The Hellenistic world became a huge religious melting pot in which a single individual might be a devotee of a number of cults. Many thoughtful people adopted the idea of "syncretism," that is, the notion that the gods of different peoples are actually various manifestations of the same god—that Zeus, Osiris, even Yahweh, all symbolize a single divine spirit. (The more orthodox among the Jews found this doctrine abominable.) Religious beliefs and religious attitudes throughout the Hellenistic world were tending to become homogenized, thereby preparing the soil for the later triumph of Christianity.

Skeptics, Cynics, Stoics and Epicureans

Many Greeks of the post-Classical age turned neither to the old Orphic and Dionysian cults nor to the salvation cults of the Orient but sought to adapt elements of the Hellenic intellectual tradition to the new conditions. One group, the Skeptics, intensified the relativism of the Sophists by denying the possibility of any knowledge whatever, either of gods, man or nature. The human mind, they maintained, is incapable of apprehending reality (if, indeed, there is any such thing as "reality"), and all beliefs and statements of fact are equally unverifiable. Mirroring the profound uncertainty of the new age, the skeptics doubted everything and thus carried rationalism to its ultimate, self-destructive limit—doubting reason itself.

Another group, the Cynics, demonstrated in various forms of eccentric behavior their contempt for conventional piety and patriotism and their rebellion against the hypocrisy that they detected in the lives and attitudes of their contemporaries. Diogenes, the most famous of the Cynics, was something of a fourth-century hippie who sought to live with integrity in a world of phonies. He rejected all official and traditional religions, all participation in civic life, marriage, the public games, and the theater. He ridiculed the prestige that was associated with wealth, power, and reputation and honored instead the simple life of courage, reason and honesty —a life of virtue—which could best be attained by a rejection of civilization and a return to nature. The man of integrity, the wise and honest man, should live like a dog, without pretensions and uncluttered by worldly possessions. Indeed, the very word *cynic* originally meant *canine* or "doglike." So Diogenes wandered the streets begging for his food, a homeless but free man. His bedchamber was a gigantic pitcher outside a temple of the Great

Mother; his latrine was the public street. He obeyed no laws, recognized no polis, and became, next to Alexander, the most illustrious man of his age. He was a colorful symbol of the great Hellenistic withdrawal from the polis into the individual soul.

The same withdrawal is evident in the two religio-ethical systems that emerged in the fourth century and influenced human thought and conduct for centuries thereafter: Stoicism and Epicureanism. Both were philosophies of resignation that taught men to fortify their souls against the harshness of life. Zeno, the founder of the Stoic School, stressed, as the Cynics did, the vanity of worldly things and the supreme importance of individual virtue. Every man, whether statesman, artist, or peasant, should pursue his calling honestly and seriously. The significant thing, however, was not individual effort; such things as politics, art, and husbandry were ultimately valueless, yet in pursuing them as best he could the individual manifested his virtue. Since virtue was all-important, the good Stoic was immune to the vicissitudes of life. He might lose his property; he might even be imprisoned and tortured, but except by his own will he could not be deprived of his virtue which was his only really precious possession. By rejecting the world the Stoic created a citadel within his own soul. Out of this doctrine there emerged a sense not only of individualism but of cosmopolitanism; the idea of the polis faded before the wider (though vaguer) concept of human brotherhood.

Ultimately the Stoic emphasis on virtue was rooted in a lofty cosmic vision based on the Greek conception of a rational, orderly, purposeful universe. The harmonious movements of the stars and planets, the growth of complex plants from simple seeds, all pointed to the existence of a divine plan which was both intelligent and good. We humans were incapable of perceiving the details of the plan as it worked in our own lives, yet by living virtuously and doing our best we could cooperate with it. The God of the universe cared about mankind, and the stern nobility of Stoic ethics was tempered and humanized by this optimistic assurance.

Epicurus, whose school was Stoicism's great rival, differed from Zeno both in his concept of human ethics and in his vision of the universe. He taught that man should seek happiness rather than virtue. Yet happiness to the Epicureans was not the pursuit of sex, liquor, and euphoria, but rather a quiet, balanced life. The life of the drunkard is saddened by countless hangovers, the life of the philanderer by countless complications. Happiness was best achieved not by chasing pleasures but by living simply and unobtrusively, being kind and affectionate to one's friends, learning to endure pain when it comes, and avoiding needless fears. In short, good Epicureans did not differ noticeably from good Stoics in actual behavior, for virtue was the pathway to happiness. But the Epicureans rejected the optimistic Stoic doctrine of divine purpose. Epicurus followed the teachings of the atomists in viewing the universe not as a great hierarchy of cosmic spheres centering on the earth, but as a vast multiplicity of atoms much the same one place as another. Our world is not the handiwork of God, but a chance configuration. The gods, if they exist, care nothing for us, and we ought to draw from this fact the comforting conclusion that we need not fear them.

Epicureanism even more than Stoicism was a philosophy of withdrawal. It was a wise, compassionate teaching that sought to banish fear, curb passions, and dispel illusions. Its doctrine of happiness was too limited and too bland to stir the millions and convert empires, yet through the lofty epic poetry of the Roman writer Lucretius (98–53 B.C.), it made its impact on the intellectual life of Rome. Although never as popular as Stoicism, it gave solace and direction, during the remaining centuries of antiquity, to an influential minority of wise and sensitive men.

Hellenistic Science

In the Hellenistic age, Greek science reached maturity. The naive generalizations of the earlier period gave way to a rigorous and highly creative professionalism. Aristotle's salutary example was followed and improved on by the Hellenistic scientists who collected and sifted data with great thoroughness before framing their hypotheses.

Alexandria was the center of scientific thought in this age. Here the Ptolemies built and subsidized a great research center—the Museum of Alexandria—and collected a library of unprecedented size and diversity containing some half-million papyrus rolls. At Alexandria and elsewhere science and mathematics made rapid strides as Greek rationalism encountered the rich, amorphous heritage of Near Eastern astrology, medical lore, and practical mathematics. The fruitful medical investigations of Hippocrates' school were carried on and expanded by Hellenistic physicians, particularly in Alexandria. Their pioneer work in the dissection of human bodies enabled them to discover the nervous system, to learn a great deal about the brain, heart, and arteries, and to perform successful surgical operations. In mathematics, Euclid organized plane and solid geometry into a systematic, integrated body of knowledge. Archimedes of Syracuse did brilliant original work in both pure and applied mathematics, discovering specific gravity, experimenting successfully with levers and pulleys to lift tremendous weights, and coming very close to the invention of calculus.

The wide-ranging military campaigns of Alexander and the subsequent cultural interchange between large areas of the world led to a vast increase in Greek geographical knowledge. Eratosthenes, the head of the Alexandrian Library in the later third century, produced the most accurate and thorough world maps that had yet been made, complete with lines of longitude and latitude and climatic zones. He recognized that the earth was a sphere and was even able to determine its circumference with an error of less than 1 percent. He did this by measuring the altitude of the sun at different latitudes, calculating from this data the length of one degree of latitude on the earth's surface, and multiplying the result by 360 (degrees).

The same painstaking accuracy and dazzling ingenuity is evident in the work of the Hellenistic astronomers. Aristarchus of Samos suggested that the earth rotated daily on its axis and revolved yearly around the sun. This heliocentric hypothesis is a startling anticipation of modern astronomical conclusions, but Aristarchus' erroneous assumption that the earth's motion around the sun was uniform and circular rendered his system inaccurate. Its failure to explain the precise astronomical observations then being made at Alexandria and its violation of the hallowed doctrine of an earth-centered universe prevented its wide acceptance. Later the great Hellenistic astronomer Hipparchus developed a complex system of circles and subcircles centered on the earth which accounted exceedingly well for the observed motions of the heavenly bodies. Hipparchus' ingenious system, perfected by the Alexandrian astronomer Ptolemy in the second century A.D., represents antiquity's final word on the subject—a comprehensive geometrical model of the universe. It was fundamentally wrong yet it corresponded satisfactorily to the best observations of the day. And it should be remembered that a scientific hypothesis must be judged not by some absolute standard of rightness or wrongness but by its success in accounting for and predicting observed phenomena. By this criterion the Ptolemaic system stands as one of the impressive triumphs of Hellenistic thought.

The Hellenistic Legacy

Greek culture exerted a fundamental influence on the Roman Empire, the Byzantine and Muslim civilizations and medieval Western Europe, but it did so largely in its Hellenistic form. The conclusions of the Hellenistic philosophers and scholars tended to be accepted by the best minds of later ages, but the Hellenistic spirit of free inquiry and intellectual daring was not matched until the sixteenth and seventeenth centuries. There is something remarkably modern about the Hellenistic world with its confident scientists, its cosmopolitanism, its materialism, its religious diversity, its trend toward increasing specialization, its large-scale business activity, and its sense of drift and disorientation. But the Hellenistic social conscience remained dormant, and Hellenistic economic organization, regardless of surface similarities, was vastly different from ours. Like all its Near Eastern predecessors, the Hellenistic economy was based on human slaves rather than on machines (which are our modern slaves). It provided only a tiny fraction of the population with the benefits of its commercial prosperity. The great majority remained servile and illiterate.

Still, the upper classes throughout the Mediterranean world and the Near East were exposed to Greek culture and the Greek language, and the Greeks themselves were deeply influenced by Oriental thought. From Syria, Asia Minor, and the Nile valley to Magna Graecia in the West, a common culture was developing with common ideas and common gods. The way was being paved for the political unification of the Mediterranean world under the authority of Rome, and its spiritual unification under the Christian Church. Alexander's dream of a homogeneous Greco-Oriental world was gradually coming into being. But if Alexander had foreseen the consequences of his work—the conquest of Hellas by an Italian city and an Oriental faith—he might well have chosen to spend his days in seclusion.

Greek Chronology

All Dates B.C.

c.3000–1400:	Minoan civilization
c.1500–1120:	Mycenaean civilization
c.1200:	Trojan war
c.1200–1000:	Dorian invasions
c.1120–800:	"Dark Age"

c.750–550:	Era of colonization
c.650 ff.:	Rise of tyrants
c.594:	Solon reforms Athenian laws
c.582–507:	Pythagoras
561–527:	Pisistratus rules Athens
508:	Cleisthenes reforms Athenian laws
490–479:	Persian Wars
477:	Delian League established
c.460–429:	Era of Pericles
454:	Delian treasury moved to Athens
432:	Parthenon completed
431–404:	Peloponnesian War
469–399:	Socrates
427–347:	Plato
384–322:	Aristotle
359–336:	Reign of Philip of Macedon
338:	Battle of Chaeronea: Philip establishes mastery over Greece
336–323:	Reign of Alexander the Great
323 ff.:	The Hellenistic Age

PART TWO
ROME

FOUR

THE RISE OF ROME: KINGDOM, REPUBLIC, EMPIRE

The rise of Rome from an inconsequential central-Italian village to the mastery of the ancient Mediterranean world is one of history's supreme success stories. The process was slow as compared with the dazzling imperialistic careers of Persia and Macedon, but it was far more lasting. There was nothing meteoric about the serious, hard-headed Romans —they built slowly and well. Their great military virtue was not tactical brilliance but stubborn endurance. They lost battles, but from their beginnings to the great days of the Empire they never lost a war. Since it was they who ultimately provided the ancient world with a viable, encompassing political framework, students of history have always been fascinated by the development of Roman political institutions. Rome's greatest contributions were in the realm of law, government, and imperial organization. In her grasp of political realities lay the secret of her triumphant career.

Republican Rome

Had Alexander lived to middle age instead of dying at thirty-two he might well have led his conquering armies westward into Italy, Sicily and North Africa. Here he would have encountered three vigorous cultures: Carthage, the city-states of Magna Graecia, and the rapidly-expanding republic of Rome. Carthage was originally a Phoenician commercial colony* but its strategic location on the North African coast, just south of Sicily, gave it a stranglehold on the western Mediterranean. It soon developed an extensive commercial empire of its own and far outstripped the Phoenician homeland in power and wealth. Carthage established a number of commercial bases in western Sicily which brought her face-to-face with the Greek city-states that dominated the eastern sections of the island.

The Greek cities of Sicily and southern Italy, known collectively as Magna Graecia, were products of the age of Greek colonization in the eighth and seventh centuries. Their political evolution ran parallel to that of the city-states in Greece. They experienced the same violent struggles between aristocratic, oligarchic, and democratic factions and the same intense cultural creativity. And like Old Greece, Magna Graecia was tormented by incessant intercity warfare. By Alexander's time the Sicilian polis of Syracuse had long been the leading power of the area, but the smaller polises guarded their independence jealously, and real unification was delayed until the Roman conquests of the third century brought these Greek cities under the sway of a common master.

Early Rome

The beginnings of Roman history are obscure. It seems likely that by about 750 B.C. settlers were living in huts on the Palatine Hill near the Tiber River. Gradually, several neighboring hills became inhabited, and around 600 these various settlements joined together to form the city-state of Rome. The strategic position of this cluster of hills, 15 miles inland on one of Italy's few navigable rivers, was of enormous importance to Rome's future growth. Ancient ocean-going ships could sail up the Tiber to Rome but no farther, and

*See p. 21, footnote.

Rome was the lowest point at which the river could be bridged easily. Hence Rome was a key river-crossing and road junction and also, at least potentially, a seaport. It was at the northern limit of a fertile agricultural district known as Latium whose rustic inhabitants, the Latins, gave their name to the Latin language. Immediately north of Rome lay the district of Etruria (the modern Tuscany) whose highly civilized inhabitants, the Etruscans, shaped the culture of the earliest Romans.

The Etruscan ruling class may have migrated to Etruria from Asia Minor around 800 B.C. bringing with it into central Italy important elements of the rich cultural heritage of the eastern Mediterranean and the Near East. The Etruscans borrowed heavily from the Greeks. Their art, their city-state political structure, and their alphabet, were all Hellenic in inspiration, but they adapted these cultural ingredients to their own needs and created out of them a vivacious, pleasure-loving civilization of considerable originality. It was in Etruscan form that Greek civilization made its first impact on Rome. The Romans adopted the Greek alphabet in its Etruscan version and perhaps through Etruscan inspiration

A Chimera, a fine Etruscan bronze.

they organized themselves into a city-state, thereby gaining an inestimable advantage over the numerous half-civilized tribes in the region between Etruria and Magna Graecia. During much of the sixth century, Rome was ruled by kings of Etruscan background whose talented and aggressive leadership made the Romans an important power among the peoples of Latium. The community grew in strength and wealth, and an impressive temple to the Roman god Jupiter was built in Etruscan style atop one of the hills. Rome was becoming a city in fact as well as in name.

About 509 B.C. the Roman aristocracy succeeded in overthrowing its Etruscan king, transforming Rome from a monarchy into an aristocratic republic. The king was replaced by two magistrates known as consuls who were elected annually by an aristocratic Senate and who governed with its advice. The consuls exercised their authority in the name of the Roman people but in the interests of the upper classes. The governing elite was composed of wealthy landowners known as patricians who zealously defended their prerogatives against the encroachments of the common people— the plebeians or plebs. Plebeian-patrician intermarriage was strictly prohibited and for a time the plebeians were almost entirely without political rights.

But step by step the plebeians improved their condition and came to play a significant role in the government. They began by organizing themselves into a deliberative body that later took the form of an important political organ known as the Tribal Assembly. They elected representatives called tribunes to be their spokesmen and represent their interests before the patrician-controlled city government. The tribunes acquired the remarkable power of vetoing anti-plebeian measures issuing from any organ of government, and anyone violating the sanctity of a tribune's person was to be punished by death. Under the leadership of their tribunes, the plebeians were able to act as a unit and to make their strength felt. On at least one occasion they seceded as a body from the Roman state, leaving the patrician governors with nobody to govern and the patrician army officers with no troops to lead.

In about 450 B.C. the Romans took the important step of committing their legal customs to writing. The result was Rome's first law code—the Twelve Tables. By later standards these laws were harsh (defaulting debtors, for example, suffered capital punishment or were delivered up for sale abroad), but they had the effect of protecting individual plebeians from the capricious authority of the patrician consuls. The Twelve Tables are exceedingly significant in Roman constitutional development, constituting as they do the first monument in the evolution of Roman law.

Having gained a measure of legal protection, the plebeians turned to the problem of land distribution and forced the government to grant them additional farms out of its own estates and from the territories of newly-conquered peoples. Gradually the Tribal Assembly of the plebeians acquired the power to initiate legislation and thereby came to play an important part in Roman government. Intermarriage was now allowed between the two classes, and a law of 367 B.C. opened the consulship itself to the plebeians. At the same time, or shortly afterward, it was stipulated that at least one of the two consuls be a plebeian. In the years that followed, plebeians became eligible for all offices of state. Collectively, these measures went far toward transforming Rome into a nominal democracy. This transformation was completed in 287 B.C. when legislation issuing from the Tribal Assembly acquired the force of law without the necessity of being ratified by the aristocratic Senate. The law was now, at least theoretically, in the hands of the people.

In the interest of simplicity and brevity we have not been able to do justice to the extreme complexity of Roman republican government. It included numerous magistrates with various functions and, at one time or another, several different assemblies. The Tribal Assembly, for example, shared power with another important public body: the Centuriate Assembly. Both were made up of the total Roman citizenry, plebeian and patrician alike, but each had its own specific power and function. Moreover, these two Assemblies differed significantly in organization. The Tribal Assembly, the more democratic of the two, was based on tribal or residential districts known as wards. Each ward had one vote, and the poorer rural wards outnumbered the urban ones. But since the patrician wards had the privilege of voting first, most matters had been decided by the time the plebeian wards cast their votes. By this means the patricians were able to limit plebeian political power within the nominally democratic framework.

The Centuriate Assembly, patterned on the organization of the Roman army, was divided into groups know as "centuries." The number of centuries allotted to each class depended on the number of men that class supplied to the army, and since wealth was the basis of Roman military service, the Centuriate Assembly was dominated by the wealthy. Empowered to elect Rome's chief magistrates and to vote on questions of war and peace, the Centuriate

Assembly remained powerful throughout the later years of the Republic. With its wealth-based organization, it further compromised the so-called "democratic" regime that was established in 287.

Roman democracy after 287 was more apparent than real. The domination of the patricians was fading, but it was giving way to a more subtle domination by a wealthy oligarchy of leading plebeian and patrician families. For during the fifth and fourth centuries a number of plebeians had accumulated extensive estates, and many of them now rivaled the patricians in wealth. By being elected to magistracies, many wealthy plebeians gained admission into the Senate which, by the third century, had ceased to be a patrician preserve. Indeed, by 287 the old division between patrician and plebeian was becoming anachronistic. It was replaced by a new division between the poor and the wealthy.* Since more and more wealthy plebeians were gaining admission into the Senate, it is conventional among historians to term the wealthy landholders of the later Republic the "senatorial aristocracy."

The complex machinery of Roman republican government offered many opportunities for the new oligarchy to retain in practice the control that in theory belonged to all the freemen of Rome. By means of political manipulation and patronage, the wealthy made their influence felt in the Tribal Assembly. They had a preponderant voice in the Centuriate Assembly, and they dominated the Senate—which lacked direct legislative power but retained enormous influence and prestige. In short, Rome in 287 was only a paper democracy. In reality, it was a plutocracy—a government of wealthy males—whose policies were controlled by the senatorial aristocracy.

Nevertheless the political realism of the Romans is well illustrated by the fact that the sweeping constitutional changes that took place between the fall of the Etruscan monarchy in 509 B.C. and the legislative supremacy of the Tribal Assembly in 287 B.C. occurred without major insurrections or excessive bloodshed. During these years much Roman blood was spilled on the battlefield but comparatively little on the city's streets. The willingness to settle internal conflicts by compromise—the ability of the patricians to bend before the winds of social change—preserved in Rome a sense of cohesiveness and a spirit of civic commitment without which its conquests would have been inconceivable.

*Women remained without political rights. And at a social level beneath that of the free poor, there existed, as in all ancient societies, a substantial slave class.

The Career of Conquest

Civic commitment was a hallmark of the early Roman. Devoted to the numerous gods of city, field, and hearth, he was hard working, respectful of tradition, obedient to civil and military authority, and dedicated to the welfare of the state. The backbone of Old Rome was the small, independent farmer who worked long and hard to raise crops on his fields and remained always vigilant against raids by tribesmen from surrounding hills. To men such as these life was intensely serious. Their stern sobriety and rustic virtues were exaggerated by Roman moralists looking back nostalgically from a later and more luxurious age, but there can be little doubt that the tenacious spirit and astonishing military success of early republican Rome owed much to the discipline and steadfastness of these citizen-farmers. As triumph followed triumph, as the booty of war flowed into Rome from far and wide, the character of her citizenry inevitably suffered. One of the great tragic themes of Roman history is the gradual erosion of social morality by wealth and power —and by the gradual expansion of huge slave-operated estates at the expense of the small farmer. But long before this process was complete the empire had been won.

The expulsion of the last Etruscan king in 509 B.C. was followed by a period of retrenchment during which the Romans fought for their lives against the attacks of neighboring tribes. In time an alliance was formed between Rome and the communities of Latium in which Rome rose to the position of senior partner. Hostile tribes were subdued after long and agonizing effort, and shortly after 400 B.C. the Etruscan cities began to fall, one by one, under Roman control. The Romans were usually generous with the Italian peoples whom they conquered, allowing them a good measure of internal self-government, and were therefore generally successful in retaining their allegiance. In time, if a conquered people proved loyal, they might hope to be granted Roman citizenship. In this generous fashion Rome was able to construct an empire far more cohesive and durable than that of Periclean Athens. (Neither Pericles nor any of his contemporaries could have conceived of granting citizenship to non-Atticans). Gradually the Roman conquests gained momentum. Battles were often lost—Rome itself was sacked in 387 B.C. by an army of Gauls from the north—but the Romans brushed off their defeats and pressed on. By 265 B.C. all Italy south of the Po Valley was under their control. Etruscan power had collapsed, and even the Italian cities of Magna Graecia acknowledged Roman supremacy. Now, midway through the third century, Rome took its place alongside Carthage and the three great Hellenistic successor states as one of the leading powers of the Mediterranean world.

Carthage and Rome stood face to face, and in 264 B.C. these two great western powers became locked in the first of three savage conflicts known as the Punic Wars (after *Poenus*, the Latin word for Phoenician or Carthaginian). Rome was now forced to build a navy and take to the sea. The wars, especially the first two, were long and bitter. Rome lost numerous battles, scores of ships, and warriors and seamen by the hundreds of thousands. During the Second Punic War (218 to 201 B.C.) the armies of the masterly Carthaginian general Hannibal swept back and forth across Italy winning victory after victory, and only the dogged determination of the Romans and the loyalty of their subject-allies saved the state from extinction. But the Romans hung on, always managing to win the last battle. At the conclusion of the Third Punic War in 146 B.C. Carthage was in ruins, and its far-flung territories in Africa, Sicily, and Spain were in Roman hands.

In the meantime Rome was drawn almost inadvertently into the rivalries among the Hellenistic kingdoms of the eastern Mediterranean. Ptolemaic Egypt, Seleucid Asia, Antigonid Macedon, and the several smaller Greek states had long been at one another's throats; Rome's victories over Carthage increased its power to the point where it was stronger than any one of them. Greek states frequently sought Roman aid against their enemies, and more often than not the Romans gave the requested support in order to maintain the balance of power in the east and to prevent any one Greek kingdom from becoming dangerously strong. Rome entered the Greek world more as a pacifier than as a conquerer, but eventually it tired of its endless task as referee and remained to rule. During the second century almost all the Hellenistic world fell either directly or indirectly under Roman control. Rome won a decisive victory over the Seleucids in 189 B.C.; it conquered Macedon in 168 B.C.; in 146 it demolished the ancient Peloponnesian city of Corinth and transformed Greece into a Roman province under the direct authority of a governor appointed by the Roman state. The remaining Hellenistic kingdoms were now completely overshadowed and had no choice but to bow to Rome's leadership. Gradually they too became provinces.

Rome followed no blueprint for conquest—indeed many of its leaders were isolationists who would have preferred to remain aloof from the Greek east—but the political conditions of the Hellenistic

Two Italian warriors carrying a dead comrade.

states exerted a magnetic attraction that was irresistible. As the second century drew toward its close, Rome was the master of the Mediterranean world. There now arose the baffling problem of adapting a government designed to rule a city-state to the needs of an empire.

Social and Political Changes (264–146 B.C.)

The years of the three Punic Wars witnessed a transformation in the structure and spirit of Rome itself. These changes can be attributed partly to the intoxicating effect of unimagined wealth and military success that gradually undermined the old civic virtue and encouraged a mood of arrogance and materialism. More specifically, as Rome was conquering the Greek world, it was falling increasingly under the influence of Hellenistic culture. Later Roman writers such as Cato and Sallust lamented that Roman soldiers were corrupted by the luxuries of eastern Mediterranean lands. Ultimately, Greece was perhaps the victor after all. The full tide of

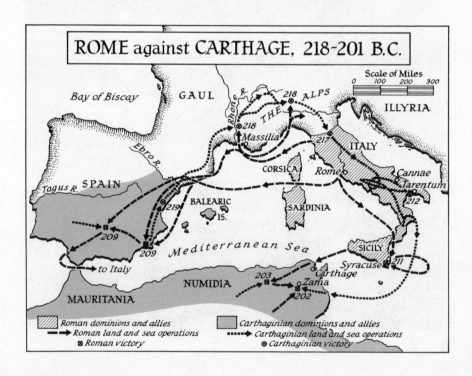

ROME against CARTHAGE, 218-201 B.C.

Scale of Miles
0   100   200   300

Bay of Biscay
GAUL
ILLYRIA
Rhone R.
THE ALPS
218
Massilia
217
ITALY
Ebro R.
CORSICA
Rome
Cannae
Tarentum
Tagus R. SPAIN
219
BALEARIC IS.
SARDINIA
212
209
Mediterranean Sea
SICILY
209
Syracuse
211
to Italy
203
Carthage
Zama
NUMIDIA
202
MAURITANIA

Roman dominions and allies
→ Roman land and sea operations
⊠ Roman victory

Carthaginian dominions and allies
⟶ Carthaginian land and sea operations
⊗ Carthaginian victory

Hellenistic skepticism and individualism, which had earlier done so much to dissolve the Greek polis, now began its corrosive work on Roman conservatism and civic dedication. As in Greece, the effects of this process were both good and bad. What Rome lost in civic virtue it gained in cultural and intellectual depth, for prior to its Hellenization, Rome was almost totally lacking in high culture. The Stoic notion of universal brotherhood was a singularly appropriate philosophy for a great empire, and it was a fortunate thing for the conquered peoples that in later years so many Roman statesmen became Stoics. But with Greek art, literature, and learning came the disquieting Hellenistic feeling of drift and alienation, aggravated by the importation of Hellenistic agricultural techniques.

The great Hellenistic successor states had emphasized the large plantation over the small independent farm, and now, as the conquests brought vast wealth and hordes of slaves into the hands of the Roman upper classes, most of central and southern Italy was converted into huge farms known as *latifundia*, worked by slaves and operated according to the latest Hellenistic techniques of large-scale scientific farming. Where the small farms had produced grain, the *latifundia* concentrated on the more lucrative production of wine and olive oil or the raising of sheep. The small farmers, whose energy and devotion had built the Roman Empire, were subjected to such heavy military demands that they found it increasingly difficult to maintain their farms. Many sold out to the *latifundia* owners and flocked into the cities, especially Rome itself, where they were joined by masses of penniless immigrants from the provinces and transformed into a chronically unemployed, irresponsible mob. In later years their riots terrorized the government. Their hunger and boredom eventually gave rise to the custom of subsidized food and free entertainment of an increasingly sadistic sort—"bread and circuses."

While Rome was engaged in its struggle with Carthage, important changes were occurring in the social structure of the Roman ruling elite. With the acceleration of commerce, a new class of businessmen and public contractors was developing that in time acquired such wealth as to rival the landed senatorial aristocracy. This new class came to be known as the equestrian order because the wealth of its members enabled them to serve in the Roman army as cavalry rather than infantry. The equestrian class was effectively excluded from the Senate. Fundamentally apolitical except in instances when its own interests were at stake, it was content to share with the senatorial aristocracy the rising living standards that were coming into Rome with military triumphs and increased contact with the Hellenistic world. As the equestrians and landed nobility came to live in increasing luxury, the gap between rich and poor steadily widened, and the pressures of social unrest began to threaten the traditional stability of Roman civilization.

Meanwhile the Roman government, which had earlier acted with restraint toward its subject allies in Italy, was proving itself incapable of governing justly its newly acquired overseas territories. Most of Rome's non-Italian holdings were organized as provinces ruled by aristocratic Roman governors and exploited by Roman tax gatherers. Infected with the selfishness and greed of Hellenistic individualism at its worst, governor and tax gatherer often worked in cruel partnership to bleed the provinces for personal advantage. The grossest kinds of official corruption were tolerated by the Roman courts of law whose aristocratic judges hesitated to condemn dishonest officials of their own class for the sake of oppressed but alien provincials. Indeed, some provincial governors made it a practice to set aside a portion of their booty to bribe the courts.

The Capitoline wolf symbol of Rome.

Violence and Revolutions: The Last Century of the Republic

The deep-seated problems that afflicted Rome brought about a century-long period of violence and unrest, between 133 and 30 B.C., which resulted ultimately in the downfall of the Republic and the advent of a new imperial government. The first steps toward revolution were taken by two aristocratic reformers, the brothers Tiberius and Gaius Gracchus, who advocated a series of popular reform measures and thereby built up a powerful faction among the Roman commoners who were struggling against the entrenched aristocracy of wealth. Tiberius Gracchus served as tribune in 133 B.C., and Gaius held the same office a decade later. The two Gracchi were deeply concerned with the ominous course of the Republic. Both recognized that the decline in able recruits for the Roman army and the deterioration of morale among the citizenry were caused by the virtual elimination of the small farm from central Italy. Their solution was to create out of the vast public lands owned by the Roman state a large number of new farms for the dispossessed. This was a courageous and compassionate program, but the virtuous Roman farmer of yesteryear could not be conjured back into existence at this late moment. As it happened, most of the public lands had long before fallen under the effective control of powerful members of the senatorial aristocracy. These wealthy men, long accustomed to farming state lands for their own profit, reacted frigidly to the proposal that they should now give up portions of these lands so that the state might create small farms for the impoverished. In the political holocaust that followed, both Gracchi were murdered—Tiberius in 133, Gaius in 121. The senatorial aristocracy demonstrated that, despite past concessions, it was still in control. But it also betrayed its political and moral bankruptcy. Violence had been introduced into Roman political affairs, and the whirlwind now unleashed was to buffet the Republic for a century and finally demolish it.

For a generation the lower classes continued to press for the Gracchan reforms, and the senatorial aristocracy found itself pitted not only against the masses but sometimes against the equestrian order as well. But the great political fact of the last republican century was the rise of individual adventurers who sought to use successful military careers as springboards to political power. During the decade of the eighties, two able military commanders, Marius and Sulla, contended against one another for political supremacy. Marius drew much of his support from the lesser classes, whereas Sulla tended to ally with the wealthier and more established, but both were motivated strongly by personal ambition. In 106 B.C. Marius had taken the portentous step of abolishing the property qualification for military service and recruiting volunteers from the poorest classes. Prior to Marius' reform, the resources of Roman military manpower had been declining alarmingly, but now the jobless masses thronged into the legions. Military service became, for many, the avenue to economic security, since soldiers of a successful and politically influential general could often expect to receive on retirement a gift of land from the Senate. The army began to acquire a more professional outlook than before, and soldiers came to identify themselves with their commanders rather than with the state. The opportunities for a ruthless and ambitious general with a loyal army at his back were limitless. But Marius was unwilling to go so far as to seize and overthrow the government. The more ruthless Sulla had no such scruples. In 83 B.C. he marched on Rome with his own devoted legions and, in the following year, made himself dictator. Once in power, he purged his enemies and proscribed a number of wealthy citizens, enriching himself from their confiscated fortunes. But Sulla had no intention of holding power indefinitely. A conservative at heart, he employed his dictatorial prerogatives to establish a series of laws that confirmed and strengthened the power of the inept Senate, then retired to affluent private life on his country estate in Campania, leaving the Republic to stagger on.

In the decade of the sixties, the great senatorial orator Cicero strove desperately to unite senators and equestrians against the growing threat of the generals and the riotous urban masses. Cicero's consummate mastery of Latin style, both in his orations and in his writings, earned him a lofty position in the field of Roman literature, but his political talents proved inadequate to the task of saving the Republic. His dream of reconciling the interests of senators and equestrians was shattered by the selfishness of each, and his efforts to perpetuate the traditional supremacy of the Senate were doomed by the Senate's own incapacity, by the smoldering unrest of the city mobs, and by the ambition of the military commanders. It was Cicero's misfortune to be a conservative in an epoch of revolutionary turbulence—a statesman in an age of generals.

Chronology of the Roman Republic

All Dates B.C.

753:	Traditional date for Rome's founding
c.616–509:	Etruscan kings rule Rome
c.450:	Twelve Tables
367:	Plebeians eligible for consulship
287:	Loss of senate's veto power over Tribal Assembly legislation
	Rome becomes a paper democracy
265:	Rome controls all Italy south of the Po
264–241:	First Punic War
218–201:	Second Punic War
149–146:	Third Punic War
146:	Macedonia becomes Roman province
133:	Tribunate of Tiberius Gracchus
123–122:	Tribunate of Gaius Gracchus
121:	Gaius Gracchus killed
106:	Marius reorganizes military recruitment
83–80:	Sulla reestablishes republican constitution
60–44:	Caesar a dominant force in Roman politics
43:	Cicero killed

The Republic was now approaching its final days in at atmosphere of chaos and naked force. The dominant political figures of Cicero's generation were military commanders such as Pompey and Julius Caesar, who bid against one another for the backing of the lower classes, seeking to convert mob support into political supremacy. Characteristically, the three great men of their age, Pompey, Cicero, and Caesar, all met violent deaths. The utter failure of republican government was now manifest, and the entire imperial structure seemed on the verge of collapse. As it turned out, however, Rome was to emerge from her crisis transformed and strengthened, and her empire was to endure for another 500 years.

Julius Caesar and Augustus

The new order, which saved Rome from the agonies of the late Republic and brought a long era of peace and stability to the mediterranean world, was chiefly the handiwork of two men: Julius Caesar and his grand-nephew, Octavian, later called Augustus. Julius Caesar was a man of many talents—a superb general, a brilliant and realistic politician, an inspiring leader, and a distinguished man of letters whose lucid and forthright *Commentaries on the Gallic Wars* was a significant contribution to the great literary surge of the late Republic. Above all, Caesar was a man of reason who could probe to the heart of any problem, work out a logical, practical solution, and then carry his plan to realization.

Caesar managed to ride the whirlwind of violence and ruthless ambition that was shattering Roman society during the mid-first century B.C. His political intuition and unswerving faith in himself and his star catapulted him to increasingly important political and military offices during the turbulent sixties. Opposed and distrusted by the conservative Senate led by the great orator Cicero, he allied himself with Pompey, a talented, disgruntled general, and Crassus, an ambitious millionaire. These three formed an extralegal coalition of political bosses, known to later historians as the "First Triumvirate," which succeeded in dominating the Roman state.

Leaving Italy in the hands of his two colleagues, Caesar spent most of the following decade (58–50 B.C.) in Gaul leading his army on a spectacular series of campaigns that resulted in the conquest of what is now France and Belgium and established his reputation as one of history's consummate military scientists. Caesar's conquest of Gaul pushed the influence of Rome far northward from the Mediterranean into the heartland of western Europe. The historical consequences of his victories were immense, for in the centuries that followed, Gaul was thoroughly Romanized. The Roman influence survived the later barbarian invasions to give medieval and modern France a romance tongue* and to provide western Europe with an enduring Greco-Roman cultural heritage.

While Caesar was winning his triumphs in Gaul his interests in Italy were suffering. His advocacy of land redistribution and of other policies dear to the hearts of the lower classes earned him the hostility of the Senate, and his spectacular military success threatened to thwart Pompey's own ambition to be first among Romans. Out of their common fear of Caesar, Pompey and the Senate now joined forces, and in 49 B.C. Caesar was declared a public enemy. His career at stake, Caesar defied the Roman constitution by leading his own loyal army into Italy. In a series of dazzling campaigns during 49 and 48 B.C., he defeated Pompey and the hostile members of the Senate. Pompey fled to Egypt and was murdered there,

---

*I.e., a language derived from Latin.

Caesar the Dictator.

and the Senate had no choice but to come to terms with the man who now towered unchallenged over Rome.

Caesar was a magnanimous victor. He restored his senatorial opponents to their former positions and ordered the execution of Pompey's murderer. He could afford to be generous, for he was now the unquestioned master of the state. The Republic had traditionally, in time of grave crisis, concentrated all power in the hands of a dictator who was permitted to exercise his virtually unlimited jurisdiction for six months only. Caesar assumed the office of dictator and held it year after year. Ultimately he forced the Senate to grant him the dictatorship for life. He also acquired the personal inviolability of the tribune and assumed several other key republican offices. Besides all these, he retained the title of *pontifex maximus* (supreme pontiff or chief priest of the civic religion), which he had held for some years. In 44 B.C. he was more-or-less deified: a temple was dedicated to his genius—the spirit of his family or clan—and the month of July was named in his honor. Most of the political institutions of the Republic survived, but they were now under his thumb. He controlled the appointment of magistrates, manipulated the assemblies, and overawed the Senate. The whole Roman electorate had become his clients.

Caesar used his power to reform the Republic along logical, realistic lines. The magnitude of his reforms defies description. He introduced a radically new calendar that, with one minor adjustment, is in almost universal use today. He organized numerous distant colonies that drained off a considerable number of Rome's unemployed masses, and halved the Roman bread dole. He did much to reform and rationalize Italian and provincial government and to purge the republican administration of its abuses. In short, he was the model of what would much later be called an "enlightened despot." Some historians have supposed that Caesar was aiming at a monarchy along Hellenistic lines, but it is more accurate to view him as a supremely talented Roman applying his intellect to the rational solution of Roman problems.

Caesar's remarkable success attests to the creative power of the human mind. His ultimate failure, however, suggests that in human affairs reason is not always enough—that the ingrained historical traditions of a people will resist the surgery of even the most skillful rationalist reformer. Caesar's reforms were immensely beneficial to the people of the Empire, but he went too far too fast. His disregard for republican institutions was too cavalier, and his assumption of the dictatorship for life alarmed powerful elements in the

Senate. On the Ides of March (March 15), 44 B.C., he was stabbed to death at a Senate meeting by a group of conservative senatorial conspirators led by Brutus and Cassius. As they rushed from the Senate the assassins shouted, "Tyranny is dead!" They were wrong: it was the Republic that was dead, and Rome now had only the choice between one-man rule and anarchy. By killing Caesar, they had given up the former for the latter.

Caesar's assassination resulted in fourteen more years of civil strife during which the conservative party of Brutus and Cassius struggled against would-be heirs to Caesar's power while the heirs struggled against one another. In the complex maneuvers of this civil war some of the most famous figures in ancient history played out their roles. Mark Antony, Caesar's lieutenant, defeated Brutus and Cassius in battle, and both committed suicide. The golden tongued Cicero, Rome's supreme literary craftsman, was murdered for his hostility to Antony. And when the fortunes of war turned against them, Antony and his exotic wife, Queen Cleopatra of Egypt, took their own lives. The ultimate victor in these struggles was a young man who had been almost unknown at the time of Caesar's death. Octavian, the later Augustus, Caesar's grand-nephew and adopted son, had woven his way through the era of strife with matchless skill. A young man of eighteen when Caesar died, Octavian proved to the world that he was in truth Caesar's heir. For although inferior to Caesar in generalship and perhaps also in sheer intellectual strength, Octavian was Caesar's superior as a realistic, practical politician. During his long, illustrious reign Octavian completed the transformation of the Roman state from republic to empire. But his reforms were more traditionalist in spirit than Caesar's, and he succeeded—where Caesar had failed—in winning the Senate's respect. He reformed the Romans and made them like it.

The Augustan Age

In 31 B.C. Octavian's forces crushed those of Antony and Cleopatra at Actium. A year later Octavian entered Alexandria as master of the Mediterranean world. He was then the same age as Alexander at the time of his death, and it might be supposed that the two world-conquerors, both young, brilliant, and handsome, had much in common. But Octavian refused to visit Alexander's tomb in Alexandria, observing, so it was said, that true greatness lies not in conquest but in reconstruction. It is appropriate, therefore, that Octavian's immense historical reputation lies not in his military victories —which were won by his generals rather than himself—but in his accomplishments as peacemaker and architect of the Roman Empire.

The reformation of Rome, completed by Octavian, gave the Mediterranean world two centuries of almost uninterrupted peace and prosperity during which classical culture developed and spread to the outermost reaches of the Empire. This unprecedented achievement caused men, in the turbulent centuries that followed, to look back longingly at the almost legendary epoch of the "Roman Peace." Octavian accomplished the seemingly impossible task of reconciling the need for one-man rule with the republican traditions of Old Rome. He preserved the Senate; indeed, increased its prestige. He retained the elected republican magistracies. He made no attempt to revive the office of dictator, for he preferred to manipulate the government in more subtle ways. He controlled the army and, like Caesar, he concentrated various key republican offices and powers in his own person—*pontifex maximus*, consul, the authority of the tribunes, and others. In 27 B.C. he was given the novel name of Augustus, a term that carried with it no specific power, but had a connotation of reverence—almost holiness. And like Caesar he was honored by having a month (August) named in his honor. It is characteristic of his philosophy of government, however, that Augustus preferred the relatively modest title of *princeps* or "first citizen." He was the leading Roman—nothing more. He lived relatively modestly, associated freely with his fellow citizens, revered the dignity of the Senate, and dressed and ate simply. It has been said that the Roman Principate (the government of the princeps) was the mirror opposite of the government of modern England; the former a monarchy with republican trappings, the latter a republic with monarchical trappings. But if the Principate was at heart a monarchy, it was by no means an arbitrary one. Augustus ruled with a keen sensitivity toward popular and senatorial opinion and a respect for traditions.

Still, Augustus was the true master of Rome. The nature of the Empire was such that the liberty of the old Republic simply could not be preserved. The Roman electorate was incapable of governing the Empire, and a democratic empire with universal suffrage was inconceivable. Roman liberty was the single great casualty of the Principate, but its loss was rendered almost painless by the political deftness of the first *princeps*. In its place Augustus provided

The Emperor Augustus.

peace, security, prosperity, and justice. The administration of the provinces was now closely regulated by the *princeps,* and the gross corruption and exploitation of the late Republic were reduced. In Rome itself an efficient imperial bureaucracy developed which was responsible to the *princeps* alone. Although class distinction remained strong, it was now possible for an able man from one of the lower classes to rise in the government service, and men with literary and artistic gifts were sought out and supported by Augustus as a matter of policy.

The stable new regime, the promise of enduring peace, the policy of "careers open to talent," and the leadership of Augustus himself combined to evoke a surge of optimism, patriotism, and creative originality. In the field of arts and letters the "Augustan Age" is the climax of Roman creative genius, surpassing even the literary brilliance of the troubled late Republic of which Cicero stands as the supreme example. Under Augustus, Roman artists and poets achieved a powerful synthesis of Greek and Roman elements. Roman architecture was obviously modeled on the Greek, but it just as obviously expressed a distinctively Roman spirit. Roman temples rose higher than those of classical Greece and conveyed a feeling that was less serene—more imposing and dynamic. Augustan poetry —the urbane and faultless lyrics of Horace, the worldly erotic verses of Ovid, the majestic cadences of Virgil—employed Greek models and ideas in original and characteristically Roman ways. Rome's supreme poem, Virgil's *Aeneid,* was cast in the epic form of Homer and dealt, as Homer's *Odyssey* did, with the voyage of an important figure in the Trojan War. But Aeneas, Virgil's hero, was also the legendary founder of Rome, and the poem is shot through with patriotic prophecies regarding the great destiny of the state which Aeneas was to found. Indeed, some readers have seen in Aeneas a symbol of Augustus himself. The *Aeneid* also contains a compassionate humanitarian strain lacking in Homer but evident in the enlightened policies of Augustus and his successors—especially the emperors of the second century. Above all, there is the feeling of hope that the Roman people—founded by Aeneas, and now led by the great peacemaker Augustus—have at last fulfilled their mission to bring enduring concord and justice to the long-tormented world:

> *But Rome! 'tis thine alone, with awful sway,*
> *To rule mankind, and make the world obey,*

Augustan art and propaganda, a detail from the Altar of Peace, symbolizing the fertility of Italy.

> *Disposing peace and war thine own majestic way;*
> *To tame the proud, the fetter'd slave to free:*
> *These are imperial arts, and worthy thee.**

Imperial Leadership after Augustus

Augustus died at the age of 76 in A.D. 14. During the decades following his death, the Principate grew steadily more centralized and more efficient. The imperial bureaucracy expanded, the provinces were reasonably well governed, taxes were relatively light and intelligently assessed, the law became increasingly humane, and the far-flung inhabitants of the Empire enjoyed unprecedented peace and prosperity. It is a tribute to Augustus's wisdom that the system

---

Aeneid, Book VI (tr. John Dryden). Rome did not, in fact, bring an end to ancient slavery.

that he created was sturdy enough to endure and flourish despite the relative incapacity of many of his imperial successors. The abilities of the first-century emperors ranged from uninspired competence to downright madness, descending on occasion to the vainglorious absurdity of a Nero or the grotesque lunacy of a Caligula, who wallowed in the pleasure of watching his prisoners being tortured to death. Caligula is reported to have allowed his favorite horse to dine at the imperial table during formal state dinners, consuming the finest food and wines from jeweled dishes and goblets. At Caligula's death he was on the point of raising the beast to the office of consul. Caligula and Nero were autocrats of the worst type, and both were removed violently from power. On the whole, however, the emperors of the early Principate retained the traditional "constitutional" attitudes exemplified by Augustus himself.

The second century A.D. witnessed a dramatic improvement in the quality of imperial leadership. Rome's rulers between A.D. 96 and 180 have been called the "five good emperors." One nineteenth-century historian described them in these words: "For eighty-four years a series of sovereigns, the best, the wisest and the most statesmanlike that the world has even seen—Nerva, Trajan, Hadrian, Antoninus, Marcus Aurelius—sat upon the throne of the world."* And although more recent historians would look askance at such sweeping praise, there can be no question that the "five good emperors" were sovereigns of rare ability.

The high level of imperial leadership that characterized this era can be attributed largely to the temporary solving of one of the knottiest dilemmas in the whole imperial system—the problem of succession. In theory the Senate chose the *princeps*, but in fact the succession usually fell to a close relative of the previous emperor and was often arranged by the emperor in advance. Too often this hereditary principle allowed the Empire to fall into the hands of an unworthy ruler; occasionally a disputed succession was settled by violence and even civil war. But none of the great second-century emperors—Trajan, Hadrian, Antoninus Pius, or Marcus Aurelius— came to power by normal hereditary succession. In each case, the previous emperor *adopted* as his son and successor a younger man of outstanding ability. The policy of adoption worked well for a time, but it did not represent a deliberate rejection of the hereditary

*Thomas Hodgkin, *The Dynasty of Theodosius* (Oxford, 1889), p. 18.

The Emperor Hadrian.

succession principle. It was simply a consequence of the fact that
none of the "five good emperors" had a son except Marcus Aurelius
—the last of them. Marcus followed the hereditary principle—which
had never consciously been abandoned—and chose his own son, the
incompetent Commodus, as his heir. With the disastrous reign of
Commodus (A.D. 180–192) the great age of imperial rule came to
an end. It was followed by a century of military despotism, assas-
sinations, economic and administrative breakdown, cultural decay,
and civil strife which almost brought an end to the Roman state.

Atlantic

Ocean

PICTS

Antonine Wall

North

Hadrian's
Wall

HIBERNIA

Sea

Baltic Sea

BRITAIN

London

12 B.C. to 9 A.D.

GERMANIA

Cologne

GERMANS

Rhine R.

Danube R.

Vienna

Loire R.

GAUL

RAETIA

NORICUM

Lyons

PANNONIA

PYRENEES

Po R.

ILLYRICUM

SPAIN

Marseilles

TUSCANS

Adriatic Sea

Cannae

Rome

CORSICA

I
T
A
L
Y

LATINS

BALEARIC IS.

SARDINIA

Naples

Tarentum

MAC

GREEKS

Actium

Mediter

SICILY

Syracuse

MAURETANIA

Carthage

Zama

ran

NUMIDIA

AFRICA

Scale of Miles

0   200   400   600   800   1000

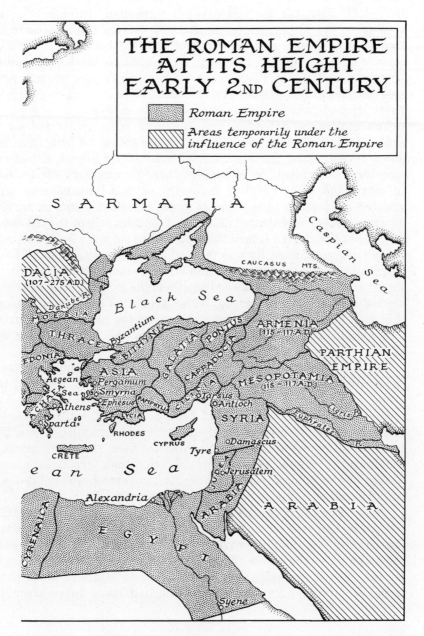

THE ROMAN EMPIRE
AT ITS HEIGHT
EARLY 2ND CENTURY

Roman Empire

Areas temporarily under the
influence of the Roman Empire

SARMATIA

Caspian Sea

CAUCASUS MTS.

DACIA
(107–275 A.D.)

Danube R.

Black Sea

MOESIA

THRACE

Byzantium

BITHYNIA

ARMENIA
(115–117 A.D.)

PARTHIAN
EMPIRE

MACEDONIA

ASIA

GALATIA

PONTUS

CAPPADOCIA

MESOPOTAMIA
(115–117 A.D.)

Aegean

Pergamum

Tigris R.

Sea

Smyrna

CILICIA

Tarsus

Euphrates R.

Athens

Ephesus

Pamphylia

Antioch

Sparta

LYCIA

SYRIA

RHODES

CYPRUS

Damascus

CRETE

Tyre

ean

Sea

Jerusalem

ARABIA

Alexandria

ARABIA

CYRENAICA

EGYPT

Syene

The Empire under the Principate

Before moving into the troubled third century, let us look briefly at the condition of the Empire at its height. During the two centuries from the rise of Augustus to the death of Marcus Aurelius (31 B.C.–A.D. 180), the Empire expanded gradually to include a vast area from the Euphrates to the Atlantic—from the Sahara to the Danube, the Rhine, and the Cheviot Hills of northern Britain. A considerable amount of territory was added to the Empire under Augustus, and several later emperors, notably Trajan, made impressive conquests. But most of the emperors were content to guard the frontiers and preserve what had earlier been won.

The burden of defending the far-flung frontiers rested on an army of some 300,000 to 500,000 men, organized on principles laid down by Augustus. Infantry legions manned by Roman citizens on long-term enlistments were supplemented by auxiliary forces, both infantry and light cavalry, made up of non-Romans who were granted citizenship at the end of their extended terms of service. The army was concentrated along the frontiers except for the small, privileged Praetorian Guard that served the emperor in Rome itself. A high degree of mobility was insured by the superb system of roads which connected the city of Rome with its most remote provinces. Paved with stones fitted closely together, these roads were nearly as eternal as the city they served. Although built for military reasons, they eased the flow of commerce as well as the movement of troops and remained in use many centuries after the Roman Peace was shattered by anarchy and barbarian invasions.

The Empire's greatest commercial artery was not built of stone; it was the Mediterranean, completely surrounded by imperial territory and referred to affectionately by the Romans as *Mare Nostrum*—"our sea." Strong Roman fleets patrolled the Mediterranean and kept it free of pirates for the first time in antiquity, permitting peaceful shipping to move unimpeded between the many ports of the Empire. Now as never before the immense territories encompassed by the Roman frontiers were well governed, well policed, and bound together by roads and protected seaways.

Under the aegis of the Roman Peace, commercial prosperity, Roman institutions, and classical culture spread far and wide across the Empire. As distant provinces became increasingly Romanized the meaning of the words "Rome" and "Roman" gradually changed. By the time of Augustus these terms were no longer confined to the imperial city and its inhabitants but had come to embrace the greater part of Italy. Now, as the decades of the Roman Peace followed one another, citizenship was progressively extended to more and more provincials until finally, in A.D. 212, every free inhabitant of the Empire was made a citizen. Emperors themselves now tended, as often as not, to be provincials: the great second-century emperor Trajan, for example, was a native of Spain. In time the terms "Rome" and "Romans" acquired a universal connotation: a Greek monarch in Constantinople, a Frankish monarch at Aachen, a Saxon monarch in Germany, a Hapsburg in Vienna could, in later centuries, all refer to themselves as "Roman emperors."

The most conspicuous effect of this process of diffusion was the urbanization of the entire Empire. The city-state, the characteristic political phenomenon of the Greco-Roman world, now spread through the outer provinces—into Gaul, Spain, the lands along the Rhine and Danube, even remote Britain. The city still retained much local self-government and normally controlled the rural territories in its vicinity. In other words, the city was the key unit of local administration—the government of the Roman state remained fundamentally urban. Paradoxically, the cities of the Empire, especially in the west, were of relatively minor importance as commercial and manufacturing centers. Rome experienced no significant industrial expansion and, although small-scale urban industry often flourished, chiefly in the east, the economy of the Empire remained fundamentally agrarian. Many of the western cities—including Rome itself—consumed far more than they produced and acted as parasites on the imperial economy. Basically they were administrative and military centers whose mercantile significance was secondary. During the first two centuries of the Empire the economy was prosperous enough to support them, but this would not always be the case. In time the cities would decline, and with them the whole political structure of the Greco-Roman world.

In the early Empire, as in the late Republic, slaves played a crucial role in the economy, especially in agriculture. But as the frontiers gradually ceased to expand and the flow of war captives diminished, the chief source of slaves was cut off. Large landholders now began to lease major portions of their estates to free sharecroppers called *coloni* who tended to fall more and more under the control of their landlords and sank slowly to a semiservile status akin to that of the medieval serfs. The *coloni*, like the impoverished masses who continued to crowd the larger cities, enjoyed little of the buoyant prosperity of the Principate. The age of the "five good emperors" was, by ancient standards, an epoch of material well-being, but it would be absurd to compare it to the abundance of the advanced industrial states of today. Roman society always included, beneath its veneer, a vast, wretched substratum of half-starved peasants and paupers.

The condition of the lower classes would have been still worse but for the humane policies of the imperial government. It was especially among the great second-century emperors that Stoic attitudes of human brotherhood, compassion, and social and political responsibility took hold. Unlike Caligula and Nero, who used their power to indulge their bizarre whims, emperors such as Hadrian and Marcus Aurelius viewed their authority as a trust, a responsibility to govern in the interests of the people whether rich or poor. The Empire of the second century is ornamented by its social conscience no less than by its leadership in military and administrative affairs.

The Silver Age

The cultural epoch from approximately the death of Augustus to the death of Marcus Aurelius is known as the Silver Age. Less illustrious than the golden Augustan Age, it nevertheless produced literary, intellectual, and artistic accomplishments of the first order. Some observers have seen in Silver Age writers such as the Stoic playwright Seneca, the satirist Lucian, and the biographer Plutarch, a decline in creative genius. They have stressed the stale conformity of second-century Roman art and literature resulting from the absence of genuine freedom, the "homogenization" of culture, and the dullness of peace and security. Such judgments are necessarily relative, and many sensitive spirits through the centuries have viewed writers of the Silver Age with enormous admiration.

Whatever one may think of the originality and excellence of Silver Age literature, there can be no question but that culture and learning spread outward and downward. Remote provincial cities built temples and baths, theaters and triumphal arches in the Roman style. Libraries and schools were scattered abundantly across the Empire, and the extent of urban literacy is demonstrated by the many irreverent and obscene scribblings and campaign slogans discovered by modern excavators on the buildings of Pompeii, buried and preserved by the eruption of Vesuvius in A.D. 79.

Alexandria, the Hellenistic metropolis, retained its commercial and intellectual importance throughout the age of the Principate, producing some of the most brilliant early Christian theologians as well as several distinguished scientists who developed and synthesized the achievements of earlier Hellenistic science. Greek and Hellenistic astronomical thought, for example, was developed into a sophisticated and comprehensive model of the universe by Ptolemy of Alexandria (*d.* about A.D. 180) who expanded the work of his predecessors into a geocentric world-system that accounted, with remarkable precision, for the observed motions of the sun, moon, and planets among the stars.* Ptolemy also wrote the most complete geography of antiquity, and Galen (A.D. 131–201), a great medical scientist from Hellenistic Pergamum, produced a series of works on biology and medicine that dominated these fields for more than a thousand years. The *Meditations* of Marcus Aurelius, the last of the "five good emperors," is a moving expression of the Stoic philosophy that deepened and humanized so much of the best thought of the era. In literature and art, science and philosophy, the Silver Age produced an effortless synthesis of Greek and Roman traditions. The rich legacies of Greece, Rome, and the ancient Orient were summarized and fused into a coherent whole.

*See above, p. 79.

FIVE

ROME
AND
JERUSALEM

Roman Law

Of all the achievements of this epoch perhaps the most far-reaching—certainly the most distinctively Roman—was the development of imperial law. The rigid code of the Twelve Tables was gradually broadened and humanized by the magistrates of the later Republic and early Empire, by the great legists of the second and third centuries A.D., and by the enlightened intervention of the emperors themselves. As the Romans became acquainted with more and more peoples, each with its unique set of laws and customs, they gradually emancipated themselves from the peculiarities of their own law and strove to replace it by a body of fundamental principles drawn from the laws of all people. The *Jus Gentium* or "law of peoples" slowly transformed the Roman code into a legal system suitable to a vast, heterogeneous empire.

The evolution of Roman law into a

universal system of jurisprudence owed something also to the Greek concept of the *Jus Naturale*—the "law of nature"—which has played a prominent role in the history of Western thought. More abstract than the *Jus Gentium*, the "law of nature" or "natural law" is based on the belief that in a divinely ordered world there are certain universal norms of human behavior which all people tend to follow, regardless. These norms, based on considerations of political and social justice, served to rationalize and humanize the law of the Empire and to provide it with a sturdy philosophical foundation. Accordingly, Roman law, a product of the Latin practical political genius influenced by Greek speculative thought, gave substance to the Augustan ideal of justice. Codified at enormous effort by the sixth-century emperor Justinian, it has become a crucial part of the Western heritage—the basis of many legal systems to this day in Europe and its former colonies.

Roman Religion

Roman religion is immensely complex, for the Romans not only recognized many gods but had numerous separate cults. Like the Greek city-states, Rome had its official civic deities—Jupiter and Juno, Minerva and Mars, and many others, who by the later Republic had become identified with parallel gods of the Greek Olympic religion. The Roman Jupiter was the Greek Zeus, the Roman Minerva was the Greek Athena, and so on. Besides these Roman state deities there were the innumerable local gods of the myriad cities and districts of the Empire. And in Rome itself as well as throughout the Empire there were countless unofficial cults that normally enjoyed the toleration of the Roman state. None of these pagan cults was exclusive; none claimed a monopoly on truth, and a single individual might without compromise associate himself with several of them.

With the coming of the Principate an important new element was added to the state religion: the cult of the emperor. Augustus, like Julius Caesar, had been honored by the deification and worship of his "Genius," and both Augustus and his successors (with a few notorious exceptions) were deified by the Senate after their deaths. In those provinces where god-kings were traditional, the *princeps* was viewed as a deity while still alive, and it soon became customary for Romans and provincials alike to participate in formal religious observances to the deified emperors as well as to the major deities of the city of Rome. These observances were at heart more patriotic than religious. They were useful in encouraging the allegiance of diverse peoples and, in accordance with religious attitudes of the day, few objected to the addition of a handful of new deities to the divine crowd that they already worshiped. To the Jews, and later the Christians, these religio-patriotic observances were another matter, for the "jealous" God of the Jews permitted the worship of no other. But Rome recognized the Jews as a people apart and usually excused them from participation in the official cults. The Christians, on the other hand, suffered gravely from their refusal to worship the emperors and gods of Rome. To the Romans such intransigence savored of both atheism and treason. It is no accident that Christianity alone of all the religions of the Empire was the object of serious Roman persecution.

The Mystery Cults

The centuries after Augustus witnessed a slow but fundamental shift in Roman religious attitudes, from the veneration of the traditional gods of household, clan, and city to the worship of transcendental deities imported from the Near East. The gods of Old Rome, like those of the Greek Olympus, had safeguarded the welfare of social and political groups; the new gods offered instead the hope of individual redemption, salvation, and eternal life. As the Roman imperial age progressed, the allegiance of the people slowly shifted from Jupiter and Minerva to the Egyptian Isis, the Persian Mithras, the Phrygian Great Mother, the Syrian Sun god, and other exotic deities who offered solace and eternal joy to people for whom the world was not enough—even the world of the Roman Peace.

This surge of mysticism was actually a continuation and expansion of a trend we have already observed among the Hellenistic Greeks. The same forces that had encouraged the widespread rootlessness and disorienteation of the Hellenistic world were now at work throughout the Roman Empire: cosmopolitanism, gradually increasing autocracy and, among the underprivileged masses, grinding poverty and loss of hope. The shift from civic god to savior god, from this world to the next, constitutes a profound transformation in mood—a repudiation of traditional Greco-Roman humanism. As the peace of the second century gave way to the anarchy of the third, the high hopes of classical humanism—the dream of a ra-

The god Mithras sacrifices the heavenly bull.

tional universe, an ideal republic, a good life—were beginning to seem like cruel illusions, and the movement toward the mystery cults gained enormous momentum.

The Emergence of Christianity

Two fundamental trends characterized religious development in the Roman Empire: the growing impulse toward mysticism that we have just examined, and the interpenetration and fusion of doctrines and practices between one cult and another—a process known as *syncretism*. The syncretic quality of Christianity itself has often been observed, for in numerous instances its beliefs and rituals were similar to those of earlier religions. Obviously, Christianity drew heavily from Judaism—nearly all the earliest Christians were Jews—but it was also anticipated in various particulars by Persian Zoroastrianism and Mithraism, the Isis-Osiris cult of Egypt, the

Greek mysteries of Dionysus and Demeter, and even Stoicism. Many Christian doctrines had long pre-Christian histories: the concept of death and resurrection, the sacramental meal, baptism, personal salvation, and the brotherhood of man under the fatherhood of God, to name but a few. Yet Christianity was far more than a new configuration of old ideas, and it would be misleading to think of it as merely another of the oriental mystery religions. It differed from them above all in two basic ways: (1) its god was the God of the Hebrews, unique in all antiquity in his claims to exclusiveness and omnipotence, and now released by Christianity from his association with a specific chosen people and universalized as the God of all mankind; (2) Christianity's founder and Savior was a vivid historic personality, Jesus, beside whom such mythical idealizations as Mithras or Isis must have seemed tepid and diffuse.

Jesus, a younger contemporary of Augustus, was a figure in the Hebrew prophetic tradition whose life and teaching show little if any Greek influence. He is depicted in the Gospels as a warm, attractive, magnetic leader who miraculously healed the sick, raised the dead, and stilled the winds. His miracles were seen as credentials of the divine authority with which he claimed to speak. His ministry was chiefly to the poor and outcast, and in Christianity's early decades it was these classes that accepted the faith most readily. He preached a doctrine of love, compassion, and humility. Like the prophets he scorned empty formalism in religion and stressed the sober, unprepossessing life of generosity toward both friend and enemy and devotion to God. He does not seem to have objected to ritual as such, but only to ritual infected with pride and complacency and divorced from charity and upright conduct. His severe criticism of the moral shortcomings of the established Jewish priesthoods, combined apparently with his claims to speak with divine authority, resulted in his crucifixion as a subversive.

According to the Gospels, Jesus' greatest miracle was his resurrection—his return to life three days after he died on the Cross. He is said to have remained on earth for a short period thereafter, giving solace and inspiration to his disciples, and then to have "ascended" into heaven with the promise that he would return in glory to judge all souls and bring the world to an end. The first generations of Christians expected this second coming to occur quickly, and it is perhaps for that reason among others that formal organization was not stressed in the primitive church.

The early Christians not only accepted Christ's ethical precepts but worshiped Christ himself as the divine incarnation of the omnipotent God. The Christ of the Gospels distinguishes repeatedly between himself—"the Son of Man"—and God—"the Father"—but he also makes the statement, "I and the Father are One," and he enjoins his disciples to baptize all persons "in the Name of the Father and the Son and the Holy Spirit." Hence, Christianity became committed to the difficult and sophisticated notion of a triune Godhead with Christ as the "Son" or "Second Person" in a Trinity that was nevertheless one God. The doctrine of the Trinity gave Christianity the unique advantage of a single, infinite, philosophically respectable god who could be worshiped and adored in the person of the charismatic, lovable, tragic Jesus. The Christian deity was both transcendent and concrete.

The Early Church

The first generation of Christianity witnessed the beginning of a deeply significant development whereby the Judeo-Christian heritage was modified and enriched through contact with the main currents of Greco-Roman culture. Christ's own apostles were no more influenced by Hellenism than their Master, and some of them sought to keep Christianity strictly within the ritualistic framework of Judaism. But St. Paul, a Hellenized Jew and early convert, suceeded in orienting the church according to his own vision of a universal brotherhood, free of the strict Jewish dietary laws and the requirement of circumcision (which were bound to discourage the conversion of non-Jews), open to all people everywhere who would accept Jesus as God and Savior—and open also to the bracing winds of Hellenistic thought. St. Paul traveled far and wide across the Empire preaching the message of Christ as he interpreted it, winning converts, and establishing Christian communities in many towns and cities of the Mediterranean world. Other Christian missionaries, among them St. Peter and his fellow apostles who had been Christ's immediate followers, devoted their lives as St. Paul did to traveling, preaching and organizing—often at the cost of ridicule and persecution. Tradition has it that St. Paul and all the apostles died as martyrs. Their work was tremendously fruitful, for by the end of the apostolic generation Christianity had become a ponderable force among the underprivileged masses of Italy and the east. Within another century the new religion had spread throughout the greater part of the Empire.

From the first, the Christians regularly engaged in a sacramental meal which came to be called the "eucharist" or "holy communion" and was viewed as an indispensable avenue of divine grace through which the Christian was infused with the spirit of Christ. By means of another important sacrament, baptism, the postulant was initiated into the brotherhood of the church, had his sins forgiven by God, and received the grace of the Holy Spirit. A person could be baptized only once, and baptized persons alone could consider themselves true Christians, but in the early church baptism was frequently delayed until adulthood. Many unbaptized persons were therefore associated with the Christian communities without being Christians in the full sense of the word.

As Christian historical documents become more common, in the second and third centuries A.D., the organization of the church begins to emerge more sharply than before. The documents of this period disclose an important distinction between the clergy, who govern the church and administer the sacraments, and the laymen, who play a more passive role. The clergy itself was divided into several ranks, the most important of which were the bishops, who served as rulers and pastors over the various urban communities, and the priests, who led the services and administered the sacraments under the jurisdiction of the bishops. And the bishops themselves were of various degrees of eminence. Above the common bishops were the metropolitans or archbishops who resided in cities of special importance and exercised control over an extensive surrounding area. At the top of the hierarchy were the bishops of the three or four greatest cities of the Empire—Rome, Alexandria, Antioch, and later Constantinople—who were known as patriarchs and who enjoyed a spiritual hegemony (often more theoretical than real) over vast areas of the Mediterranean world.* As time went on, the bishop of Rome—the pope—came to be regarded more and more as the highest of the patriarchs, but the actual establishment of papal authority over even the Western church was to require the efforts of many centuries.

Christianity and Hellenism

Medieval and modern Christian theology is a product of both the Hebrew and the Greek traditions. The synthesis of these two intellectual worlds began not among the Christians but among the Jews

*For a time there was also a patriarch of Jerusalem.

themselves, especially those who had migrated in large numbers to Alexandria. Here Jewish scholars—in particular a religious philosopher of the early first century A.D. named Philo Judaeus—worked toward the reconciliation of Jewish revelation and Greek philosophy. Drawing heavily from Aristotle, the Stoics, and particularly Plato, Philo developed a symbolic interpretation of the Old Testament that was to influence Christian thought across the centuries.

Following many of the fruitful leads of Philo, Christian theologians strove to demonstrate that their religion was more than merely an immensely appealing myth—that it could hold its own in the highest intellectual circles. The Savior Christ, for example, as true God and true man, constituted a unique synthesis of the material and spiritual worlds. In Greek terms, Christ reconciled Plato's dualism, for Christ was at once a particular person and an archetype. Christianity differed from most of the Near Eastern mystery religions—especially those emanating from Persia—in its refusal to reject the material world. Matter could not be evil of itself, for it was the handiwork of God; the human body could not be wholly corrupt, for Christ himself was a human in the fullest sense. Christianity was therefore not so radically at odds with Greek humanism as, say, Mithraism—although its concept of sin and its doctrine of the fall of man through the disobedience of Adam were obviously far removed from the traditional humanistic viewpoint of the Greeks.

The fusion of matter and spirit, so fundamental to orthodox Christianity, did not escape challenge among the early Christians. Once the expectation of an immediate second coming began to fade, many Christians began to examine their faith more philosophically than before and to raise difficult questions about the nature of Christ and the Trinity. A diversity of opinions emerged, some of which seemed so inconsistent with the majority view that they were condemned as heresies. As questions were raised and orthodox solutions agreed on, the Christian faith became increasingly precise and increasingly elaborate. The early heresies sought to simplify the nature of Christ and the Trinity. One group, known as the Gnostics, interpreted Christ in the light of the Persian notion that matter was evil. They insisted that Christ was not really human—only a divine phantom—that a good God could not assume a physical body. Others maintained that Christ was not fully divine—not an equal member of the triune Godhead. The latter position was taken up by the fourth-century Arians, whom we shall meet later in this chapter. The orthodox position lay midway between these two views: Christ was fully human and fully divine—a coequal member of the Holy Trinity. He had always existed and always would but had become incarnate in human form at a particular moment in time, and walked the earth, taught, suffered, and died, as the man Jesus. Thus the synthesis of matter and spirit was strictly preserved, and Christ remained the bridge between the two worlds.

The Christian apologists—the defenders of orthodoxy against pagan attacks from without and heterodox attacks from within—played a crucial role in formulating and elaborating Christian doctrine, coping with problems that had not even occurred to the apostolic generation. It is of the highest significance that a great many serious Christian thinkers worked within the framework of the Greek philosophical tradition. This is especially true of the greatest of them, the Alexandrian theologian Origen (d. 254) who created a coherent, all-inclusive Christian philosophical system on Platonic foundations. Origen was one of the foremost thinkers of his age and is widely regarded as one of the supreme minds in the entire history of the church. His religious system did not win over the pagan intellectual world at a blow—indeed, several of his conclusions were rejected by later Christian orthodoxy—but he and other Christian theologians succeeded in making Christianity meaningful and intellectually attractive to men whose thinking was cast in the Greco-Roman philosophical mold. The greatest of the Greek philosophers, so these Christian writers said, had been led toward truth by the subconscious inspiration of the Christian God.

Christianity and the Empire

At the very time that Christian theology was being Hellenized, pagan thought itself was shifting increasingly toward otherworldliness. Origen's greatest pagan contemporary was the Neo-Platonist Plotinus. Indeed, the two had even been schoolmates for a time. One of the deepest and subtlest minds of the age, Plotinus popularized the doctrine of a single god, infinite and beyond reasoning, unknowable and unapproachable except through an ecstatic trance. Plotinus taught that God was the source of reality and existence. All being, both physical and spiritual, radiated outward from him like concentric ripples in a pool. The Neoplatonists taught that the gods of the pagan cults were all symbols of the one unknowable god and that each pagan cult therefore had validity.

The growth of a transcendental outlook throughout the ancient world created an atmosphere highly nourishing to a salvation religion such as Christianity. The Christian viewpoint was becoming increasingly in tune with the times; it appealed to an age hungry for a profound and consoling doctrine of personal redemption. Yet its triumph was by no means assured, for it faced other salvation religions such as Mithraism and the Isis cult—and traditional Greco-Roman paganism in its new, otherwordly, Neoplatonic guise. Against these rivals Christianity could offer the immense appeal of the historic Jesus, the ever-increasing profundity of its theology, the infinite majesty of its God, and the compassion and universalism of its message preserved and dramatized in its canonical books—the Old and New Testaments. Few social groups were immune to its attraction. The poor, humble, and underprivileged made up the bulk of its early converts, and it was to them that Jesus directed much of his message. Thoughtful men were drawn by its Hellenized theology, men of feeling were captivated by its mysticism, and men of affairs were attracted by the ever-increasing effectiveness of its administrative hierarchy. For in administration no less than in theology the church was learning from the Greco-Roman world.

Before the collapse of the Roman Empire in the West, Christianity had absorbed and turned to its own purposes much of Rome's heritage in political organization and law, carrying on the Roman administrative and legal tradition into the medieval and modern world. Roman civil law was paralleled by the canon law of the church. The secular leadership of the Roman Empire gave way to the spiritual leadership of the Roman pope, who assumed the old republican and imperial title of *pontifex maximus*—supreme pontiff—and preserved much of the imperial ceremonial of the later Empire. As imperial governors and local officials gradually disappeared in the west, their traditions were carried on, in a new spiritual dimension, by metropolitans and bishops. Indeed, the *diocese*, the traditional unit of a bishop's jurisdiction, was originally an imperial administrative district. In this organizational sense, the medieval church has been described as a ghost of the Roman Empire. Yet it was far more than that. For the church reached its people as Rome never had, giving the impoverished masses a sense of participation and involvement that the Empire had failed to provide.

From the beginning the Christians of the Empire were a people apart, convinced that they alone possessed the truth and that the truth would one day triumph, eager to win new converts to their faith, uncompromising in their rejection of all other religions, willing to learn from the pagan world but unwilling ever to submit to it. Their stark seriousness of purpose, their cohesiveness (which doubtless appeared to their enemies as conspiratorial), their sense of destiny, and their refusal to worship the state gods proved exceedingly aggravating to their pagan contemporaries. Consequently, the Christians were often objects of suspicion, hatred, and persecution. The emperors themselves followed a rather inconsistent policy toward them. Violent persecutions, such as those under Nero and Marcus Aurelius, alternated with long periods of inaction. On the whole, the church throve on the blood of its martyrs; the persecutions were neither sufficiently ruthless nor sufficiently lengthy to come near wiping out the entire Christian community.

Most of the emperors, if they persecuted Christians at all, did so reluctantly. The "good emperor" Trajan instructed a provincial governor neither to seek Christians out nor to heed anonymous accusations. (Such a procedure, Trajan observed, is inconsistent with "the spirit of the age.") Only if a man should be denounced as a Christian, tried and found guilty, and then should persist in his refusal to worship the imperial gods, was he to be punished. One can admire the Christian who would face death rather than worship false gods, but one can also sympathize with emperors such as Trajan who hesitated to apply their traditional policy of religious toleration to a people who seemed bent on subverting the Empire.

The persecutions of the first and second centuries, although occasionally severe, tended to be limited in scope to specific local areas. The great empire-wide persecutions of the third and early fourth centuries were products of the crisis that Roman civilization was then undergoing. The greatest imperial persecution—and the last —occurred at the opening of the fourth century under the Emperor Diocletian. By then Christianity was too strong to be destroyed, and the failure of Diocletian's persecution must have made it evident that the Empire had no choice but to accommodate itself to the church. A decade after the outbreak of this last persecution, Constantine, the first Christian emperor, undertook a dramatic reversal of religious policy. Thereafter the Empire endorsed Christianity rather than fighting it, and by the close of the fourth century the majority of the urban inhabitants of the Empire had been brought into the Christian fold. Rome and Jerusalem had come to terms at last.

The Beginnings of Imperial Decline: The Third Century

The turbulent third century—the era of Origen and Plotinus—brought catastrophic changes to the Roman Empire. The age of the "five good emperors" (A.D. 96–180) was followed by a hundred troubled years during which anarchy alternated with military despotism. The army, now fully conscious of its strength, made and unmade emperors. One military group fought against another for control of the imperial title—a man might be a general one day, emperor the next, and dead the third. No less than 19 emperors reigned during the calamitous half-century between 235 and 285, not to mention innumerable usurpers and pretenders whose plots and machinations contributed to the general chaos. In this 50-year period every emperor save one died violently—either by assassination or in battle. The Silver Age had given way to what one contemporary historian describes as an age "of iron and rust."

A crucial factor in the chaos of the third century was the problem of the imperial succession. All too often, a competent emperor would be followed by an incompetent son. As the power of the army increased and military rebellions became commonplace, the imperial succession came more and more to depend on the whim of the troops. Perhaps the most successful emperor of the period, Septimius Severus (193–211), maintained his power by expanding and pampering the army, opening its highest offices to every class, and broadening its recruitment. A military career was now the logical avenue to high civil office, and the bureaucracy began to display an increasingly military cast of mind. The old ideals of Republic and Principate were less and less meaningful to the new governing class, many of whom rose from the lower orders of society through successful army careers to positions of high political responsibility. These new administrators were often men of strength and ability, but they were not the sort who could be expected to cherish the old Roman political traditions. Septimius Severus increased imperial taxes to fatten his treasury and appease his troops. Soldiers prospered at the expense of an increasingly impoverished civilian population as the Empire drifted more and more toward military absolutism. Septimius' dying words to his sons are characteristic of his reign and his times: "Enrich the soldiers and scorn the world."

But Rome's troubles in the third century cannot be ascribed entirely to the problem of imperial succession. As early as the reign of Marcus Aurelius (161–180) the Empire had been struck by a devastating plague that lingered on for a generation and by an ominous irruption of Germanic barbarians who spilled across the Rhine-Danube frontier as far as Italy itself. Marcus Aurelius, the philosopher-emperor, was obliged to spend the greater part of his reign campaigning against the invaders, and it was only by enormous effort that he was able to drive them out of the Empire. During the third century the Germans attacked repeatedly, penetrating the frontiers time and again, forcing the cities of the Empire to erect protective walls, and threatening for a time to submerge the state under a barbarian flood. And the Germanic onslaught was accompanied by attacks from the east by the recently reconstituted Persian Empire led by the able kings of its new Sassanid dynasty (226–651 A.D.).

Rome's crucial problems, however, were internal ones. During the third century, political disintegration was accompanied by social and economic breakdown. The ever-rising fiscal demands of the mushrooming bureaucracy and the insatiable army placed an intolerable burden on the inhabitants of town and country alike. Peasants fled from their fields to escape the hated tax collector, and the urban middle classes became shrunken and demoralized. The self-governing town, the bedrock of imperial administration and, indeed, of Greco-Roman civilization itself, was beginning to experience serious financial difficulties, and as one city after another turned to the emperor for financial aid, civic autonomy declined. These problems arose partly from the parasitical nature of many of the Roman cities, partly from rising imperial taxes, and partly from the economic stagnation that was slowly gripping the Empire. Long before the death of Marcus Aurelius, Rome had abandoned its career of conquest in favor of a defensive policy of consolidation. The flow of booty from conquered lands had ceased, and the Empire as a whole was thrown back on its own resources and forced to become economically self-sufficient. For a while all seemed well, but as administrative and military expenses mounted without a corresponding growth in commerce and industry, the imperial economy began to suffer. The army, once a source of riches from conquered lands, was now an unproductive encumbrance.

By the third century, if not before, the Roman economy was shrinking. Plagues, hunger, and a sense of hopelessness resulted in a gradual decline in population. At the very time when imperial expenses and imperial taxes were rising, the tax base was contracting. Prosperity gave way to depression and desperation, and the flight of peasants from their farms was accompanied by the flight of the savagely-taxed middle classes from their cities. The Empire was now clogged with beggars and bandits, and those who remained at their jobs were taxed all the more heavily. It was the western half of the Empire that suffered most. What industry there was had always been centered in the East, and money was gradually flowing eastward to productive centers in Syria and Asia Minor and beyond, to pay for luxury goods, some of which came from outside the Empire altogether—from Persia, India, and China. In short, the Empire as a whole, and the western Empire especially, suffered from an unfavorable balance of trade that resulted in a steady reduction in Rome's supply of precious metals.

The increasingly desperate financial circumstances of the third-century Empire forced the emperors to experiment in the devaluation of coinage—adulterating the precious metals in their coins with baser metals. This policy provided only temporary relief. In the long run, it resulted in a runaway inflation that further undermined the economy. Between A.D. 256 and 280 the cost of living rose 1000 percent.

The third-century anarchy reached its climax during the 260s. By then the Roman economy was virtually in ruins. Barbarian armies were rampaging across the frontiers. Gaul and Britain in the west and a large district in the east had broken loose from imperial control and were pursuing independent courses. The population was speedily shrinking, and countless cities were in an advanced state of decay. Rome's demise seemed imminent. As it turned out, however, the Empire was saved by the tremendous efforts of a series of stern leaders who rose to power in the later third century. The Roman state survived in the west for another two centuries and in the east for more than a millennium. But the agonies of the third century left an indelible mark on the reformed Empire. The new imperial structure that brought order out of chaos was profoundly different from the government of the Principate: it was a naked autocracy of the most thorough-going sort.

The Reforms of Diocletian

Even at the height of the anarchy there were emperors who strove desperately to defend the Roman state. After A.D. 268 a series of able, rough-hewn emperor-generals from the Danubian provinces managed to turn the tide, restoring the frontiers, smashing the invading armies of Germanic barbarians and Persians, and recovering the alienated provinces in Gaul and the East. At the same time measures were undertaken to arrest the social and economic decay that was debilitating the Empire. These policies were expanded and brought to fruition by Diocletian (284–305) and Constantine (306–337) to whom belong the credit—and responsibility—for reconstituting the Empire along authoritarian lines. No longer merely a *princeps,* the emperor was now *dominus et deus*—lord and god—and it is appropriate that the new despotic regime that replaced the Principate should be called the "Dominate."

In the days of Augustus it had been necessary, so as not to offend republican sensibilities, to disguise the power of the emperor. In Diocletian's day the imperial title had for so long been dishonored and abused that it was necessary to exalt it. Diocletian and his successors glorified the office in every way imaginable. The emperor became a lofty, remote, unapproachable figure clothed in magnificent garments, a diadem on his head. An elaborate court ceremonial was introduced, somewhat similar to that of Persia, which included the custom of prostration in the emperor's sacred presence.

Diocletian's most immediate task was to bring to a close the turbulent era of shortlived "barracks emperors" and military usurpers. In order to stabilize the succession and share the ever-growing burden of governing the Empire, he decreed that there would thenceforth be two emperors—one in the east, the other in the west—who would work together harmoniously for the welfare and defense of the state. Each of the two would be known by the title *Augustus,* and each would adopt a younger colleague—with the title *Caesar*—to share his rule and ultimately to succeed him. The Empire was now divided into four parts, each supervised by an Augustus or a Caesar. Well aware of the increasing importance of the eastern over the western half of the Empire, Diocletian made his capital in the east and did not set foot in Rome until the close of his reign. A usurper would now, presumably, be faced with the perplexing task of overcoming four widely-scattered personages instead of one. The chances of military usurpation were further reduced by Diocletian's rigorous separation of civil and military authority. The army was considerably enlarged, chiefly by the incorporation of barbarian forces who now assumed much of the burden of guarding the frontiers, but it was organized in such a way that the emperor (or emperors) could control it far more effectively than before.

Imperial control was the keynote of this new, centralized regime. The Senate was now merely ornamental, and the emperor ruled through his obedient and ever-expanding bureaucracy—issuing edict after edict to regulate, systematize, and regiment the state. The shortage of money was circumvented by a new land tax to be collected in kind (that is, goods), and the widespread flight from productive labor was reduced by new laws freezing peasants, craftsmen, and businessmen to their jobs. A system of hereditary social orders quickly developed; sons were required by law to take up the careers and tax burdens of their fathers. Peasants were bound to the land, city dwellers to their urban professions. Workers in the mines and quarries were literally branded. The system was more theoretical than real, for these measures were difficult to enforce, and a degree of social mobility remained. Nevertheless, the Dominate was a relatively regimented society. Economic collapse was temporarily averted, but at the cost of social petrification and loss of hope. The once-autonomous cities now lay under the iron hand of the imperial government. Commitment to the Empire was rapidly waning among the tax-ridden urban commercial elite, who had formerly been among its most enthusiastic supporters but were now (as one historian has put it) condemned for life to the Chamber of Commerce.

But it was Diocletian's mission to save the Empire whatever the cost, and it may well be that authoritarian measures were the only ones possible under the circumstances. For every problem Diocletian offered a solution—often autocratic and heavy-handed, but a solution nevertheless. A thoroughgoing currency reform had retarded inflation but had not stopped it altogether, so Diocletian issued an edict fixing the prices of most commodities by law. To the growing challenge of Christianity, Diocletian responded, regretfully, by inaugurating a persecution of unprecedented severity. As it turned out, neither the imperial price controls nor the imperial persecution achieved their purposes, but the very fact that they were attempted illustrates the lengths to which the Emperor would go in his effort to preserve by force the unity and stability of the state.

The division of the Empire among the two Augustuses and the two adopted Caesars worked satisfactorily only so long as Diocletian himself was in command. Once his hand was removed, a struggle for power brought renewed civil strife. The principle of adoption, which the sonless Diocletian had revived without serious difficulty, was challenged by the sons of his successors. The era of chaos ran from the end of Diocletian's reign in 305 to the victory of Constantine over the last of his rivals in 312 at the battle of the Milvian Bridge near Rome.

The Reign of Constantine (A.D. 306–337)

Constantine's triumph at the Milvian Bridge marked the return of political stability and the consummation of Diocletian's economic and political reforms. Diocletian's policy of freezing occupations and making them hereditary was tightened by Constantine in an edict of A.D. 332. Imperial ceremonial was further elaborated, and authoritarianism grew. In certain respects, however, Constantine's policies took radical new directions. In place of the abortive principle of adoption, Constantine founded an imperial dynasty of his own. For a time he shared his authority with an imperial colleague (his brother-in-law), but in 324 he conquered him and thereafter ruled alone. Nevertheless, the joint rule of an eastern and a western emperor became common in the years after Constantine's death, and he himself contributed to the division of the Empire by building the magnificent eastern capital of Constaninople on the site of the ancient Greek colony of Byzantium.

Constantinople was a second Rome. It had its own senate, its own imposing palaces, and public buildings, and its own hungry proletariat fed by the bread dole and diverted by chariot races in its enormous Hippodrome. A few decades after its foundation it even acquired its own Christian patriarch. Constantine plundered the Greco-Roman world of its artistic treasures to adorn his new city and lavished his vast resources on its construction. Founded in A.D. 330, Constantinople was to remain the capital of the Eastern Empire for well over a thousand years, impregnable behind its great walls, protected on three sides by the sea, perpetually renewing itself through its control of the rich commerce flowing between the Black Sea and the Mediterranean. The age-long survival of the Eastern Empire owes much to the superb strategic location of its capital, which dominated the straits between these two seas.

Even more momentous than the building of Constantinople was Constantine's conversion to Christianity and his reversal of imperial policy toward the church. Although he put off baptism until his dying moments, Constantine had been committed to Christianity ever since his triumph in 312. From that time onward he issued a continuous series of pro-Christian edicts insuring full toleration, legalizing bequests to the church (which accumulated prodigiously over the subsequent centuries), and granting a variety of other privileges. Christianity was now an official religion of the Empire. It was not yet *the* official religion, but it would become so before the fourth century was ended.

The Emperor Constantine, a fragment of the colossal statue.

Several explanations have been offered for Constantine's conversion. He has been portrayed as an irreligious political schemer bent on harnessing the vitality of the church to the failing state. But there seems no reason to doubt that, in fact, his conversion was sincere if somewhat superficial. Strictly speaking, there were no irreligious men in the fourth century.

The Christian Empire

The respite gained by Diocletian's reforms and the subsequent conversion of Constantine made it possible for the church to develop rapidly under the benevolent protection of the Empire. The years between Constantine's victory at the Milvian Bridge in 312 and the final suppression of the Western Empire in 476 were momentous ones in the evolution of Christianity. For one thing, the fourth century witnessed mass conversions to the Christian fold. Perhaps 10 percent of the inhabitants of the Western Empire were Christians in 312 (in the east the figure would be considerably higher) whereas by the century's end the now respectable Christians were in the majority. But, as is so often the case, triumph evoked internal dissension, and the fourth century witnessed a violent struggle between orthodoxy and heresy. Here, too, the Christian emperors played a determining role, and it was with strong imperial support that the greatest of the fourth-century heresies, Arianism, was at length suppressed within the Empire.

The Arians maintained that the purity of Christian monotheism was compromised by the orthodox doctrine of the Trinity. Their solution to this conflict was the doctrine that God the Father was the only true god—that Christ the Son was not fully divine. The orthodox Trinitarians regarded this doctrine as subversive to one of their most fundamental beliefs: the equality and codivinity of Father, Son, and Holy Spirit. Constantine sought to heal the Arian-Trinitarian dispute by summoning an ecumenical (universal) council of Christian bishops at Nicaea in A.D. 325. He had no strong convictions himself, but the advocates of the Trinitarian position managed to win his support. With imperial backing, a strongly anti-Arian creed was adopted almost unanimously. The three divine Persons of the Trinity were declared equal: Jesus Christ was "of one substance with the Father."

But Constantine was no theologian. In after years he vacillated, sometimes favoring Arians, sometimes condemning them, and the same ambiguity characterized imperial policy throughout the greater part of the fourth century. Indeed, one of Constantine's fourth-century successors, Julian "the Apostate" reverted to paganism. At length, however, the uncompromisingly orthodox Theodosius I came to the throne (378–395) and broke the power of the Arians by condemning and proscribing them. It was under Theodosius and his successors that Christianity became the one legal religion of the Empire. Paganism itself was now banned and persecuted and quickly disappeared as an organized force.

Orthodox Christianity now dominated the Empire, but its triumph, won with the aid of political force, was far from complete. For one thing, the mass conversions of the fourth century tended to be superficial—even nominal. Conversion to Christianity was the path of least resistance, and the new converts were on the whole a far cry from the earlier society of saints and martyrs. It was at this time that many ardent Christians, discontented with mere membership in a respectable, work-a-day church, began taking to the desert as hermits or flocking into monastic communities.

Moreover, the imperial program of enforced orthodoxy proved difficult to carry out. Old heresies lingered on and vigorous new ones arose in the fifth century and thereafter. Even Arianism survived, not among the citizens of the Empire, but among the Germanic barbarians. For during the mid-fourth century, at a time when Arianism was still strong in the Empire, large numbers of barbarians had been converted to Christianity in its Arian form, and the Trinitarian policies of Theodosius I had no effect on them whatever. Accordingly, when the barbarians ultimately formed their kingdoms on the ruins of the Western Empire, most of them were separated from their Old Roman subjects not only by language and custom but by a deep religious chasm as well.

Finally, by accepting imperial support against paganism and heresy, the church sacrificed much of its earlier independence. The Christians of Constantine's day were so overwhelmed by the emperor's conversion that they tended to glorify him excessively. As a Christian, Constantine could no longer claim divinity, but contemporary Christian writers such as the historian Eusebius allowed him a status that was almost quasi-divine. To Eusebius and his contemporaries, Constantine was the thirteenth apostle; his office was commissioned by God; he was above the church. His commanding position in ecclesiastical affairs is illustrated by his domination of the Council of Nicaea, and the ups and downs of Arianism in the following decades depended largely on the whims of his successors.

In the east, this glorification of the imperial office ripened into the doctrine known as *caesaropapism*—that the emperor is the real master of both church and state, that he is both caesar and pope—and caesaropapism remained a dominant theme in the Eastern or Byzantine Empire throughout its long history. Church and state tended to merge under the sacred authority of the emperor. Indeed, the Christianization and sanctification of the imperial office were potent forces in winning for the eastern emperors the allegiance and commitment of the masses of their Christian subjects. Religious loyalty to the Christian emperor provided indispensable nourishment to the East Roman state over the ensuing centuries. Conversely, widespread hostility toward imperial orthodoxy in districts dominated by heretical groups resulted in the alienation and eventual loss to the Byzantine Empire of several of its fairest provinces.

Caesaropapism was far less influential in the west, for as the fifth century dawned the Western Empire was visibly failing. Western churchmen were beginning to realize that Christian civilization was not irrevocably bound to the fortunes of Rome. Gradually the Western church began to assert its independence of state control—with the result that church and state in medieval Western Europe were often at odds and never fused.

The Doctors of the Latin Church

During the later fourth and early fifth centuries, as a time when the Christianization of the Roman state was far advanced but before the Western Empire had lost all its vitality, the long-developing synthesis of Judeo-Christian and Greco-Roman culture reached its climax in the west with the work of three gifted scholar-saints: Ambrose, Jerome, and Augustine. These men came to be regarded as "Doctors of the Latin Church," for their writings deeply influenced medieval thought. Each of the three was thoroughly trained in the Greco-Roman intellectual tradition; each devoted his learning and his life to the service of Christianity; each was at once an intellectual and a man of affairs.

Ambrose (c. 340–397) was bishop of Milan, which by the later fourth century had replaced Rome as the western imperial capital. He was famed for his eloquence and administrative skill, for his vigor in defending Trinitarian orthodoxy against Arianism, and for the ease and mastery with which he adopted the literary traditions of Cicero and Virgil and the philosophy of Plato to his own Christian purposes. Above all, he was the first churchman to assert that in the realm of morality the emperor himself is accountable to the Christian priesthood. When the powerful Emperor Theodosius I massacred the inhabitants of rebellious Thessalonica, Ambrose barred him from the Church of Milan until he had formally and publicly repented. Ambrose's bold stand and Theodosius' submission constituted a stunning setback for the principle of caesaropapism and a prelude to the long struggle between church and state in the Christian west.

Jerome (c. 340–420) was a masterly scholar and a restless, inquisitive reformer with a touch of acid in his personality. He once remarked to an opponent, "You have the will to lie, good sir, but not the skill to lie." Wandering far and wide through the Empire, he founded a monastery in Bethlehem where he set his monks to work copying manuscripts, thereby instituting a custom that throughout the middle ages preserved the tradition of Latin letters and transmitted it to the modern world. Like other Christian thinkers he feared that his love of pagan literature might dilute his Christian fervor, and he tells of a dream in which Jesus banished him from heaven with the words, "Thou art a Ciceronian, not a Christian." But in the end he managed to reconcile pagan culture and Christian faith by using the former only in the service of the latter. His greatest contribution to Christian thought was in the field of biblical translation and commentary—above all, in his scholarly translation of the Scriptures from Hebrew and Greek into Latin. Jerome's Latin Vulgate Bible has been used ever since by Roman Catholics and has served as the basis of innumerable translations into modern languages. (English-speaking Catholics use the Douay translation of Jerome's Vulgate.) It was an achievement of incalculable significance to Western Civilization.

The most profound of the Latin Doctors was Augustine (354–430), who spent his final 40 years as bishop of the North African city of Hippo. Like Jerome, Augustine worried about the dangers of pagan culture to the Christian soul, finally concluding, much as Jerome did, that Greco-Roman learning, although not to be enjoyed for its own sake, might properly be used to elucidate the Faith. Augustine was the chief architect of medieval theology. Even more than his contemporaries he succeeded in fusing Christian doctrine with Greek thought—especially the philosophy of Plato and the Neoplatonists. It has been said that Augustine baptized Plato. As a Platonist he stressed the importance of ideas or archetypes over intangible things, but instead of locating his archetypes in the abstract Platonic "heaven" he placed them in the mind of God. The human mind had access to the archetypes through an act of God which Augustine called "divine illumination."

As a bishop, Augustine was occupied with the day-to-day cares of his diocese and his flock. His contribution to religious thought arises not from the dispassionate working-out of an abstract system of theology but rather from his responses to the burning issues of the moment. His thought is a fascinating mixture of profundity and immediacy—of the abstract and the human. His *Confessions*, the first psychologically sensitive autobiography ever written, tells of his own spiritual journey through various pagan and heretical cults to Christian orthodoxy. Implicit in this book is the hope that others as misguided as he once was might also be led by God's grace to the truth in Christ.

Against the several heretical doctrines that threatened Christian orthodoxy in his day Augustine wrote clearly and persuasively on the nature of the Trinity, the problem of evil in a world created by God, the special character of the Christian priesthood, and the nature of free will and predestination. His most influential work, the *City of God*, was prompted by a barbarian sack of Rome in A.D. 410, which the pagans ascribed to Rome's desertion of her old gods. Augustine responded by developing a Christian theory of history which interpreted human development not in political or economic terms but in moral terms. As the first Christian philosopher of history, Augustine drew heavily on the historical insights of the ancient Hebrews. Like the Hebrew prophets of old, he asserted that kingdoms and empires rose and fell according to a divine plan, but he insisted that this plan lay forever beyond human comprehension. Augustine rejected the theory, common in antiquity, that history was an endless series of cycles, arguing on the contrary that history was moving toward a divinely appointed goal. This linear view of history set something of a precedent for the modern secular concept of historical progress. Augustine also rejected the Hebrew notion of tribal salvation, putting in its place the Christian notion of *individual* salvation. The ultimate units of history were not tribes and empires but individual immortal souls.

The salvation of souls, Augustine stated, depends not on the fortunes of Rome but on the grace of God. Christ is not dependent on Caesar. And if we look at history from the moral standpoint—from the standpoint of souls—we see not the clash of armies or the rivalry of states but a far more fundamental struggle between good and evil which has raged through history and which rages even now within each soul. Humanity is divided into two classes: those who live in God's grace and those who do not. The former belong to what Augustine called the "City of God," the latter to the "Earthly City." The members of the two cities are hopelessly intermixed in this world, but they will be separated at death by eternal salvation or damnation. It is from this transcendental standpoint, Augustine believed, that the Christian must view history. Only God could know what effect Rome's decline would have on the City of God. Perhaps the effect would be beneficial, perhaps even irrelevant.

Augustine is one of the two or three seminal minds in Christian history. His Christian Platonism governed medieval theology down into the twelfth century and remains influential in Christian thought today. His emphasis on the special sacramental power inherent in the priestly office remains a keystone of Catholic theology. His emphasis on divine grace and predestination, although softened considerably by the medieval church, reemerged in the sixteenth century to dominate early Protestant doctrine. And his theory of the two cities, although often in simplified form, had an enormous influence on Western historical and political thought over the next millennium.

Ambrose, Jerome, and Augustine were at once synthesizers and innovators. The last great minds of the Western Empire, they operated at a level of intellectual sophistication that the Christian West would not reach again for 700 years. The strength of the classical tradition that underlies medieval Christianity and Western civilization owes much to the fact that these men, and others like them, found it possible to be both Christians and Ciceronians.

SIX

THE WANING OF THE WESTERN EMPIRE

"Decline and Fall"

The catastrophe of Rome's decline and fall has always fascinated historians, for it involves not only the collapse of mankind's most impressive and enduring universal state but also the demise of Greco-Roman civilization itself. The reasons are far too complex to be explained satisfactorily by any single cause: Christianity, disease, slavery, lead-poisoning, soil-exhaustion, or any of the other "master-keys" that have been proposed from time to time. One must always bear in mind that the Roman Empire "fell" only in the west. It endured in the east, although there, too, Greco-Roman civilization was significantly changed. The civilization of the Eastern Empire during the medieval centuries is normally described not as "Roman" or even "Greco-Roman" but as "Byzantine," and the change in name betokens a profound alteration in mood. In other words, Greco-Roman culture was gradually

143

transformed in both east and west, but its transformation in the west was accompanied by the dismemberment of the Roman state whereas its transformation in the east occurred despite an underlying political continuity in which emperor followed emperor in more-or-less unbroken succession.

In the west, then, we are faced with two separate phenomena—political breakdown and cultural transformation. The political collapse culminated in the deposition of the last western emperor in A.D. 476, but the true period of crisis was the chaotic third century. The recovery under Diocletian and Constantine was only partial and temporary: the impending death of the body politic was delayed, but the disease remained uncured. The impoverished masses in town and countryside had never participated meaningfully in Roman civilization, and the third-century anarchy resulted in the spiritual disengagement of the middle classes as well. Initiative and commitment ebbed in the atmosphere of economic and political upheaval and were stifled by the autocracy that followed. Fourth-century Rome was an authoritarian, highly centralized state that robbed its subjects of their independence and watched over them through a network of informers and secret agents. The collapse of such a state cannot be regarded as an unmitigated disaster; to many it must have seemed a blessing.

The west had always been poorer and less urbanized than the east, and its economy, badly shaken by the political chaos of the third century, began to break down under the growing burden of imperial government and the defense of hard-pressed frontiers. Perhaps the fatal flaw in the western economy was its inability to compensate for the cessation of imperial expansion by more intensive internal development. There was no large-scale industry, no mass production; the majority of the population was far too poor to provide a mass market. Industrial production was inefficient, and technology progressed at a snail's pace. The economy remained fundamentally agrarian, and farming techniques advanced little during the centuries of the Empire. The Roman plow was rudimentary and inefficient; windmills were unknown and water mills exceptional. The horse could not be used as a draught animal because the Roman harness crossed the horse's windpipe and tended to strangle him under a heavy load. Consequently, Roman agriculture was based on the less efficient oxen and on the muscles of slaves and *coloni*.

Economic exhaustion brought with it the twin evils of population decline and growing poverty. At the very time that the manpower shortage was becoming acute and impoverishment was paralyzing the middle classes, the army and bureaucracy were expanding to unprecedented size and the expenses of government were soaring. One result of these processes was the deurbanization of the west. By the fifth century the once vigorous cities were becoming ghosts of their former selves, drained of their wealth and much of their population. Only the small class of great landowners managed to prosper in the economic atmosphere of the late Western Empire, and these men now abandoned their town houses, withdrew from civic affairs, and retired to their estates where they often assembled sizable private armies and defied the tax collector. The aristocracy, having now fled the city, would remain an agrarian class for the next thousand years. The rural nobility of the middle ages had come into being.

The decline of the city was fatal to the urbanized administrative structure of the Western Empire. More than that, it brought an end to the urban-oriented culture of Greco-Roman antiquity. The civilization of Athens, Alexandria, and Rome could not survive in the fields. It is in the decay of urban society that we find the crucial connecting link between political collapse and cultural transformation. In a very real sense Greco-Roman culture was dead long before the final demise of the Western Empire, and the deposition of the last emperor in 476 was merely the faint postscript to a process that had been completed long before. By then the cities were moribund; the rational, humanist outlook had given way completely to transcendentalism and mysticism; the army and even the civil government had become barbarized as the desperate emperors, faced with a growing shortage of manpower and resources, turned more and more to Germanic peoples to defend their frontiers and preserve order in their state. In the end, barbarians abounded in the army, entire tribes were hired to defend the frontiers, and Germanic military leaders came to hold positions of high authority in the Western Empire. Survival had come to depend on the success of half-hearted Germanic defenders against plunder-hungry Germanic invaders.

Despite the deurbanization, the mysticism, and the barbarism of the late Empire, it is nevertheless true that in a certain sense the Greco-Roman tradition never died in the west. It exerted a profound influence, as we have seen, on the Doctors of the Latin Church and, through them, on the mind of the Middle Ages. It was the basis of repeated cultural revivals, great and small, down through the centuries. And if in one sense the Roman state was dead long before the line of western emperors ended in 476, in another sense it survived long thereafter—in the ecclesiastical organization of the Roman Catholic Church and in the medieval Holy Roman Empire. Roman law endured to inspire Western jurisprudence; the Latin tongue remained the language of educated Europeans for more than a millennium while evolving in the lower levels of society into the Romance languages: Italian, French, Spanish, Portuguese, and Rumanian. In countless forms the rich legacy of classical antiquity was passed on to the Middle Ages. Europeans for centuries to come would be nourished by Greek thought and haunted by the memory of Rome.

The Germanic Peoples

Medieval civilization owed much to its Greco-Roman heritage, but it drew sustenance also from the Judaeo-Christian culture and the Germanic cultural traditions. We have already observed the fusion of Greco-Roman and Christian culture in the Roman Empire, culminating in the work of Ambrose, Jerome, and Augustine. By the fifth century the fusion of these two traditions was essentially complete, but their integration with Germanic culture had only begun. Throughout the turbulent centuries of the Early Middle Ages the Greco-Roman-Christian tradition was preserved by the Church, whereas the Germanic tradition dominated the political and military organization of the barbarian states which established themselves on the carcass of the Western Empire. The Germanic invaders soon became at least nominal Christians, but for centuries a cultural gulf remained between the Church, with its Greco-Roman-Christian heritage, and the Germanic kingdoms with their primitive, war-oriented culture. The Church of the Early Middle Ages was able to preserve ancient culture only in a simplified and debased form, for as time went on ecclesiastical leaders and aristocratic laymen came more and more to be drawn from the same social milieu. Still, it remained the great task of the early medieval Church to civilize and Christianize the Germanic peoples. In the end the Classical-Christian-Germanic synthesis was achieved and a new Western European civilization came into being.

Most of the tribes that invaded the Western Empire seem to have come originally from the Scandinavian area, the homeland of the later Vikings. Gradually they migrated into Eastern and Southeastern Europe and began to press against the Rhine and Danube frontiers. It is hazardous to make broad generalizations regarding their culture and institutions, for customs varied considerably from tribe to tribe. The Franks, the Angles, and the Saxons, for example, were agrarian peoples whose movements were slow, but who, once settled, were difficult to displace. Little influenced by Roman civilization they came into the empire as heathens. The Visigoths, Ostrogoths, and Vandals, on the other hand, were far more mobile. All three had absorbed Roman culture to some degree before they crossed the frontiers, and all had been converted in the fourth century to Arian Christianity.

A good contemporary account of early Germanic institutions is to be found in a short book entitled *Germania* written by the Roman historian Tacitus in A.D. 98. This work is not entirely trustworthy; it is a morality piece written with the intention of criticizing the "degeneracy" of the Romans by comparing them unfavorably with the simple and upright barbarians. Nevertheless, it is an invaluable source of information on early Germanic customs and institutions. We can certainly accept Tacitus' description of the Germans as large men with reddish-blond hair and blue eyes, living in simple villages, but his eulogy of their virtue and chastity is a gross exaggeration. On the whole they appear to have been drunks, liars, and lechers, whose vices were certainly no less numerous than those of the Romans, only cruder. Their standards of personal hygiene are suggested by the observation of a fifth-century Roman gentleman: "Happy the nose that cannot smell a barbarian."*

Although the Germans used iron tools and weapons, their social and economic organization was in many ways reminiscent of the Neolithic culture stage. Their chief activities were tending crops or herds and fighting wars. The key social unit within the tribe had traditionally been the kindred group or clan, which protected the welfare of its members by means of the blood feud. When a man was killed, his clan was bound to avenge his death by conducting a feud—declaring war, as it were—against the killer and his clan. In the boisterous atmosphere of the tribe, killings were only too common, and in order to keep the social fabric from being torn asunder by blood feuds it became customary for the tribe to establish a *wergeld*, a sum of money that the killer might pay to the relatives of his victim to appease their vengeance. Wergeld sched-

---

*The author, some of whose best friends are of Frankish and Anglo-Saxon descent, disclaims any sort of ethnic bias. The crudeness of the barbarians was due entirely to their lack of social and educational opportunities.

ules became quite elaborate, the amount of money to be paid by the killer varying in accordance with the social status of his victim. Smaller wergelds were established for lesser injuries such as the cutting off of a victim's arm, leg, thumb, or finger. There was no guarantee, however, that the man who did the killing or maiming would agree to pay the wergeld, or that the victim or his clan would agree to accept it. In spite of the wergeld system, blood feuds continued far into the Middle Ages.

The ties of kinship were strong among the early Germans, but they were rivaled by those of another social unit, the war band or *comitatus*. Kinship played no part in this institution; it consisted rather of a group of warriors bound together by their loyalty to a chief or king. The comitatus was a kind of military brotherhood based on honor, fidelity, courage, and mutual respect between the leader and his men. In warfare the leader was expected to excel his men in courage and prowess, and should the leader be killed, his men were honor-bound to fight to the death even if their cause should appear hopeless. The heroic virtues of the comitatus persisted throughout the Early Middle Ages as the characteristic ideology of the European warrior nobility.

The comitatus and the clan were subdivisions of a larger unit, the tribe, whose members were bound together by their allegiance to a king and by their recognition of a body of customary law. Germanic law was arbitrary and childish compared with the majestic legal edifice of Rome. Procedural formalities were all important, and guilt or innocence was often determined by requiring the accused to grasp a bar of red-hot iron or to plunge his hand into a cauldron of boiling water. Nevertheless, throughout the Early Middle Ages the legal structure of the Western European states tended to be Germanic rather than Roman. It was not until the twelfth century that Roman law was revived in the West and began to make its influence felt once again. In the meantime, Germanic law, for all its crudeness, implanted one singularly fruitful idea in the Western mind: that law was a product not of the royal will but of the immemorial customs of the people. And if law could not be altered by the king, then royal authority could not be absolute. In the Early Middle Ages a number of Germanic kings had the customs of their people put into writing, but they rarely claimed the power to legislate on their own.

The centuries immediately preceding the invasions witnessed the development of relatively stable royal dynasties among many of the Germanic tribes. Perhaps an unusually gifted warrior with a particularly large comitatus might start such a dynasty, but before many generations had gone by the kings were claiming descent from some divine ancestor. When a king died, the assembly of the tribe chose as his successor the ablest member of his family. This might or might not be his eldest son, for the tribal assembly was given considerable latitude in its power to elect. The custom of election persisted in most Germanic kingdoms far into the Middle Ages. Its chief consequence during the fifth-century invasions was to insure that the barbarian tribes were normally led by clever, battleworthy kings or chieftains at a time when the Western Empire was ruled by weaklings and fools.

Historians of previous centuries made much of the fact that certain Germanic institutions seemed to contain the seeds of constitutionalism and popular sovereignty. Democracy, so it was said, had its genesis in the forests of Germany. It should be obvious, however, that the veneration of a customary "law of the folk" or the political prominence of a tribal assembly is not uniquely Germanic but is common to many primitive peoples. The noteworthy thing about these institutions is not their existence among the Germanic barbarians but their endurance and development in the centuries that followed.

The Barbarian Invasions

The Germanic peoples had long been a threat to the Empire. They had defeated a Roman army in the reign of Augustus; they had probed deep into the Empire under Marcus Aurelius and again in the mid-third century. But until the later fourth century, the Romans had always managed eventually to drive the invaders out or settle them under Roman rule. Beginning in the mid-370s, however, an exhausted Empire was confronted by renewed barbarian pressures of an unprecedented magnitude. Lured by the relative wealth, the good soil, and the sunny climate of the Mediterranean world, the barbarians tended to regard the Empire not as something to destroy but as something to enjoy. Their age-long yearning for the fair lands across the Roman frontier was suddenly transformed into an urgent need by the westward thrust of an Asian tribe of nomads known as the Huns. These fierce horsemen conquered one Germanic tribe after another and turned them into satellites. The Ostrogoths fell before their might and became a subject people. The other great Goth tribe, the Visigoths, sought to avoid a similar fate by appealing for sanctuary behind the Roman Danube frontier. The Eastern Emperor Valens, a fervent Arian, sympathized with the Arian Visigoths, and in 376 they all crossed peacefully into the Empire.

There was trouble almost immediately. Corrupt imperial officials cheated and abused the Visigoths, and the hot-tempered tribesmen retaliated by going on a rampage. At length, Emperor Valens himself took the field against them, but the Emperor's military incapacity cost him his army and his life at the battle of Adrianople in 378. Adrianople was a military debacle of the first order. Valens' successor, the able Theodosius I, managed to pacify the Visigoths, but he could not expel them. When Theodosius died in 395, the Roman Empire was split between his two incompetent sons and, as it happened, the eastern and western halves were never again rejoined. A vigorous new Visigothic leader named Alaric now led his people on a second campaign of pillage and destruction that threatened Italy itself. In 406 the desperate Western Empire recalled most of its troops from the Rhine frontier to block Alaric's advance, with the disastrous consequence that the Vandals and a number of other tribes swept across the unguarded Rhine into Gaul. Shortly thereafter the Roman legions abandoned distant Britain, and the defenseless island was gradually overrun by Angles, Saxons, and Jutes. In 408 the only able general in the West was executed by the frantic, incompetent Emperor Honorius, who then took refuge behind the marshes of Ravenna. The Visigoths entered Rome unopposed in 410 and Alaric permitted them to plunder the city for three days.

The sack of Rome had a devastating impact on imperial morale, but in historical perspective it appears as a mere incident in the disintegration of the Western Empire. The Visigoths soon left the city to its blundering emperor and turned northward into southern Gaul and Spain where they established a kingdom that endured until the Muslim conquests of the eighth century. Meanwhile other tribes were carving out kingdoms of their own. The Vandals swept through Gaul and Spain and across the Straits of Gibraltar into Africa. In 430, the very year of St. Augustine's death, they took his city of Hippo. A new Vandal kingdom arose in North Africa, centering on ancient Carthage. Almost immediately the Vandals began taking to the sea as buccaneers, devasting Mediterranean shipping and sacking one coastal city after another. Vandal piracy shattered the age-long peace of the Mediterranean and dealt a crippling blow to the waning commerce of the Western Empire.

Midway through the fifth century the Huns themselves moved

against the west, led by their pitiless leader Attila, the "Scourge of God." Defeated by a Roman-Visigothic army in Gaul in 451, they returned the following year, hurling themselves toward Rome and leaving a path of devastation behind them. The western emperor abandoned Rome to Attila's mercies, but the Roman bishop, Pope Leo I, traveled northward from the city to negotiate with the Huns on the wild chance that they might be persuaded to turn back. Oddly enough, Pope Leo succeeded in his mission. Perhaps because the health of the Hunnish army was adversely affected by the Italian climate, perhaps because the majestic Pope Leo was able to overawe the superstitious Attila, the Huns retired from Italy. Shortly afterward Attila died, the Hunnish empire collapsed, and the Huns themselves vanished from history. They were not mourned.

In its final years the Western Empire, whose jurisdiction now scarcely extended beyond Italy, fell under the control of hard-bitten military adventurers of Germanic birth. The emperors continued to reign for a time but their Germanic generals were the powers behind the throne. In 476 the barbarian general Odovacar, who saw no point in perpetuating the farce, deposed the last emperor, sent the imperial trappings to Constantinople, and asserted his sovereignty over Italy by confiscating a good deal of farmland for the use of his Germanic troops. Odovacar claimed to rule as an agent of the Eastern Empire but, in fact, he was on his own. A few years later the Ostrogoths, now free of Hunnish control and led by a skillful king named Theodoric, advanced into Italy, conquered Odovacar, and established a strong state of their own.

Theodoric ruled Italy from 493 to 526. More than any other barbarian king he appreciated and respected Roman culture, and in his kingdom the Arian Ostrogoths and the Orthodox Romans lived and worked together in relative harmony, repairing aqueducts, erecting impressive new buildings, and bringing a degree of prosperity to the long-troubled peninsula. The improved political and economic climate gave rise to a minor intellectual revival that contributed to the transmission of Greco-Roman culture into the middle ages. The philosopher Boethius, a high official in Theodoric's regime, produced philosophical works and translations which served as fundamental texts in western schools for the next 500 years. His *Consolation of Philosophy*, an interesting mixture of Platonism and Stoicism, was immensely popular throughout the middle ages. Theodoric's own secretary, Cassiodorus, was another scholar of considerable distinction. Cassiodorus spent his later years as abbot of a monastery and set his monks to the invaluable task of copying

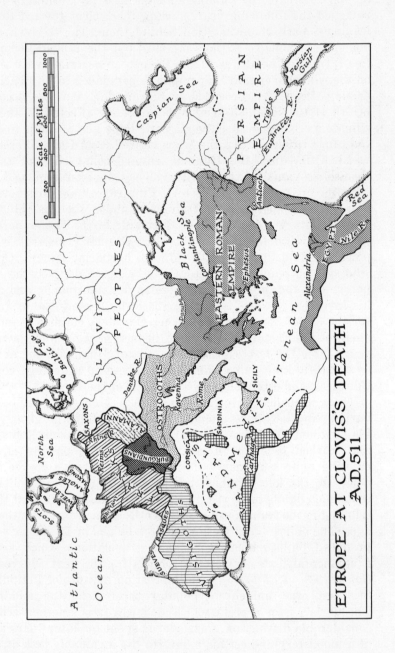

EUROPE AT CLOVIS'S DEATH
A.D. 511

and preserving the great literary works of antiquity, both Christian and pagan.

During the years of Theodoric's beneficent rule in Ostrogothic Italy, another famous barbarian king, Clovis (481–511), was creating a Frankish kingdom in Gaul. Clovis was far less Romanized, far less enlightened, far crueler than Theodoric, but his kingdom proved to be the most enduring of all the barbarian successor states. The Franks were good farmers as well as good soldiers and they established deep roots in the soil of Gaul. Moreover, the Frankish regime was buttressed by the enthusiastic support of the Roman Catholic church. For Clovis, who had been untouched by Arianism, was converted directly from heathenism to Catholic Christianity. He remained a brutal barbarian to the end, yet the church came to regard him as another Constantine—a defender of orthodoxy in a sea of Arianism. As the centuries went by, the royal name Clovis was softened to "Louis" and the "Franks" became the "French." And the friendship between the Frankish monarchy and the Church developed into one of the great determining elements in European politics.

Europe in A.D. 500

As the sixth century dawned, the Western Empire was only a memory. In its place was a group of barbarian successor states that foreshadowed in certain respects the nations of modern Western Europe. Theodoric headed a tolerant and relatively enlightened Ostrogothic-Arian regime in Italy. The barbaric but orthodox Clovis was completing the Frankish conquest of Gaul. The Vandal monarchy, Arian in religion and increasingly corrupt and intolerant, lorded it over the restive population of North Africa. The Arian Visigoths were being driven out of southern Gaul by the Franks, but their regime continued to dominate Spain for the next two centuries. And the Angles and Saxons were in the process of establishing a group of small heathen kingdoms in Britain that would one day coalesce into "Angleland" or England.

At the very time that the Germanic kingdoms were establishing themselves in the West, the Roman papacy was beginning to play an important independent role in European society. We have seen how the great mid-fifth century pope, Leo I (440–461), assumed the task of protecting the city of Rome from the Huns, thereby winning for himself the moral leadership of Italy. Leo and his successors declared that the papacy was the highest authority in the Church, and, following the example of St. Ambrose, they insisted on the supremacy of Church over state in spiritual matters. In proclaiming its doctrines of papal supremacy in the Church and ecclesiastical independence from state control, the papacy was hurling a direct challenge at Byzantine Caesaropapism. In the fifth century these papal doctrines remained little more than words, but they were to result in an ever-widening gulf between the Eastern and Western Church. More than that, they constituted the opening phase of the prolonged medieval struggle between the rival claims of Church and state. The mighty papacy of the High Middle Ages was yet many centuries away, but it was already foreshadowed in the bold independence of Leo I. The Western Empire was dead, but eternal Rome still claimed the allegiance of the world.

Chronology Of The Roman Empire

44 B.C.:	Assassination of Julius Caesar
31 B.C.–A.D. 14:	
	Reign of Augustus
96–180:	The Age of the great second-century emperors
235–284:	Height of the anarchy
185–254:	Origen
205–270:	Plotinus
284–305:	Reign of Diocletian
306–337:	Reign of Constantine
325:	Council of Nicaea
330:	Founding of Constantinople
354–430:	St. Augustine of Hippo
376:	Visigoths cross Danube
378:	Battle of Adrianople
378–395:	Reign of Theodosius I
395:	Final division of Eastern and Western Empires
410:	Alaric sacks Rome
430:	Vandals capture Hippo
451–452:	Huns invade Western Europe
440–461:	Pontificate of Leo I
476:	Last Western emperor deposed by Odovacar
493–526:	Theodoric the Ostrogoth rules Italy
481–511:	Clovis rules Franks, conquers Gaul

PART THREE

THE EARLY MIDDLE AGES: THE GENESIS OF WESTERN CIVILIZATION

SEVEN

PART THREE
THERAPY
AND DEATH:
THE GENESIS
OF WESTERN
CIVILIZATION

BYZANTIUM, ISLAM, AND WESTERN CHRISTENDOM

Medieval Western Eurasia: A General View

In A.D. 500 the western portion of the Eurasian land mass contained two great civilized powers: the Eastern Roman or "Byzantine" Empire centered on Constantinople and, to its east, the Persian Empire under the rule of the Sassanid dynasty. During the centuries that followed, two other civilizations arose— Western Christendom and Islam. In the seventh century Islam conquered and absorbed Sassanid Persia, and the Eastern Roman Empire had to fight for its life against this explosive new threat from the Arabian Desert. But the Eastern Roman Empire stood its ground against the full force of youthful, militant Islam. Important Byzantine provinces were lost permanently to the Arabs, but Byzantium survived as an empire and a civilization for another 800 years. And as Islam and Byzantium struggled with one another, the civilization of Western Christendom was gradually, painfully arising among the former western provinces of the Roman Empire. In 800 the Frankish monarch Charlemagne was crowned Roman Emperor in the West, thereby endowing this new civilization with the dignity and prestige of the ancient imperial title. By 800 the three great civilizations of medieval and Western Eurasia—Islam, Byzantium, and Western Christendom—were firmly rooted. For the remainder of the Middle Ages these three would continue to dominate Europe, North Africa, and the Middle East.

It was not until the eleventh century, however, that Western Christendom began to achieve sufficient political stability, economic well-being, and creative power to rival Byzantium and Islam. From A.D. 500 to about 1050, Western Christendom was an underdeveloped society struggling for its survival against invaders—and against its own poverty and ignorance. It was in no sense comparable to the civilizations of the Byzantines and Arabs. It commands our attention less for its military, political, intellectual, and artistic achievements than for its success in creating the beginnings of certain institutions and habits of mind that contributed to the rise of a great civilization in twelfth- and thirteenth-century Western Europe—a civilization that, later on, extended its power, techniques, styles, and ideologies across the globe.

The peoples of the three civilizations fought not only among themselves and between each other, but also against external nomadic or seafaring "barbarians." Germanic, Viking, Berber, and Slavic tribes were an incessant threat, and even more dangerous were the Altaic invaders from Central Asia who came westward in recurring waves for nearly a millennium. The Huns, who had preyed on the faltering Roman Empire of the fifth century, were followed westward in subsequent centuries by kindred Altaic peoples: Bulgars, Avars, Magyars (Hungarians, Turks, and finally, in the twelfth and thirteen centuries, the dreaded Mongols. These Asian invaders possessed ruthlessly efficient military organizations based on light cavalry. Their nomadism made them difficult to attack, and their remarkable military mobility posed a grave threat to the sedentary civilizations that they assailed. Some of these Altaic peoples were eventually absorbed into the religious and cultural frameworks of the defending civilizations. The Bulgars adopted Eastern Orthodox Christianity and submitted to the patriarch and the emperor in Constantinople; the Magyars eventually were converted to Roman Catholicism, and their king became a papal vassal. The Avars were ultimately annihilated as a political force by Charlemagne; and the Huns faded back into the East.

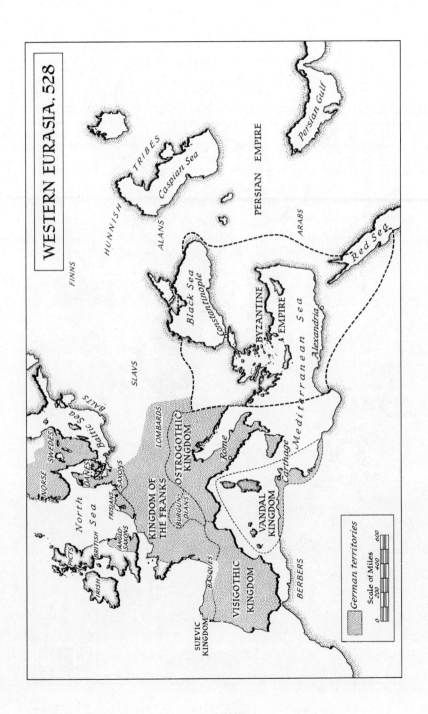

WESTERN EURASIA, 528

FINNS

HUNNISH   TRIBES

Caspian Sea

ALANS

PERSIAN   EMPIRE

Persian Gulf

Black Sea

Constantinople

BYZANTINE

EMPIRE

ARABS

Red Sea

Alexandria

SLAVS

BALTS

SWEDES

NORSE

Baltic Sea

DANES

SAXONS

FRISIANS

PICTS

IRISH

BRITISH

ANGLO-
SAXONS

North Sea

LOMBARDS

KINGDOM OF
THE FRANKS

OSTROGOTHIC
KINGDOM

BURGUN-
DIANS

Rome

Mediterranean Sea

Carthage

VANDAL
KINGDOM

BASQUES

VISIGOTHIC
KINGDOM

SUEVIC
KINGDOM

BERBERS

German territories

Scale of Miles
0   200   400   600

159

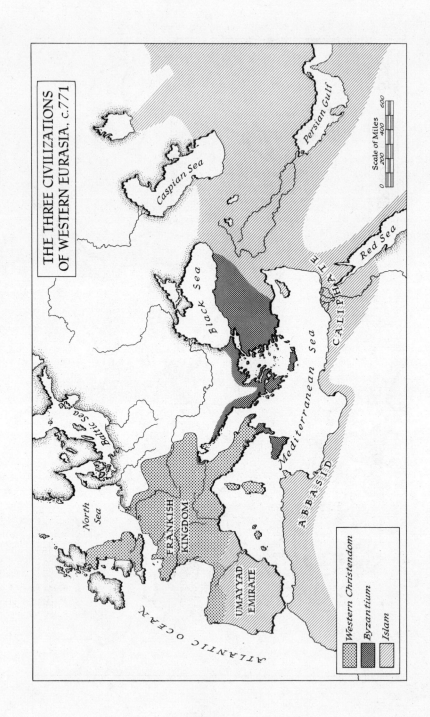

THE THREE CIVILIZATIONS
OF WESTERN EURASIA. c.771

Scale of Miles

0   200   400   600

Caspian Sea

Persian Gulf

Black Sea

Red Sea

CALIPHATE

Mediterranean Sea

ABBASID

Baltic Sea

North Sea

FRANKISH
KINGDOM

UMAYYAD
EMIRATE

ATLANTIC OCEAN

Western Christendom

Byzantium

Islam

After 1050 the Seljuk Turks (and the Ottoman Turks four centuries later) were to assume political control of much of Islam and become militant Muslims. But whether repelled, assimilated, or destroyed, these Altaic peoples were for centuries a source of turbulence and terror, and on occasion they threatened the very survival of the civilizations of Europe and Asia.

The cultural sources of Byzantium, Islam, and Western Christendom were by no means limited to the classical and Hebrew traditions. Western Christendom was a fusion of classical, Christian, and Germanic culture; Islam was at least as oriental as it was Greco-Roman, and the culture of Islamic Baghdad owed much to the traditions of ancient Persia; Byzantium drew inspiration not only from its Greco-Roman past but also from the Ancient-Near-Eastern heritage, which had permeated the Greek world long before, in Hellenistic times. The solemn and magnificent court ceremonial of ancient Persia, which was borrowed in part by the Roman emperors of the late third and fourth centuries, influenced both the imperial rites of Constantinople over the next millennium and the rituals of the Roman papacy that continue to the present day.

Again, late-Roman religious thought was influenced by the concepts of Persian Zoroastrianism. The universal conflict between the Zoroastrian god of good and evil was projected into the world as a series of dualisms: good versus evil, light versus matter. Spirit-matter dualism is to be found in the religious traditions of the Hebrews and even of the Greeks, but it was manifested most clearly and powerfully in Persian thought. Dualism became the dominant note in three great religious movements of the Roman Empire—Gnosticism, Mithraism, and Manichaeism—and through these movements it affected Christianity itself. There were many influential Christian Gnostics in the early history of the church; St. Augustine of Hippo had been a Manichaean before he was a Christian; and Mithraism was one of Christianity's chief rivals among the mystery cults of the third century. Christian orthodoxy consistently resisted the more extreme implications of dualism. Yet Christianity's distinctive vision of a universal synthesis between spirit and matter, soul and body, was modified in the early church, under dualistic influences, into an attitude of renunciation and withdrawal from the world. God had created the earth, and He had dignified the human body by assuming it unto himself in the incarnate Christ. Yet early Christians, living in a religious atmosphere profoundly affected by the dualistic viewpoint—and in an age of vast political and cultural upheaval—tended to renounce the body and flee the world.

Byzantium

By about A.D. 500 the former western provinces of the Roman Empire had become a cluster of political fragments ruled by Germanic tribes, but the Eastern Roman emperors, with their capital at Constantinople, retained control of an immense, crescent-shaped empire girdling the eastern Mediterranean from the Balkans through Asia Minor, Syria, and Palestine, to Egypt. The last western emperor was deposed in 476, and the western provinces had by then been lost, but since the reign of Diocletian (284–305) the political power of the Roman Empire had been concentrated in the East. During the fourth and fifth centuries the Empire changed internally and contracted geographically, yet it survived as an apparently indestructible state and, centered on Constantine's eastern capital, it lived on for another millennium.

Nevertheless, the culture of classical antiquity was gradually transformed in the East, just as in the West, even though the line of eastern emperors continued without significant interruption from the time of Diocletian to 1453. Historians recognize this cultural transformation by giving a new name to the Eastern Roman Empire from about the sixth century onward. It is called the Byzantine Empire, after the ancient Greek town of Byzantium on whose site Constantinople was built. But the cultural change was exceedingly gradual, and one might equally well argue that the era of most significant transition was the third and fourth centuries rather than the sixth.

Byzantine civilization was built on a fusion of three ingredients: Roman government, Christian religion, and Greco-Oriental culture. From Rome, and most particularly from the authoritarian empire of Diocletian and Constantine, Byzantium inherited its autocracy, its administrative system, and its fusion of religious and political power, which has been termed caesaropapism. The celebrated Byzantine emperor Justinian (527–565) sent his armies westward to bring Italy and North Africa back under imperial control, and although these conquests were both expensive and short-lived, they testify to Justinian's dream of reviving the Roman Empire of old. This same concern for the Roman past impelled Justinian to set a group of talented Byzantine lawyers to assemble the huge mass of legal precedents, judicial opinions, and imperial edicts that constituted the age-long legacy of Roman law. These materials were arranged into a huge, systematic collection known as the *Corpus Juris Civilis* the "body of civil law." Justinian's *Corpus* not only became the basis for all future Byzantine jurisprudence, but it also served as the vehicle in which Roman law returned to Western Europe in the twelfth century to challenge the traditional domination of Germanic legal custom. The appearance of the *Corpus Juris Civilis* in the medieval West was of incalculable importance to the development of rational legal systems in the European states. Its effect is still evident in the legal codes of modern nations.

The prevailing Byzantine mood, like the mood of the fourth and fifth century empire, was one of defense—of self-preservation. To the Byzantines, their state was the ark of civilization in an ocean of barbarism—the political embodiment of the Christian faith—and, as such, it had to be preserved at all costs. The virtues appropriate to such a state were entrenchment, not conquest; caution, not daring. If Justinian is the most famous of the long line of Byzantine emperors, he is also the least typical.

The Byzantine Legacy

Throughout the Middle Ages, Constantinople remained Europe's eastern bastion against the Muslims. Its impregnable walls protected not only the Byzantine Empire but Western Europe as well, from the ravages of Asiatic invaders. And the West was indebted to Byzantium for far more than its soldiers and its walls. The Eastern Empire served Western Europe and the world as a custodian of classical culture. The writings of the Greek philosophers, for example, were with a few exceptions unknown in the early medieval West but were preserved and studied in Constantinople. The Byzantines systematized and perpetuated the Roman legal heritage. Byzantine art influenced the work of medieval and Renaissance architects and painters. Byzantine missionaries Christianized and civilized the Slavs and laid the political and theological foundation for Czarist Russia. Indeed, when Constantinople fell in 1453, Moscow became the third Rome: its rulers assumed the Byzantine mantle as Caesars or Czars, lording it over both Church and state just as their Byzantine predecessors had. It has even been suggested that the present rulers of Russia, with their control of both the State and the Communist ideological apparatus, are carrying on the tradition of Byzantine caesaropapism in a secularized form.

Yet the Byzantine achievement had its limitations. Byzantium remained an autocracy to the end, and its creative genius was often inhibited by its profound conservatism. For much of its long history it was a society under siege, and so much of its energy was devoted to its own survival that little was left for social, political, or technological experimentation or bold philosophical speculation. It performed the priceless service of preserving the thought and letters of Greco-Roman antiquity, but perhaps its classical heritage was also a kind of burden; perhaps the Byzantines were so awed by the achievements of their Greco-Roman forebears that they were hesitant to strike out in new directions. In this sense the Byzantines were prisoners of their own past. The sophistication of Constantinople stands in sharp contrast to the ignorance and barbarism of the early medieval West, but the West, for all its barbarism, had the inestimable advantage of a fresh start. Its relapse into intellectual twilight and semi-savagery resulted ultimately in its liberation from the dead hand of the past. The spirit of Greco-Roman antiquity inspired and enriched Western Christendom but did not shackle it.

Islam

Each of Rome's three "heirs"—Byzantium, Islam, and Western Christendom—has affected world history down to the present day. The impact of Western Christendom on today's world is obvious enough. Byzantium shaped the future of Russia and the Balkans. Islam remains a distinctive culture and a living religion extending across an immense area in South Asia, the Middle East, and North Africa—from the East Indies to Pakistan to the Arab world of Southwest Asia and Mediterranean Africa. This vast Islamic belt was created by a militant, compelling religion that burst into the world in seventh-century Arabia.

The new faith was called "Islam" (the Arabic word for "surrender"). Created by the Arab prophet Mohammed out of Christian, Hebrew, and Zoroastrian elements, it was centered on the worship of the omnipotent God of the Hebrews, whom the Muslims called Allah. Mohammed did not claim divinity for himself; rather, he claimed to be the last of and greatest of a long line of prophets running back through Jesus to the Hebrew prophets of old. There was no trinity; Allah was, in the purest sense, One God. Thus, the central dogma of the Islamic faith declares, "There is no god but Allah, and Mohammed is His prophet."

Islam respected the Old and New Testament and was relatively tolerant toward Jews and Christians—the "people of the book." But the Muslim's had a book of their own, the Koran, which superseded its predecessors and was believed to contain the pure essence of divine revelation. The Koran is the comprehensive body of Mohammed's writings, the bedrock of the Islamic faith: "All men and jinn in collaboration," so it was said, "could not produce its like." Muslims regarded it as the word of Allah dictated to Mohammed by the angel Gabriel from an original "uncreated" book located in heaven. Accordingly, its divine inspiration and authority extend not only to its precepts but also to its every letter (of which there are 323, 621). Thus, it loses its authority when translated into another language. Every good Muslim must read the Koran in its original Arabic. As Islam spread, the Arabic language necessarily spread with it.

Mohammed's religion spread outward from Arabia with remarkable speed. In the hundred years following the Prophet's death in 632, Islamic armies shattered the Christian domination of the Mediterranean, destroyed the Persian Empire, seized Byzantium's richest provinces, and nearly took Constantinople. Far to the west, the Muslims swept across North Africa, crossed into Visigothic Spain and conquered it, and pressed deeply into France until they were turned back by the Frankish Christian leader, Charles Martel, in 732, on a battlefield between Tours and Poitiers.

The vast territories that the Arabs conquered were united by a common tongue, a common faith, and a common culture. The untutored Arab from the desert became the cultural heir of Greece, Rome, Persia, and India and, within less than two centuries after Mohammed's death, Islamic culture had reached the level of a mature, sophisticated civilization. Its swift rise was a consequence of the Arabs' success in absorbing the great civilized traditions of their conquered peoples and employing these traditions in a cultural synthesis—both new and unique. Islam borrowed, but never without digesting. What it drew from other civilizations it transmuted and made its own.

During his lifetime Mohammed had become both the religious and the political leader of Arabia. The fusion of religion and politics that he created remained a fundamental characteristic of Islamic society for centuries thereafter. There was no Muslim priesthood; there was no Muslim "church" apart from the Islamic state itself. Mohammed's political successors, the caliphs, were defenders of the faith and guardians of the faithful. The creative tension between church and state, which was to provoke such violence and such creativity in medieval Western Europe, was quite unknown in the Muslim world.

The Islamic Impact

And yet the world of Islam was deeply creative. From Cordova in Spain to Baghdad in Iraq and far to the east, Muslim scholars and artists developed the legacies of past civilizations. Architects molded Greco-Roman forms into a brilliant, distinctive new styles. Philosophers studied and elaborated the writings of Plato and Aristotle, despite the hostility of narrowly orthodox Islamic theologians. Physicians expanded the ancient medical doctrines of Galen and his Greek predecessors, describing new symptoms and identifying new curative drugs. Astronomers tightened the geocentric system of Ptolemy, preparing accurate tables of planetary motions, and giving Arabic names to the stars—names such as Altair, Deneb, and Aldebaran—which are still used. The renowned astronomer poet of eleventh-century Persia, Omar Khayyam, devised a calendar of singular accuracy. Muslim mathematicians borrowed creatively from both Greece and India. From the Greeks they learned geometry and trigonometry, and from the Hindus they appropriated the so-called Arabic numerals, the zero, and algebra, which were ultimately passed on to the West to revolutionize European mathematics.

The Arab conquests during the century after Mohammed changed the historical course of North Africa and Southwest Asia decisively and permanently. The Arabs conquered their vast territories thrice over: with their armies, their faith, and their language. In the end, the term "Arab" applied to every Muslim from Morocco to Iraq, regardless of his ethnic background. Within its encompassing religious and linguistic framework, Arab culture provided a new stimulus and a new orientation to the long-civilized peoples of former empires. With its manifold ingredients, the rich Islamic heritage would one day provide invaluable nourishment to the voracious mind of the twelfth and thirteenth-century west. Later, Islamic armies would bring Byzantium to an end and make Constantinople

Mausoleum in Islamic style, Bukhasa, Central Asia, tenth century.

a Muslim city. Later still, in the sixteenth and seventeenth centuries, they would be at the gates of Vienna. Only in the nineteenth century did Islam become clearly subordinate to the West militarily and politically. And today there are clear signs that this subordination is ending.

Western Christendom

During the half millennium following A.D. 500, while Byzantium struggled to preserve its territory and culture, and while Islamic civilization rose and flowered, Western Europe underwent an agonizing process of decline and rebirth. Classicial civilization collapsed almost totally, and on its ruins there arose, slowly, the new civilization of Western Christendom.

Although many Roman towns survived in the Barbarian West, as the headquarters of important bishoprics and the sites of cathedral churches,* they played a drastically reduced role in the economy of the New Germanic states. The important economic centers of the age were the monastery, the peasant village, and the great farm or villa owned by some wealthy Roman or Germanic aristocrat and divided into small plots worked by semifree tenant farmers. A small-scale international luxury trade persisted, but by and large the sixth and seventh centuries were characterized by economic localism. Small agrarian communities produced most of their own needs and were very nearly self-sufficient.

Except in Britain and the western Rhineland, the Germanic invaders were gradually absorbed by the more numerous native populations. Among the Franks, Visigoths, and Burgundians the free farmers often sank to the level of semi-servile *coloni* within a few generations. The Germanic warrior nobility was to retain its separate identity much longer, especially in Italy, where a Germanic tribe known as the Lombards held sway from the late sixth to the late eighth century. Even after the old and new upper classes became fused through intermarriage, the aggressive, rough-and-ready values of the Germanic aristocracy prevailed.

The barbarian kings, with the exception of the Ostrogoth, Theodoric, in Italy (493–526), proved incapable of carrying on the Roman administrative traditions they inherited. The Roman tax system broke down almost completely, the privilege of minting coins fell into private hands, and the power and wealth of the government declined accordingly. The Germanic kings lacked any conception of responsible government and regarded their kingdoms as private estates to be exploited or alienated according to their whims. They made reckless gifts of land and political authority to the nobility and the church and used what was left for their own personal enrichment. They managed to combine the worst features of anarchy and tyranny.

Since the Germanic kings were doing nothing to enhance the economy or ameliorate the general impoverishment, the Church strove to fill the vacuum. It dispensed charity; offered eternal salvation to the poor, and glamorized the virtue of resignation. But even the Church was ill-equipped to cope with the chaos of the barbarian West. The Roman popes claimed leadership over the Church yet seldom asserted real power beyond central Italy. Elsewhere ecclesi-

---

*Technically, the term *cathedral* denotes the seat of a bishopric—literally, the bishop's throne. A church, whether large or small, is a "cathedral" if it serves as a bishop's headquarters.

astical organization was confined largely to the almost deserted towns and the walled monasteries. Only gradually were rural parishes organized to meet the needs of the countryside, and not until the eighth century did they become common. Until then a peasant was fortunate if he saw a priest once a year. The monarchy and the Church, the two greatest landholders in the barbarian kingdoms, were better known among the peasantry as acquisitive landlords than as fountains of justice and divine grace. The countryside was politically and spiritually adrift, and peasant life was harsh, brutish, and short.

Monasticism and Early Medieval Culture

What little high culture there was in the Early Middle Ages was centered in the monasteries. Ireland had been won for Christianity by St. Patrick in the fifth century, and, by about 600, Irish monasteries had developed a richly creative Celtic-Christian culture. Irish scholars were studying both Greek and Latin literature at a time when Greek was unknown elsewhere in the West. Irish artists were producing superb sculptured crosses and illuminated manuscripts in the flowing, curvilinear Celtic style. Irish Christianity, isolated from the continental Church by the pagan Anglo-Saxon kingdoms, developed its own distinctive organization and spirit, centered on the monastery rather than the diocese. Irish monks were famous for their learning, the austere severity of their lives, and the vast scope of their missionary activities. They converted large portions of Scotland to their own form of Christianity and by the early 600s were doing missionary work on the continent itself.

Meanwhile a very different kind of monastic order, spreading northward from Italy, was making a deep impact on the life of dark-age Europe. This movement was organized in the early sixth century by St. Benedict of Nursia (c. 480–c. 544), a contemporary of Justinian. St. Benedict founded the great monastery of Monte Cassino, between Rome and Naples, and framed a rule of monastic life that inspired and energized the medieval Church. Pope Gregory the Great (590–604) described the Benedictine Rule as "conspicuous for its discretion." Rejecting the harsh asceticism of earlier Christian monasticism, it provided for a busy, closely regulated life, simple but not austere. Benedictine monks were decently clothed, adequately fed, and seldom left to their own devices. Theirs was a life dedicated to God and to the quest for personal sanctity, guided by the obligations of chastity, poverty, and obedience to the abbot. Yet it was also a life that was available to any dedicated Christian, not merely to the spiritual hero. Its ideals were service and prayer under moderate, compassionate leadership.

In the two centuries after St. Benedict's death his order spread throughout Western Christendom. The result was not a vast, hierarchical monastic organization, but rather hundreds of individual, autonomous monasteries sharing a single rule and way of life. Benedict had pictured his monasteries as spiritual sanctuaries into which pious men might withdraw from the world, but the chaotic, illiterate society of the barbarian west, desperately in need of the discipline and learning of the Benedictines, could not permit them to renounce secular affairs.

The Benedictines had an enormous impact on the world they had sought to abandon. Their schools produced the majority of literate Europeans during the Early Middle Ages. They served as a vital cultural link with the writings of Latin antiquity. They spearheaded the penetration of Christianity into pagan England at the end of the sixth century, into Germany two centuries later, and, in the tenth century, into Scandinavia, Poland, and Hungary. They served as scribes and advisers to kings and were drafted into high ecclesiastical offices. As recipients of gifts of land from pious donors over many generations, they held and managed vast estates that became models of intelligent agricultural management and technological innovation. As islands of peace, security, and learning in an ocean of barbarism, the Benedictine monasteries became the spiritual and intellectual centers of the developing Classical-Christian-Germanic synthesis that underlay European civilization. In short, Benedictine monasticism was the supreme civilizing influence in the Barbarian West.

Pope Gregory the Great (590–604)

The Benedictines carried out their great civilizing mission with the enthusiastic and invaluable support of the papacy. The alliance between these two institutions was consummated by the monk-pope, Gregory the Great, who recognized immediately how effective the Benedictines might be in spreading the Catholic faith and extending papal leadership far and wide across Christendom.

Pope Gregory was an important early-medieval scholar—a popularizer of Augustinian thought. But his theology, although highly influential in subsequent centuries, failed to rise much above the intellectual level of his age. His real genius lay in his keen understanding of human nature and his ability as an administrator and organizer. His *Pastoral Care*, a treatise on the duties and obligations of a bishop, is a masterpiece of practical wisdom and common sense. It answered a great need of the times and became one of the most widely read books in the Middle Ages.

Gregory loved the monastic life and ascended the papal throne with genuine regret. On hearing of his election he went into hiding and had to be dragged into the Roman basilica of St. Peter's to be consecrated. But once resigned to his new responsibilities, Gregory devoted all his energy to the extension of papal authority. Following in the tradition of Pope Leo I, Gregory the Great believed fervently that the pope, as successor of St. Peter, was the rightful ruler of the Church. He reorganized the financial structure of the papal estates and used the increased revenues for charitable works to ameliorate the wretched poverty of his age. His integrity, wisdom, and administrative ability won for him an almost regal position in Rome and central Italy, towering over the contemporary Lombards and Byzantines who were then struggling for control of the peninsula. The reform of the Frankish Church was beyond his immediate powers. But he set in motion a process that would one day bring both France and Germany into the papal fold when he dispatched a group of Benedictine monks to convert heathen England.

The Conversion of England

The mission to England was led by the Benedictine St. Augustine (not to be confused with the great theologian of an earlier day, St. Augustine of Hippo). In 597, Augustine and his followers arrived in the English kindom of Kent and began their momentous work. England was then divided into a number of independent barbarian kingdoms of which Kent was momentarily the most powerful, and Augustine was assured a friendly reception by the fact that the king of Kent had a Christian wife. The conversion progressed speedily, and on Whitsunday, 597, the king and thousands of his subjects were baptized. The chief town of the realm, "Kent City" or Canterbury, became the headquarters of the new Church, and Augustine himself became Canterbury's first archbishop.

During the decades that followed, the fortunes of English Benedictine Christianity rose and fell with the varying fortunes of the barbarian kingdoms. Kent declined, and by the mid-600s political power had shifted to the northernmost of the Anglo-Saxon states, Northumbria. This remote outpost became the scene of a deeply significant encounter between the two great creative forces of the age: Irish-Celtic Christianity moving southward from its monasteries in Scotland, and Roman-Benedictine Christianity moving northward from Kent.

Although the two movements shared a common faith, they had different cultural backgrounds, different notions of monastic life and ecclesiastical organization, and even different systems for calculating the date of Easter. At stake was England's future relationship with the Continent and the papacy; a Celtic victory might well have resulted in the isolation of England from the main course of Western Christian development. But at the Synod of Whitby in 664, the king of Northumbria decided in favor of Roman-Benedictine Christianity, and papal influence in England was assured. Five years later, in 669, the papacy sent the scholarly Theodore of Tarsus to assume the archbishopric of Canterbury and reorganize the English Church into a coherent hierarchical system. As a consequence of Northumbria's conversion and Archbishop Theodore's tireless efforts, England, only a century out of heathenism, became Europe's most vigorous and creative Christian society.

The Irish-Benedictine encounter in seventh-century Northumbria produced a significant cultural surge known as the Northumbrian Renaissance. The two traditions influenced and inspired one another to such an extent that the evolving civilization of the barbarian West reached its pinnacle in this remote land. Boldly executed illuminated manuscripts in the Celtic curvilinear style, a new script, a vigorous vernacular epic poetry, an impressive architecture—all contributed to the luster of Northumbrian civilization in the late 600s and the early 700s. This Northumbrian Renaissance centered in the great monasteries founded by Irish and Benedictine missionaries, particularly in the Benedictine monastery of Jarrow. Here the supreme scholar of the age, St. Bede the Venerable, spent his life.

Bede entered Jarrow as a child and remained there until his death in 735. The greatest of his many works, the *Ecclesiastical History of England,* displays a keen critical sense far superior to that of Bede's medieval predecessors and contemporaries. The *Ecclesiastical History* is our chief source for early English history. It reflects a remarkable cultural breadth and a penetrating mind, and establishes Bede as the foremost Christian intellectual since Augustine.

Cross Page from the Lindisfarne Gospels (c. A.D. 700), illustrating the artistic illuminations typical of the Northumbrian Renaissance.

By Bede's death in 735 the Northumbrian kings had lost their political hegemony, and Northumbrian culture was beginning to fade. But the tradition of learning was carried from England back to the Continent during the eighth century by a group of intrepid Anglo-Saxon Benedictine missionaries. In the 740s the English monk St. Boniface reformed the Church in Frankland, infusing it with Benedictine idealism and binding it more closely to the papacy. Pope Gregory had now been in his grave for 140 years, but his spirit was still at work. St. Boniface and other English missionaries founded new Benedictine monasteries among the Germans east of the Rhine and began the long and difficult task of Christianizing and civilizing these savage peoples, just as Augustine and his monks had once Christianized heathen Kent. By the later 700s the cultural center of Christendom had shifted southward again from England to the rapidly rising empire of the Frankish leader Charlemagne, whose career will be traced in the following chapter. Significantly, the leading scholar in Charlemagne's kingdom was Alcuin, a Benedictine monk from Northumbria.

The Church and Western Civilization

The Barbarian West differed from the Byzantine and Islamic East in innumerable ways, the most obvious being its far lower level of civilization. But even more important is the fact that the Western Church was able to reject caesaropapism and to develop more or less independently of the state. Church and state often worked hand in hand, yet the two were never merged as they were in Byzantium, Islam and most ancient civilizations. The early Christian West was marked by a profound dichotomy—a separation between cultural leadership, which was ecclesiastical and monastic, and political power, which was in the hands of the barbarian kings. This dualism underlay the fluidity and dynamism of Western culture. It produced a creative tension that tended toward change rather than crystallization, toward an uninterrupted series of cultural climaxes, and toward ever-new intellectual and spiritual configurations. The heroic warrior culture of the Germanic states and the classical-Christian culture of Church and monastery remained always in the process of fusion yet never completely fused. The interplay between these two worlds governed the development of medieval civilization.

EIGHT

CAROLINGIAN, EUROPE AND THE NEW INVASIONS

The Rise of the Carolingians

Just as the new Europe was aroused spiritually by the wide-ranging Benedictines, it was united politically by the new Carolingian dynasty of Frankish monarchs.* The original Frankish dynasty—the Merovingians—had declined over the centuries since Clovis's days, from bloodthirsty autocrats to crowned fools. Their policy of dividing royal authority and crown lands among all the sons of a deceased king further weakened Merovingian authority and, by the later 600s, all real power had passed to the aristocracy. The greatest Frankish noble family at this time, the Carolingians, had risen to power in northeastern Frankland and had established a firm grip on the chief viceregal office in the

---

*The dynasty has been termed "Carolingian" by later historians, after its greatest ruler, Charlemagne (Latin: *Carolus Magnus*).

kingdom. The Carolingians became hereditary "mayors of the palace" of the Merovingian kings. In reality, they were, by the late 600s, the military and political masters of Frankland, leading their own armed retainers against internal rivals and commanding the Frankish host against foreign enemies. So it was that Charles Martel (714–741), a masterful and ruthless Carolingian mayor of the palace, led the Franks to victory over the Muslims at Tours in 732. Charles Martel's son, Pepin the Short, won for his family the Frankish crown itself, and Pepin's son, Charlemagne, won an empire.

The Coronation of Pepin (751)

By around 750, the Carolingian mayor, Pepin the Short (741–768), had hopes of establishing his own dynasty upon the Frankish throne in place of the incompetent Merovingians. But the Merovingian kings, with all their weaknesses, retained the enormous prestige that Germanic royal dynasties always enjoyed. If the Carolingians aspired to replace them, they would have to call upon the most potent spiritual sanction available to their age; papal consecration. As mayors of the palace, the Carolingians had supported the re-forming activities of St. Boniface and his English Benedictine monks in Frankland and had thereby established a warm relationship with the Benedictines' great ally, the papacy. Now, seeking papal support for a dynastic revolution, Pepin the Short could reasonably expect a favorable response from Rome.

The popes, for their part, had been seeking a defender against the Byzantines and the aggressive Lombards, who had long been contending for political supremacy in Italy. The Carolingians would have seemed strong candidates for the role of papal champion. And by the mid-eighth century the pope was in desperate need of such a champion. The Lombards, although they had by now adopted trinitarian Christianity, were an ominous threat to papal independence. And by 750, they were on a rampage, threatening not only the Byzantine territories in Italy but the lands of the pope himself. The Byzantines seemed neither able nor inclined to protect the papacy. Over the years the Eastern and Western Churches had been drifting apart and, by 750, they were separated by major theological differences. If Pepin the Short needed the papacy, the papacy needed Pepin even more.

So, the alliance was struck. Pepin was anointed King of the Franks by the Pope's representative, St. Boniface, in 751 and by the pope himself three years later. Thus Pepin became a king not by mere force and usurpation but by the supernatural potency of the royal anointing. The last of the Merovingians were packed off to a monastery and, shortly thereafter, Pepin paid his debt by leading an army into Italy. Defeating the Lombards in battle, he granted the pope a large territory around Rome. This "Donation of Pepin" had the immediate effect of relieving the papacy of the dangerous Lombard pressure. More important, the lands that the pope received from Pepin became the nucleus of the Papal States, which would dominate central Italy until the late nineteenth century.

Charlemagne (768–814)

Pepin, for all his accomplishments, was overshadowed by his far more celebrated son. Charles the Great, or Charlemagne, was a phenomenally gifted military commander, a statesman of rare skill, a friend of learning, and a monarch possessed of a deep sense of responsibility for the welfare of his society. Like all successful rulers of his time, he was a warrior-king. He led his armies on yearly campaigns as a matter of course; the decision to be made each year was not whether to fight but whom to fight. Only gradually did Charlemagne develop a notion of Christian mission and a program of unifying and systematically expanding the Christian west. At the behest of the papacy, he conquered Lombard Italy in 774 and incorporated it into his growing empire. He carved out at Muslim expense a "Spanish March" on the Iberian side of the Pyrenees, centered in Barcelona. He conquered and absorbed Bavaria, organizing its easternmost district into a forward defensive barrier against the Slavs. This East March or *Ostmark* became the nucleus of a new state later to be called Austria. Most important of all, he campaigned intermittently for more than 30 years in northern Germany against the pagan Saxons (772–804). By the early ninth century the Frankish control of Saxony was assured, and in subsequent decades, through the tireless work of Benedictine monks, the Saxons were thoroughly Christianized. A century and a half later, Christian Saxons were governing the most powerful and enlightened state in Europe.

Charlemagne's armies, by incorporating central Germany into

Contemporary bronze figure of Charlemagne.

the new civilization, had succeeded where the Roman emperors had failed. By 800, Charlemagne was the master of Western Christendom. Only a few small Christian kingdoms in the British Isles and northwestern Spain remained outside his jurisdiction. On Christmas Day, 800, his accomplishment was given formal recognition when the pope placed the imperial crown on his head and acclaimed him "Emperor of the Romans." From the standpoint of

THE CAROLINGIAN EMPIRE

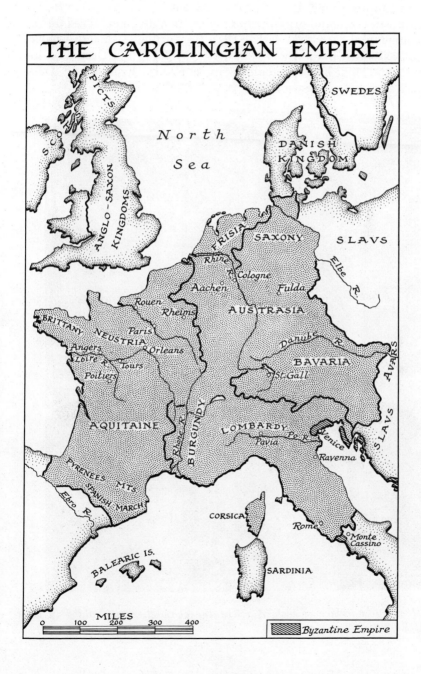

legal theory, this coronation reconstituted the Roman Empire in the west after an interregnum of 324 years.

But Carolingian Europe differed radically from the Western Roman Empire of old. It was a land without large cities, thoroughly agrarian in economic organization, with its culture centered on the monastery and cathedral rather than the forum. Although Charlemagne extended his authority into Italy, Spain, and Germany, his capital and his heart remained in northern Frankland. Thus,

Charlemagne's Palace church, Aachen; the chandelier was added in the twelfth century.

St. Peter giving symbols of authority to Pope Leo III and Charlemagne—
the pallium to Leo III, the imperial standard to Charlemagne. Mosaic in
St. John's Lateran, Rome.

Carolingian Europe no longer faced the Mediterranean. The axis of western culture had shifted northward. And this northward shift shaped Europe's development far into the future.

Agrarian Technology

The relative brightness of Charlemagne's age resulted from creative processes that had been at work during the preceding darker centuries. One of the most important of these processes was the development of a new agrarian technology that eventually increased the productivity of northern European farmlands well beyond the level of the old Roman Empire.

By the opening of the eighth century, the ineffective scratch plow of Roman times had been replaced in the northern districts of Western Europe by a heavy compound plow with wheels, colter, plowshare, and moldboard, which cut deeply into the soil, pulverized it, and turned it aside into ridges and furrows. This heavy plow—which may have been introduced from the Slavic lands in Eastern Europe—could be used in vast areas of rich, heavy soil where the Roman scratch plow was ineffective. It also accentuated the tendency toward dividing fields into long strips cultivated by the eight-ox teams the heavy plow required. Peasants now pooled their oxen and their labor in order to exploit the heavy plow, and in doing so they laid the foundation for the cooperative agricultural communities of medieval Europe, with their strong village councils regulating the division of labor and resources.

The coming of the heavy plow resulted in a significant change in the method of crop rotation. By the Carolingian age, much of northern Europe was beginning to adopt the three-field system in place of the two-field system characteristic of Roman times. Formerly, a typical farm had been divided into two fields, each of which, in turn, was planted one year and left fallow the next. This pattern continued in southern Europe throughout the Middle Ages. But the rich northern soils, newly opened by the heavy plow, did not require a full year's rest between crops. They were often divided now into three fields, each of which underwent a three-year cycle system of autumn planting, spring planting, and fallow. The three-field system increased food production significantly and brought unprecedented prosperity to northern Europe, perhaps contributing to the northward shift of the Carolingian era.

Meanwhile, the water mill, which was used only occasionally in antiquity for grinding grain, had come into fairly widespread use on Carolingian farms. During the centuries following Charlemagne's death the water mill was put to new uses—to power the rising textile industry of the eleventh century and to drive trip hammers in forges. Thus, technological progress continued over the medieval centuries. By A.D. 1000 the coming of the horseshoe and a new, efficient horse collar—both apparently imported from Siberia or Central Asia—made possible the very gradual substitution of the horse for the less efficient ox on the richer north European farms. And in the twelfth century the windmill made its debut in the European countryside. These post-Carolingian advances resulted in the greater productivity underlying the vital civilization of the twelfth and thirteenth centuries. Carolingian Europe profited from the earlier phase of this steady advance in agrarian technology.

The Carolingian Renaissance

The significant intellectual revival known as the "Carolingian Renaissance" was largely a product of Charlemagne's concern for the welfare of the church and the perpetuation of Classical-Christian culture. Charlemagne assembled scholars from all over Europe. These Carolingian writers produced no lofty abstract throught, no original philosophical or theological systems, and no institutions of higher learning. Rather, they sought to revive and preserve the rudiments of the Classical-Christian intellectual tradition. Under the leadership of the Englishman Alcuin of York they set about to rescue continental culture from the pit of ignorance into which it was sinking. Alcuin prepared an accurate new edition of the Bible, purged of the scribal errors that had crept into it over the centuries, thereby saving Western Christian culture from the confusion arising from the corruption of its fundamental text. Carolingian scholars also purified the church liturgy and encouraged the preaching of sermons. They carried further the monastic reforms begun in Frankland by earlier Benedictines and saw to it that every major monastery had a school. They developed a new, standardized script—the Carolingian minuscule—to replace the varied and sometimes illegible scripts previously employed. And throughout the realm, monks set about copying manuscripts on an unprecedented scale.

With the gradual disintegration of Western European unity after Charlemagne's death in 814, the momentary fusion of political and spiritual energies slowly dissolved, yet the intellectual revival continued. In ninth- and tenth-century monasteries and cathedrals (particularly those of the recently conquered German districts), documents continued to be copied and schools continued to function. By the eleventh century, Europe was ready to build soaring and original intellectual edifices on its sturdy Carolingian foundations.

Carolingian Chronology

714–741:	Rule of Charles Martel.
733:	Arabs defeated at Tours.
741–768:	Rule of Pepin the Short.
751:	Pepin crowned king of the Franks. Merovingian Dynasty ends.
768–814:	Reign of Charlemagne.
772–804:	Charlemagne's Saxon Wars.
800:	Charlemagne crowned Roman Emperor.
843:	Treaty of Verdun.

The Carolingian Breakdown

The economic and cultural revival under Charlemagne was reversed after his death by an internal political breakdown and new invasions from without. During the ninth and tenth centuries Europe struggled grimly against the attacks of Hungarians (Magyars) from Central Asia, Saracens (Muslims) from North Africa, and Vikings from Scandinavia. In addition to these external pressures, the empire suffered an internal breakdown under Charlemagne's immediate successors. In the Treaty of Verdun (843) the empire was divided among his three grandsons, and the division became permanent.

The three kingdoms created by the Treaty of Verdun foreshadowed the political division of later Western Europe. The East Frankish realm became the nucleus of modern Germany; the West Frankish realm evolved directly into the kingdom of France. The Middle Kingdom stretched northward from Italy through Burgundy, Alsace, Lorraine, and the Netherlands and included considerable parts of what are now western Germany and eastern France; its territories soon became fragmented and were to be the source of disputes between France and Germany over the next millennium.

Saracens and Magyars

The Saracens of the ninth and tenth centuries, unlike their Muslim predecessors in the seventh and eighth, came as brigands rather than conquerors and settlers. From their pirate nests in Africa, Spain, and the Mediterranean islands they attacked shipping, plundered coastal cities, and sailed up rivers to carry their devastation far inland. In 846 Saracen brigands raided Rome itself, and as late as 982 a Saracen force routed the army of King Otto II of Germany in southern Italy. But by then the raids were tapering off. Southern Europe, now bristling with fortifications, had learned to defend itself and was beginning to challenge Saracen dominion of the western Mediterranean.

The Hungarians (Magyars), fierce Altaic mounted nomads from the Asiatic steppes, settled in Hungary and, between the late 800s and 955, terrorized Germany and northern Italy. Hungarian raiding parties ranged far and wide, seeking defenseless settlements to plunder, avoiding fortified towns, and outriding and outmaneuvering the armies sent against them. But in time they became more sedentary, gave more attention to their farms, and lost much of their nomadic savagery. In 955, King Otto I of Germany crushed a large Hungarian army at the Battle of Lechfeld in southern Germany and brought the raids to an end at last. Within another half century the Hungarians had adopted Christianity and were becoming integrated into the community of Christian Europe.

The Vikings

The Vikings, or Norsemen, were the most fearsome invaders of all. These redoubtable warrior seafarers came from Scandinavia, the very land that had, centuries before, disgorged many of the Germanic barbarians into Europe. But to the ninth-century European—the product of countless Germanic-Celtic-Roman intermarriages, warlike still, but civilized by the church and by centuries of settled life—the pagan Vikings seemed a savage and alien people.

Then, as now, the Scandinavians were divided roughly into Swedes, Danes, and Norwegians, and each group had its own area of enterprise. The Danes concentrated on Northern France and England, the Norwegians on Scotland, Ireland, and the North Atlantic, and the Swedes on the Baltic shores and Russia. Yet the three Norse peoples were much alike, and one can regard their raids,

THE VIKING, HUNGARIAN AND MUSLIM INVASIONS

Atlantic Ocean

ICELAND

VIKINGS

NORWAY

SWEDEN

SCOTLAND

IRELAND

DENMARK

ENGLAND

Rhine R.

Dnieper R.

Kiev

Aachen

Rouen

Paris

Seine

Loire R.

Tours

Danube R.

HUNGARIANS

Danube R.

Black Sea

LOMBARDY

PROVENCE

Marseilles

CORSICA

Rome

Monte Cassino

Naples

Constantinople

SARDINIA

BALEARIC IS.

SICILY

MUSLIMS

Mediterranean Sea

	Vikings
	Muslims
	Hungarians

MILES

0   200   400   600   800

explorations, and commercial activities as a single great international movement. They conquered much of England, terrorized France, and even sailed around Spain into the Mediterranean. In the East, they overran Finland and established a powerful state in Russia—the grand duchy of Kiev. Far to the west, they settled Iceland, discovered Greenland, and planted a short-lived colony on the coast of North America.

In the course of the tenth century, Christianity was beginning to penetrate the Norse world. In about 911, a Carolingian king of the West Franks, Charles the Simple, struck a bargain with a Viking leader named Rollo, whose band had settled around the mouth of the River Seine. The Viking settlers adopted Christianity, and Rollo swore his allegiance to Charles the Simple in return for the king's official recognition of the settlement as a legitimate royal dependency. Expanding gradually over subsequent generations, this Norse settlement came to be known as the duchy of Normandy. Little by little, its inhabitants absorbed French culture and adopted the French tongue, yet they retained much of their former vitality and wanderlust. By the eleventh century, Normandy was producing some of Europe's ablest knights, crusaders, administrators, and monks; and its armies and statebuilders were carrying French Christian culture into faraway lands—England, Southern Italy, Sicily, Antioch, and Muslim Spain.

Meanwhile, in Scandinavia itself, centralized monarchies were developing in Denmark, Norway, and Sweden and, as their political authority grew, the Viking spirit was gradually tamed. Around the year 1000, Christianity was winning converts all across the Viking world. In Iceland, in Russia*—even in the kingdoms of Scandinavia itself—the ferocious Northmen were adopting the religion of the monks who had once so feared them. Scandinavia was becoming a part of Western European culture.

*The grand duke of Kiev adopted Byzantine Christianity here in about 988.

NINE

EUROPE SURVIVES THE SIEGE

The invasions of the ninth and tenth centuries wrought notable changes in the political and social organization of West⸗ern Europe. Generally speaking, political authority tended to crumble into small, local units as cumbersome royal armies proved incapable of coping with the lightning raids. This was decidedly true in France, but less so in Germany where the monarchy, after a period of relative weakness, recovered spectacularly in the tenth century. In England, paradoxically, the hammer blows of the Danes ultimately led to the union of several Anglo-Saxon states into a single English kingdom.

The Unification of England

In the late eighth century, on the eve of the Viking invasions, England was poli⸗tically fragmented, as it had been ever since the Anglo-Saxon conquests. Its conversion to Christianity in the sixth

191

and seventh centuries had produced a degree of ecclesiastical centralization but no political unity. Over the centuries, however, the smaller kingdoms had gradually been passing under the control of three larger ones—Northumbria in the north, Mercia in the midlands, and Wessex in the south. The Danish attacks of the ninth century destroyed the power of Wessex's rivals, clearing the field for the Wessex monarchy and thereby hastening the trend toward consolidation that was already underway.

King Alfred the Great

The Danes might well have conquered Wessex itself had it not been that at the moment of crisis a remarkable leader rose to the Wessex throne. Alfred the Great (871–899) did everything in his power to save his kingdom from the Vikings, fighting them, bribing them, constructing fortress-sanctuaries throughout the land, directing the building of an English fleet. And in the end, Wessex not only endured but expanded significantly under Alfred's leadership. In the 880s a peace treaty between Alfred and the Danes gave Wessex most of southern and western England. The remainder of England —the "Danelaw"—remained hostile, but all non-Danish England was now united under King Alfred.

Like all successful leaders of the age, Alfred was an exceedingly able warrior. But he was far more than that. He was a brilliant, imaginative organizer who systematized military recruitment and founded the English navy, seeing clearly that Christian Europe could not hope to drive back the Vikings without challenging them on the seas. He filled his land with fortresses which served both as defensive strongholds and as places of sanctuary for the agrarian population in time of war. And gradually, as the Danish tide was rolled back, new fortresses were built to secure the territories newly reconquered. Alfred clarified and rationalized the laws of his people, enforced them strictly, and ruled with an authority such as no Anglo-Saxon king had exercised before his time.

This remarkable monarch was also a scholar and a patron of learning. His intellectual environment was even less promising than Charlemagne's had been. The great days of Bede, Boniface, and Alcuin were far in the past, and by Alfred's time, Latin—the key to classical Christian culture—was almost unknown in England. Like Charlemagne, Alfred gathered scholars from far and wide—Eng-

ENGLAND ABOUT 885

Scale of Miles
0 20 40 60 80 100

SCOTS

Picts

Tay

North

Firth of Forth

ENGLISH NORTHUMBRIA

•LINDISFARNE

Sea

Picts

IRELAND

Whitby

York

Irish Sea

Tees

DANELAW

WALES

ENGLISH MERCIA

Trent R.

Severn R.

Ouse

EAST ANGLIA

Thames London
R.

SURREY

KENT

Canterbury

DEVON

WESSEX

SUSSEX

CORNWALL

English Channel

land, Wales, the Continent—and set them to work teaching Latin and translating Latin classics into the Anglo-Saxon language. Alfred himself participated in the work of translation, rendering such works as Boethius' *Consolation of Philosophy,* Pope Gregory's *Pastoral Care,* and Bede's *Ecclesiastical History* into the native tongue. In his translation of Boethius, Alfred added a wistful comment of his own: "In those days one never heard tell of ships armed for war." And in his preface to the *Pastoral Care* he alluded with nostalgia to the days "before everything was ravaged and burned, when England's churches overflowed with treasures and books." Alfred's intellectual revival, even more than Charlemagne's, was a salvage operation rather than an outburst of originality. He was both modest and accurate when he described himself as one who wandered through a great forest collecting timber with which others could build.

Alfred's task of reconquest was carried on by his able successors in the first half of the tenth century. Midway through the century all England was in their hands, and the kings of Wessex had become the kings of England. Great numbers of Danish settlers still remained in northern and eastern England—the amalgamation of Danish and English customs required many generations—but the creative response of the Wessex kings to the Danish threat had transformed and united the Anglo-Saxon world. Out of the agony of the invasions the English monarchy was born.

French Feudalism

In England the invasions stimulated the trend toward royal unification; in France they encouraged a shattering of political authority into small local units. This paradox can be explained in part by the fact that France, unlike England, was far too large for the Vikings to conquer. Although many of them settled in Normandy, the chief Norse threat to France came in the form of plundering expeditions rather than large conquering armies. Distances were too great, communications too primitive, and the national territorial army too unwieldy for the king to take the lead in defending his realm. Military responsibility descended to local lords who alone could hope to protect the countryside from the swift and terrible Viking assaults. The French Carolingians became increasingly powerless until at length, in 987, the crown passed to a new dynasty—the

Capetians.* During the twelfth and thirteenth centuries the Capetian family produced some of France's most illustrious kings, but for the time being the new dynasty was as powerless as the old one. After 987, as before, the nobles overshadowed the king. About all one can say of the French monarchy in these dark years is that it survived.

The Viking Age witnessed the birth of feudalism in France. In a very real sense feudalism was a product of France's response to the invasions. Yet in another sense the Franks had long been drifting in a feudal direction. The roots of feudalism ran deep: one root was the honorable bond of fidelity and service of a warrior to his lord, which characterized the lord-vassal relationship of late-Merovingian and early-Carolingian times, and the still earlier comitatus of the Germanic barbarians. Another root was the late-Roman and early-medieval concept of land-holding in return for certain services to the person who granted the land. An estate granted to a tenant in return for service was known as a *benefice*.

The Carolingians took an important step toward feudalism by joining the institutions of benefice and vassalage. There were several reasons for this step. For one thing money was in very short supply throughout the Early Middle Ages so that it was difficult for a ruler to support his soldiers with wages. Often the vassals of an important Frankish lord were fed and sheltered in his household. Indeed, the "household knight" persisted throughout the feudal age. But as their military importance grew these warrior-vassals exhibited an ever-increasing hunger for land. Their lords were therefore under considerable pressure to grant them estates—benefices—in return for their loyalty and service.

This tendency was associated with a shift in Frankish military tactics. In Merovingian times the Franks had fought chiefly with foot soldiers and light cavalry. Thereafter, heavy cavalry became increasingly important. By the tenth century the Frankish warrior *par excellence* was the armored, mounted knight. A warrior of this sort needed for a fine mount, heavy armor and weapons, several attendants, and many years of training. Hence the tendency for a lord to support his knightly vassals by granting them estates in

---

*The decline of the later Carolingian kings of France and Germany is suggested by the various nicknames they received: Charles the Bald, Louis the Stammerer, Charles the Simple, Louis the Blind, Charles the Fat, Louis the Child, etc. One late Carolingian was called simply Boso.

return for their service. The knight did not, of course, labor on his own fields; rather, he administered them and collected dues, chiefly in kind from his peasants.

The Carolingian military vassal was typically a knight. As knightly tactics came more and more to dominate warfare the custom of vassalage spread widely. The great Frankish magnates of Charlemagne's time pledged their allegiance to their emperor and thereby recognized that they were his vassals and he their lord. Moreover, these royal vassals had vassals of their own who owed primary allegiance to their immediate lords rather than to the emperor. Charlemagne himself approved of this practice and encouraged the free men of his realm to become vassals of his magnates. In time of war these vassals of vassals (or subvassals) were expected to join their lord's contingents in the royal army. The centrifugal tendencies implicit in such an arrangement are obvious. Yet Charlemagne, lacking a civil service or adequate funds to hire a professional army of his own, was obliged to depend on this potentially unstable hierarchy of authority and allegiance.

With the removal of Charlemagne's commanding personality and under the pressure of the invasions, the rickety hierarchy began to crumble into its component parts. Charlemagne's old territorial officials, the dukes, counts, and margraves, backed by their own vassals, tended increasingly to usurp royal rights, revenues, and prerogatives. They administered justice and collected taxes without regard for the royal will. In time, they built castles and assumed all responsibility for the defense of their districts. Nominally, these feudal magnates remained vassals of the kings of France, but they soon became too powerful to be coerced by the crown. Their authority was limited chiefly by the independence of their own vassals who began to create subvassals or sub-subvassals of their own. At the height of the feudal age the lord-vassal relationship might run down through some ten or twenty levels; there was scarcely a vassal to be found who was not the lord of some still lower vassal.

The ultimate consequences of these developments have been described as "feudal anarchy." In a sense the term is well chosen, but it should not mislead us into thinking of feudalism simply as a "bad thing." Given the instability of the Carolingian Empire and the desperate plight of France in the Viking era, feudalism emerges as a realistic accommodation to the hard facts of the age. It should never be forgotten that whereas Roman Europe succumbed to barbarian invasions, Feudal Europe survived its invaders and ultimately absorbed them.

French feudalism reached its height in the tenth and eleventh centuries. Its key institution was the military benefice, the estate granted by a lord to his vassal in return for allegiance and service— primarily knightly military service. This military benefice was commonly known as a *fief* (rhyming with beef).* It was a logical response to the desperate requirements of local defense, the perpetuation of at least some degree of political authority, and the scarcity of money which necessitated paying for service in land rather than wages. A great lord would grant an estate—a fief—to his vassal. The vassal might then grant a part of the estate— another fief—to a vassal of his own. And so on and on, down and down, the process of enfeoffment went. The result was a hierarchically organized landed knightly aristocracy. Each knight gave homage and fealty—that is, the pledge of his personal allegiance— to his immediate lord; each lived off the labor and dues of a dependent peasantry which tilled the fields that his fief embraced; each administered a court and dispensed justice to those below him.

Such were the essential ingredients of feudalism. The term is extremely difficult to define and has been frequently abused and misunderstood. If we wish to put the whole institution in a nutshell, we can do no better than repeat a description of medieval feudalism's greatest modern scholar, the French historian Marc Bloch:

A subject peasantry; widespread use of the service tenement (that is, the fief) instead of a salary, which was out of the question; the supremacy of a class of specialized warriors; ties of obedience and protection which bind man to man and, within the warrior class, assume the distinctive form called vassalage; fragmentation of authority—leading inevitably to disorder; and in the midst of all this, the survival of other forms of association, family and state . . . —such then seem to be the fundamental features of European feudalism.†

With this description in mind it may be helpful to emphasize some of the things that feudalism was not. It was not, for one thing, a universal and symmetrical system. Born in northern France in the Viking age it spread across Europe, taking on many different forms as it expanded into other lands. In northern France itself it varied widely from one region to another. It by no means encompassed all the land, for even at its height many landowners owed

*The Latin word for "fief" is *feudum*: hence our modern term, "feudalism"—a system based on the *feudum* or fief.
†Bloch, *Feudal Society*, II, 446.

no feudal obligations and had no feudal ties. The feudal hierarchy or feudal "pyramid" was riddled with ambiguities: a single vassal might hold several fiefs from several lords; a lord might receive a fief from his own vassal, thereby putting himself in the extraordinary position of being his vassal's vassal. The degree of confusion possible in feudalism can best be appreciated by examining a typical document of the age:

I, John of Toul, affirm that I am the vassal of the Lady Beatrice, countess of Troyes, and of her son Theobald, count of Champagne, against every creature living or dead, excepting my allegiance to Lord Enjourand of Coucy, Lord John of Arcis, and the count of Grandpré. If it should happen that the count of Grandpré should be at war with the countess and count of Champagne in his own quarrel, I will aid the count of Grandpré in my own person, and will aid the count and countess of Champagne by sending them the knights whose services I owe them from the fief which I hold of them.

So much for feudal order.

Feudalism was not, in its heyday, associated with the romantic knight errant, the many-turreted castle, or the lady fair. The knight of the ninth, tenth, and eleventh centuries was a rough-hewn warrior. His armor was simple, his horse was tough, his castle was a crude wooden tower atop an earthen mound, and his lady fair was any available wench. Chivalry developed after a time, to be sure, but not until the foundations of the old feudal order were being eroded by the revival of commerce and a money economy, and by stronger monarchies. Only then did the knight seek to disguise his declining usefulness by turning to elaborate shining armor, lace and ruffles, courtly phrases, and wedding-cake castles.

Feudalism was not entirely military. The vassal owed his lord not only military service but a variety of additional obligations as well. Among these were the duty to join his lord's retinue on tours of the countryside; to serve, when summoned, in his lord's court of justice; to feed, house, and entertain his lord and his lord's retinue on their all-too-frequent visits; to give money to his lord on a variety of specified occasions; to contribute to his lord's ransom should he be captured in battle. Early in its history the fief became hereditary. The lord, however, retained the right to confiscate it should his vassal die without heirs, to supervise and exploit it during a minority, and to exercise a power of veto over the marriage of a female fief-holder. In return for such rights as these the lord was obliged to protect and uphold the interests of his vassals. The very essence of feudalism was the notion of reciprocal rights and obligations. Consequently the feudal outlook played a key role in steering medieval Europe away from autocracy.

Feudalism was both a military system and a political system. With military responsibility went political power. As the kings of West Frankland demonstrated an ever-increasing incapacity to cope with the invasions or keep peace in the countryside; sovereignty tended to descend to the level of the greater feudal lords. Although nominally royal vassals, these magnates were in effect powers unto themselves, ruling their own territories without royal interference and maintaining their own courts and administrative systems as well as their own armies. In the days of the Viking raids many of these magnates had extreme difficulty in controlling their own turbulent vassals; feudal tenants several steps down in the pyramid were often able to behave as though they had no real superiors. Subvassals with their own courts and armies were frequently in a position to defy their lords. It is difficult therefore to identify the real locus of political power in early feudal France. Sovereignty was spread up and down the aristocratic hierarchy, and a lord's real power depended upon his military prowess, his ambition, and the firmness of his leadership.

The feudal chaos of the ninth and tenth centuries, with its extreme fragmentation of sovereignty and its incessant private wars, gradually yielded to a more orderly regime as dukes and counts consolidated their authority over large districts such as Anjou, Normandy, and Flanders. In the eleventh and twelfth centuries royal governments grew stronger, yet the feudal lords remained powerful, drawing their strength from their fiefs. Their prerogatives, and their contractual relationship with the monarchy gave them a degree of autonomy that was based on both legal theory and political reality. Often they cooperated with the monarchy in governing society, but at times it acted, in its own interest, to curb the autocratic impulses of an ambitious king. Like the church, the feudal aristocracy helped to shield medieval Western Europe from the royal absolutism common to most civilizations. The politics of high-medieval Christendom were marked not by the unchallenged rule of priest-kings but by the ever-changing power relationships and creative tensions between monarchy, landed aristocracy, and international church.

The Decline and Revival of the German Monarchy

East Frankland—which evolved directly into the kingdom of Germany—was attacked first by the Vikings and later by Hungarian horsemen of the east. The late-Carolingian kings of Germany—the successors of Charlemagne's grandson who had gained East Frankland in 843 at the Treaty of Verdun—proved incapable of coping with the Hungarian raids. As in France, real authority descended to the great magnates of the realm. Since much of Germany had been only recently incorporated into Western Christendom, the tribal consciousness of Saxons, Bavarians, and Swabians was still strong, and when the kings faltered, it was the dukes of these "tribal duchies" who seized power.

The German Carolingian line ended in 911, and within a few years the dukes of Saxony had established a new royal dynasty. It was under the Saxon dynasty, and particularly under its greatest representative, Otto I, that the particularistic trend was reversed and the king won supremacy.

Otto I—"the Great" (936–973)—based his power on three significant achievements. First, he defended Germany against the Hungarians and crushed them militarily at the Battle of Lechfeld (955), thus opening Germany's eastern frontier to gradual eastward penetration by German-Christian culture. Second, he established royal supremacy over the other tribal duchies, putting down rebellions and recovering royal rights and revenues. And third, he extended German royal control into the crumbling, unstable Middle Kingdom that had been created by the Treaty of Verdun in 843 and had begun to disintegrate soon afterward. The dukes of Swabia and Bavaria had notions of seizing the Burgundian and Italian portions of this defunct state. Otto the Great, anxious to forestall them, led his own armies into Italy and, in 962, was crowned Roman emperor by the pope.

It is the coronation of Otto I in 962, rather than the coronation of Charlemagne in 800, that marks the true genesis of the medieval Holy Roman Empire. Otto's empire differed from Charlemagne's chiefly in the fact that it was German or German-Italian—not a universal empire as Charlemagne's had pretended to be. Otto and his imperial successors exercised no jurisdiction over France nor the remainder of Western Christendom. The medieval Holy Roman Empire had its roots deep in the soil of Germany, and most of the emperors subordinated imperial interests to those of the German monarchy.

THE HOLY ROMAN EMPIRE IN 962

North Sea

Baltic Sea

K. OF DEN.

FRISIA

SAXONY

SLAVS

Rhine R.

LORRAINE

Elbe R.

FRANCONIA

BOHEMIA

FRANCE

SWABIA

Lechfeld

BAVARIA

Danube R.

CARINTHIA

HUNGARIANS

KINGDOM OF BURGUNDY

Rhone R.

Venice

KDM. OF CROATIA

SERVIA

KDM. OF ITALY

CORSICA

Rome

BENEVENTO

APULIA

SARDINIA

CALABRIA

SICILY

0   100   200   300 MILES

▨ The Holy Roman Empire
░ The Five Stem Duchies

Otto and his heirs were never very successful in ruling Italy, but in Germany the emperor was supreme. The great magnates were, for the most part, his obedient vassals. The church was in his power, and he controlled the important ecclesiastical appointments, hand-picking his great bishops and abbots, and using them as his trusted lieutenants in the royal administration. After 962 the German monarchy was even moderately successful in appointing popes. The emperor was regarded as *rex et sacerdos*, king and priest, sanctified by the holy anointing at his coronation. He was the vicar of God, the living symbol of Christ the King, the "natural" leader of the imperial church. There would come a time when the church, under papal leadership, would rebel against this imperial system and ideology, but in Otto the Great's age the time was still far-off.

Otto's remarkable reign gave rise to an intellectual revival that flowered under his two successors, Otto II (973–983) and Otto III (983–1002). This "Ottonian Renaissance" produced talented artists and a group of able administrators and scholars, the most brilliant of whom was Gerbert of Aurillac—later Pope Sylvester II (*d.* 1003). Gerbert visited Spain and returned with a good grasp of Islamic science. The Arab intellectual legacy was beginning to filter into Western Christendom at last. A master of classical literature, logic, mathematics, and science, Gerbert astonished his age by teaching the Greco-Arab doctrine that the earth was spherical. Rumors circulated that he was a wizard in league with the devil, but the rumors were dampened by his elevation to the papacy. Gerbert was no wizard. Rather, he was a herald of the intellectual awakening that Europe was about to undergo—a harbinger of the High Middle Ages.

Europe on the Eve of the High Middle Ages

By 1050 both England and Germany were relatively stable, well-organized kingdoms. The French monarchy remained weak, but its hour was approaching, and meanwhile French feudal principalities such as Normandy, Flanders, and Anjou were achieving political cohesion. Warfare was still endemic, but it was beginning to lessen as Europe advanced toward political stability. Above all, the invasions were over—the siege had ended—and Western Europe would remain untroubled by outside invaders for the next millennium. Hungary and the Scandinavian world were being absorbed into Christendom, and Islam was by now on the defensive.

The Ottonian Crown, tenth century.

Throughout Western Christendom, food production continued to rise with the gradual improvements in agricultural technology and the slowly increasing pacification of the countryside. Beneath the level of the ecclesiastical, political, and military aristocracy, 80 to 90 percent of the population continued to labor on the land. Agrarian organization was almost infinitely diverse: medieval agricultural units ranged from small independent farms to large manors divided between the peasants' fields and the lord's demesne fields.* The

*Manorialism, which regulated the peasants' lives and their relations with their lords, should not be confused with feudalism, which regulated the relations of the nobles with their king and among themselves.

Chronology of the Age of Siege and Its Aftermath

England	France	Germany
c.787: First Danish raid	814: Charlemagne's death	814: Charlemagne's death
871–899: Reign of Alfred	843: Treaty of Verdun	843: Treaty of Verdun
c.954 Reconquest of Danelaw completed	c. 911: Duchy of Normandy established	936–973: Reign of Otto the Great
		955: Otto defeats Hungarians at Lechfeld
		962: Otto crowned
	987: Capetians replace Carolingians as Kings of France	973–983: Reign of Otto III
		983–1002: Reign of Otto III
		1003: Gerbert of Aurillac dies

peasants themselves varied from slaves to freemen, although slaves were sharply declining in number between the ninth and eleventh centuries and the majority of peasants—the serfs or villeins—were neither completely free nor completely enslaved. Like the old Roman *coloni*, they were bound to their land. They owed their manorial lord various dues, chiefly in crops, and were normally expected to labor for a certain number of days per week on their lord's fields. But they were not slaves—they could neither be sold nor be deprived of their hereditary fields. After paying manorial dues, they could keep the remaining produce of their lands, and an efficient serf with good land might hope to prosper. Although hardly affluent, they appear to have been distinctly better off than the peasantry of the ancient civilizations and of medieval Byzantium and Islam. Western Europe was developing into the first major non-slave civilization in human history.

By the mid-eleventh century Western Christendom was beginning to draw abreast of its two neighboring civilizations in political power and in intellectual and cultural vitality. Byzantium and Islam, having dominated Western Eurasia and North Africa during the early middle ages, were both entering periods of political turbulence and decline. But in Western Europe agricultural productivity was increasing, the population was expanding, commerce was quickening, political cohesion was growing, great Romanesque churches were rising, minds were awakening. In the church an impulse toward renewal was galvanizing the spiritual life of the west. Reform monasteries were spreading across the land, and the papacy was about to emerge from its long passivity to challenge the traditional secular dominion over the Church. Western Christendom was on the threshold of an immense creative surge.

PART FOUR

THE HIGH MIDDLE AGES: THE FIRST FLOWERING OF EUROPEAN CULTURE

TEN

ECONOMIC REVOLUTION AND NEW FRONTIERS

The High Middle Ages: 1050–1300

History, it has often been said, is a seamless web. But the human mind can only cope with the flow of historical reality by dividing it into arbitrary chronological units—forcing it into compartments of the historian's own making. In this sense every historical "period" is a kind of falsehood—an affront to the continuity of human development. Yet, unless we concoct historical epochs, unless we invent ages, or unless we force the past into some relatively tidy chronological framework, we cannot make history intelligible to the human mind. Thus, the historian speaks of "Classical Antiquity," "The Early Middle Ages," and "The Renaissance," and the like. These are all historical lies to be sure, but they are necessary lies—white lies —without which the past would have little meaning. It is possible, of course, to subdivide the past into totally different eras than the traditional ones (for

209

example: "Europe in the Making: A.D. 250–1000," "Pre-Industrial Europe: 1100–1789"). But we cannot do without eras altogether; nor should we ever forget that they are inventions of our own.

The term *High Middle Ages* has been applied to the great cultural surge of the later eleventh, twelfth, and thirteenth centuries. The surge did not occur everywhere in Western Christendom at a single moment. Its coming was gradual and uneven. Ever since the ebbing of the Viking, Hungarian, and Saracen invasions, many decades prior to 1050, Western Europe had been pulsing with new creative energy. But, broadly speaking, the scope and intensity of the revival did not become evident until the later eleventh century. By the century's end, Europe's lively commerce and bustling towns, her intellectual vigor and growing political cohesion, her military expansion and her heightened religious enthusiasm left no doubt that potent new forces were at work—that Western Christendom had at last become a mature civilization.

The causes of an immense culture awakening such as occurred in the High Middle Ages are varied and obscure. One essential element was the ending of the invasions and the increasing political stability that followed. We know that in the eleventh century Europe's population was beginning to rise sharply and that its food production was growing. Whether increased productivity led to increased population or vice versa is difficult to say, but productivity could not have risen as it did without the improvements in agrarian technology that had occurred during the preceding centuries.

The Growth of Towns

The growth in productivity and population was accompanied by a significant commercial revival and a general reawakening of urban life. And the new towns, in turn, became the centers of a reinvigorated culture. The frequent human contacts arising from town life stimulated thought and art. The cathedral and the university, two of the supreme achievements of high-medieval culture, were both urban phenomena; the Franciscan order, the most dynamic religious institution of the age, devoted itself primarily to urban evangelism. Yet the towns were also, and above all, centers of commercial and industrial enterprise. The high-medieval economy remained fundamentally agrarian, but the towns were the great economic and cultural catalysts of the era.

The new towns, unlike the administrative-military towns of the

Western Roman Empire or the episcopal towns of the Early Middle Ages, were economically self-supporting. Instead of depending on the labor and taxes of the countryside, the towns lived off the fruits of their own merchant and industrial activities. Small, foul, disease-ridden, and often torn by internal conflict, they were Western Europe's first cities in the modern sense.

The growth of the towns corresponded to the general upsurge of commerce. Sometimes the towns originated as suburbs of older cathedral towns, sometimes as trading posts outside the walls of castles. By 1100 they were springing up all over Europe, but they were concentrated most densely in Flanders and northern Italy, where the opportunities of international commerce were first exploited.

The greatest Italian city of the age was Venice, long a Byzantine dependency but by this time an independent commercial republic that carried on a lucrative trade with Constantinople and the east. Other Italian coastal towns—Genoa, Pisa, and Amalfi—soon followed Venice into the profitable markets of the eastern Mediterranean, and their commerce brought vigorous new life to inland towns such as Florence and Milan. The Muslims were all but driven from the seas, and Italian merchants dominated the Mediterranean.

The Flemish towns grew rich from the commerce of the North, trading with northern France and the British Isles, the Rhineland, and the Baltic coast. Both they and the northern Italian towns became manufacturing as well as commercial centers, producing woolen cloth in large quantities. Textile production developed into the major manufacturing enterprise of the age. As the twelfth and thirteenth centuries progressed, towns were rising and prospering in England, France, and Germany. While the Germans were pushing eastward along the Baltic shore, the thriving towns of old Germany were sending out numerous commercial colonies into the new territories—colonies which themselves became important towns. The North German towns, working collectively, came in time to dominate the Baltic trade and developed far-flung commercial links that stretched from Western Europe into Russia. Eventually, these towns formed themselves into an interurban confederation known as the Hanseatic League, establishing commercial colonies in such western cities as Bruges and London. Even before the advent of the German Hanseatic League, the towns of northern Italy had organized for mutual protection into a Lombard League.

This tendency toward confederation illustrates the townsmen's need to combine forces against the repression of the old order. The

Lombard League struggled for independence from the Holy Roman Empire. And, on a smaller scale, a great many towns had to fight for their autonomy against the monarchs, bishops, or feudal lords on whose lands the town had risen. Only by collective action could the town merchants win the privileges essential to their new vocation: personal freedom from servile status, freedom of movement, freedom from inordinate tolls at every bridge or feudal boundary; the right to own property in the town, to be judged by the town court, to execute commercial contracts, and to buy and sell freely. Collective action expressed itself through tightly regulated merchant guilds, and during the twelfth and thirteenth centuries a number of lords, either through farsightedness or through coercion —or for a price—were issuing town charters that guaranteed many of these rights. Indeed, some lords began founding and chartering new towns on their own initiative.

The charters tended to transform the towns into semiautonomous political and legal entities, each with its own government, its own court, its own tax-collecting agencies, and its own laws. Taxes continued to be paid to the lords in most cases, but they were paid collectively rather than individually.

Within the towns themselves, class distinctions were sharpening. The guilds, composed of merchants who engaged in long-distance trade, tended to dominate, and the craftsmen were, at least at first, in a subordinate status. Before long, however, craftsmen were making their weight felt by combining into various craft guilds. As time progressed, an urban working class grew increasingly numerous; and as conflicts between townsmen and their external lords gradually eased, class conflicts among townsmen grew increasingly severe.

Yet throughout the greater part of the High Middle Ages the towns were avenues to personal freedom and commercial success, astir with new life and bursting with energy. The wealth that they produced was beginning to transform the European economy. Feudalism changed as kings and lords acquired the wealth necessary to replace landed knights with mercenaries in their armies and to replace feudal magnates with professional judges and bureaucrats in their courts and administration. The feudal aristocracy remained strong, but the traditional feudal concept of service in return for land tenure was dissolving.

Agrarian life, too, was changing. Capital and labor were now available to carve out extensive new farm sites from forest and marsh. The great primeval forests of northern Europe were reduced to scattered woods, swamps and marshes were drained, and vast new territories were reopened to cultivation. Agricultural surpluses could now be sold to townsmen and thereby converted into cash. Slavery all but vanished, and serfs were freed on a large scale. With the opening of new lands a competition developed for peasant settlers, and peasant communities were often granted the status and privileges of chartered communes. High-medieval Europe was a buoyant, prosperous society—a society in process of change and growth, which expanded inwardly through the clearing of forest and swamp, and outwardly through the conquest and settlement of vast new territories.

Territorial Expansion

The open, expanding frontier is one of the most characteristic aspects of Europe in the high middle ages. Considerable areas of the Arab, Byzantine, and Slavic worlds were incorporated within the ballooning boundaries of Western Christendom, intensifying Europe's spirit of enterprise and adding wealth to its flourishing economy.

Western Christendom had been expanding ever since 732, and since about 1000 it had pushed far to the north and east through the conversion of regions such as Scandinavia, Hungary, Bohemia, and Poland. North of the Balkans and west of Russia, most Slavic peoples accepted Catholic Christianity rather than Byzantine Orthodoxy. Indeed, Hungary, Bohemia, and Poland, at one time or another, all acknowledged the political lordship of the pope.

During the High Middle Ages, the population boom produced multitudes of landless aristocratic younger sons who sought land and glory on Christendom's frontiers. The church always eager for new converts, supported them. The townsmen, seeking ever larger fields for commercial enterprise, encouraged and sometimes financed them. And the proliferating peasantry served as a potential labor force for the newly conquered lands.

Reconquest of Spain

Thus it was that knightly adventurers from all over Christendom—and particularly from feudal France—streamed southward into Spain in the eleventh century to aid the Iberian Christian kingdoms in their struggle with Islam. The great Muslim caliphate of Cordova had disintegrated after 1002 into small, warring fragments, and the Christians seized the opportunity. Often the reconquest was delayed by wars among the Christian kingdoms themselves. But at length, in 1085, the Christian Kingdom of Castile captured the great Muslim city of Toledo, which thenceforth became a crucial contact point between Islamic and Christian culture. Here, numerous Arabic scientific and philosophical works were translated into Latin and then disseminated throughout Europe to challenge and invigorate the Western mind.

Early in the twelfth century the Christian Kingdom of Aragon, contesting Castile's supremacy, took the offensive against the Moors.* In 1140 Aragon strengthened itself by uniting with Catalonia—the wealthy state around Barcelona which had once been Charlemagne's Spanish March. But further inter-Christian warfare delayed the reconquest until 1212, when Pope Innocent III proclaimed a crusade against the Moors. Advancing from Toledo with a pan-Iberian army, the king of Castile won a decisive victory at Las Navas de Tolosa, permanently crippling Moorish power. Cordova fell to Castile in 1236, and by the 1260s the Moors were confined to the small southern Kingdom of Granada, where they remained until 1492. Castile now dominated central Spain, and Christian peasants were imported en masse to resettle the conquered lands. Aragon, meanwhile, occupied the Muslim islands of the western Mediterranean and won a powerful maritime empire. Thus, the High Middle Ages witnessed the Christianization of nearly all the Iberian Peninsula and its division into two strong Christian kingdoms and several weaker ones.

Southern Italy and Sicily

Probably the most vigorous and militant force in Europe's eleventh-century awakening was the warrior-aristocracy of Normandy—largely Viking in ancestry but now thoroughly adapted to French culture. These Norman knights—French in tongue, Christian in faith, feudal in social organization—plied their arms across the length and breadth of Europe in the reconquest of Spain, on the Crusades to the Holy Land, on the battlefields of England and

---

*By then most of Muslim Spain was ruled by North African Berbers who, having also conquered Morocco, were called Moors in Europe.

THE RECONQUEST OF SPAIN

Map 1 (1000): LEON, FRANCE, NAVARRE, BARCELONA, CALIPHATE OF CORDOVA, Moslem Possessions — **1000**

Map 2 (1100): LEON AND CASTILE, PORTUGAL, ARAGON, BARCELONA, Lisbon, MOORISH STATES, Guadalquivir, BALEARIC IS., Miles 100 200 — **1100**

Map 3 (1212): Compostella, LEON, NAVARRE, ARAGON, Saragossa, CATALONIA, PORTUGAL, CASTILE, Toledo, Valencia, Lisbon, Cordova, Las Navas de Tolosa, Seville, Granada, Mediterranean Sea — **1212**

Map 4 (1300): GALICIA, LEON AND CASTILE, NAVARRE, ARAGON, Barcelona, PORTUGAL, Toledo, Valencia, Cordova, Seville, GRANADA, TO CASTILE 1492 — **1300**

France, and in southern Italy and Sicily. Normandy itself was growing in prosperity and political centralization, and an ever-increasing population pressure drove the greedy and adventurous Norman warriors far and wide on distant enterprises.

During the course of the eleventh century the Normans became masters of southern Italy and Sicily. They came first as mercenaries to serve in the chaotic south-Italian political struggles between Byzantine coastal cities, Lombard principalities, and rising seaport republics such as Naples and Amalfi. Within a few decades the Normans had overthrown their paymasters. By the close of the eleventh century they had won southern Italy for themselves and had conquered Muslim Sicily as well. And in 1130, the Norman leader Roger the Great (d. 1154) fused Sicily and southern Italy into a single kingdom and became its first king.

Roger the Great and his successors ruled firmly but tolerantly over the kingdom of Sicily and southern Italy, with its variety of peoples, faiths, customs, and tongues. Here, a synthesis was achieved of Byzantine, Islamic, Lombard, and northern French cultural traditions and a highly effective political structure was created out of the Byzantine and Islamic administrative machinery that the Normans inherited and shaped. The Sicilian capital of Palermo, with its superb harbor and bustling international commerce, its impressive palace and luxurious villas, was known as the city of the threefold tongue. Islamic, Byzantine, and Western scholars worked under royal patronage, providing Western Christendom with Latin translations of Arabic and Greek texts, and doing important original work of their own. East and west met in Roger the Great's glittering, sundrenched realm, and worked creatively together to make this kingdom the most sophisticated state of its day.

The Crusades

The Crusades to the Holy Land were the most self-conscious acts of Western Christian expansionism in the High Middle Ages, although not the most lasting. They arose in response to the conquests in the Near East of the recently Islamized Seljuk Turks and, in particular, a great Turkish victory over Byzantium at Manzikert (1071), which gave the Turks control of Anatolia. When Constantinople appealed to the west for help, Western Christendom, under the leadership of a reinvigorated papacy, responded emphatically.

The Crusades represented a fusion of three characteristic impulses of medieval man: sanctity, pugnacity, and greed. All three were essential. Without Christian idealism the Crusades would have been inconceivable, yet the pious dream of liberating Jerusalem from the infidel was mightily reinforced by the lure of adventure, new lands, and riches. And to the Italian towns, which financed and provided transportation for many of the Crusades, the Near East offered alluring commercial opportunities.

Accordingly, when in 1095 Pope Urban II urged the European nobility to undertake a crusade to liberate the Holy Land, the response was overwhelming. A great international army—with a large contingent of knights from France, Normandy, and Norman Sicily—poured into Syria and, in 1099, captured Jerusalem. A long strip of territory along the eastern Mediterranean, previously under Islamic rule, was now divided into four Crusader States, the chief of which was the Kingdom of Jerusalem. The king of Jerusalem was the theoretical feudal overlord of the four states, but he had trouble enforcing his authority outside his own realm. Indeed, the knightly settlers in the Holy Land were far too proud and independent for

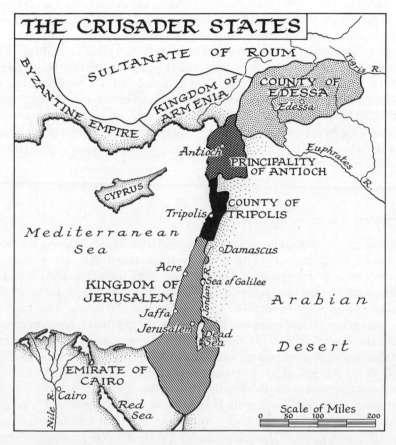

THE CRUSADER STATES

their own good, and from the beginning the Crusader States were torn by internal dissension.

Gradually, the Muslims recovered their strength and began the reconquest of their lost lands. Jerusalem fell to them in 1187, and though in later years such illustrious Christian monarchs as Richard the Lion-Hearted, Emperor Frederick Barbarossa, and St. Louis led crusading armies against the Muslims, the Crusader States continued to crumble. In 1291 they came to an end with the fall of Acre, the last Christian bridgehead on the Syrian coast.

For a time during the Crusading era Constantinople itself was ruled by westerners. The Fourth Crusade (1202–1204) was diverted from Jerusalem to Constantinople by the greed of its Venetian financial backers. The Crusaders took the city by siege in 1204, succeeding where so many before them had failed, and a dynasty of western emperors ruled Constantinople for half a century, until a Byzantine dynasty replaced them in 1261.

The Crusades were more than merely a colorful failure. For nearly two centuries Christians ruled portions of the Holy Land. There, and in Constantinople, they broadened their perspectives by contacts with other cultures. Western merchants established footholds in Syria, vastly enlarging their role in international commerce and bringing wealth and vitality to the Italian cities. When the Crusades withdrew at last from the Holy Land, the Italian merchants remained.

Germanic Expansion in Eastern Europe

The High Middle Ages also witnessed the incorporation of vast areas of Eastern Europe into the civilization of Western Christendom. The Slavic peoples of the Balkans and Russia passed into the sphere of Byzantine Orthodox Christianity, but those north of the Balkans and west of Russia became Roman Catholics. The process of converting these peoples had begun in the tenth century when Otto the Great (936–973) defeated the Hungarians at Lechfeld and established his supremacy over the Slavic lands between the Elbe and Oder rivers. For a time thereafter, the dual processes of Christianization and Germanization went hand in hand. But by the year 1000 the Slavs and Hungarians, while accepting Catholic Christianity, were vigorously resisting German colonization and political suzerainty. Hungary, under its illustrious king, St. Steven (997–1038) adopted Christianity and turned from nomadism to a settled agrarian society of the western type. But St. Stephen and his successors rejected German influences, submitting instead to a tenuous papal overlordship, and the same course was followed by the Catholic Kings of Poland.

In the early twelfth century, Germany began once again to expand its authority and commerce eastward in partnership with Christian evangelism. This new German eastward push—the *Drang nach Osten*—concentrated on the lands along the southeastern shore of the Baltic Sea. It was not a product of active royal policy but, rather, a movement led by enterprising local aristocrats. They succeeded, over a long period running from about 1125 to 1350, in moving the eastern boundary of Germany from the Elbe River past the Oder to the Vistula at Slavic expense. They consolidated their gains by building innumerable agrarian villages and encouraging a massive eastward migration of German peasants. New towns were established that maintained close commercial ties with the older North German towns and that eventually joined with them in the Hanseatic League. The league itself, with its flourishing outposts to the east, was able to dominate the rich trade between Western Europe and the Baltic and Russia. Thus as the new lands were conquered, they were in large part Christianized and Germanized.

The later phases of the *Drang nach Osten* were spearheaded by the Teutonic Knights, a semimonastic German crusading order which transferred its activities from the Holy Land to northern Germany. The Teutonic Knights penetrated far northward into Lithuania, Latvia, and Estonia and even made an unsuccessful bid to conquer the Russian principality of Novgorod in 1242. During the fourteenth and fifteenth centuries the Teutonic order was obliged to forfeit some of its conquests, yet much of the German expansion proved to be permanent.

By the late thirteenth century the great European expansion was drawing to an end. The internal frontiers of forest and swamp had by then been won, and the external frontiers were hardening, sometimes even receding, as in the Holy Land. The German eastward push continued to the mid-fourteenth century, yet as early as the 1240s the Mongols swept out of Asia to seize most of Russia and, for a brief, terrifying moment pierced into the heart of Catholic Central Europe.

The closing of the frontiers was accomplished by diminishing prosperity and a drying up of high medieval culture. The brilliant cultural achievements of the High Middle Ages were products of a buoyant, expanding frontier society, fired by a powerful faith, driven by immense ambitions, and beguiled by a world in which, so it seemed, anything was possible. This world came to an end when the frontiers closed.

Chronology of the European Frontier Movement

Spain	Sicily	Holy Land
1002: Breakup of Caliphate of Cordova	1016: Norman infiltration begins	
	1060–1091: Sicily conquered	
1085: Capture of Toledo		1095: Calling of First Crusade
1140: Aragon unites with Catalonia	1130: Coronation of Roger the Great	1099: Crusaders take Jerusalem
	1154: Death of Roger the Great	
		1187: Crusaders lose Jerusalem
1212: Great Christian victory at Las Navas de Tolosa		1204: Crusaders take Constantinople
1236: Castile takes Cordova		1291: Crusaders driven from Holy Land
1260: All Spain except Granada is under Christian rule		

The High Middle Ages: First Flowering of European Culture

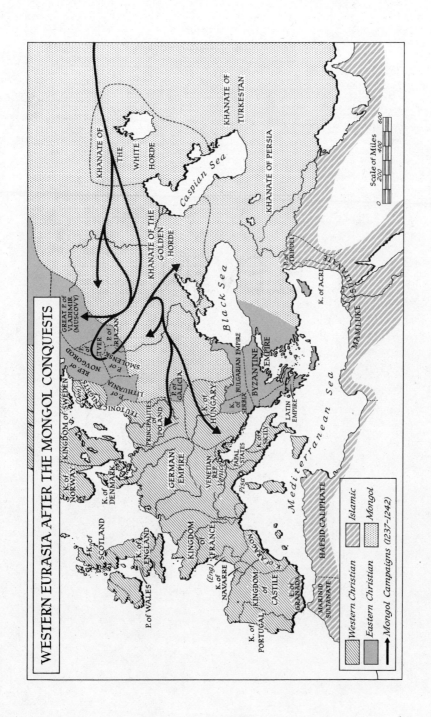

WESTERN EURASIA AFTER THE MONGOL CONQUESTS

KHANATE OF THE WHITE HORDE

KHANATE OF TURKESTAN

KHANATE OF PERSIA

Caspian Sea

KHANATE OF THE GOLDEN HORDE

Black Sea

Scale of Miles
0   200   400   600

GREAT P. of VLADIMIR (MUSCOVY)

REP. of NOVGOROD

P. of TVER

P. of SMOLENSK

P. of RIAZAN

LITHUANIA

K. of SWEDEN

KINGDOM of NORWAY

TEUTONIC KNIGHTS

(Den.)

K. of DENMARK

PRINCIPALITIES of POLAND

P. of GALICIA

K. of HUNGARY

BULGARIAN EMPIRE

SERBIA

BYZANTINE EMPIRE

LATIN EMPIRE

K. of SICILY

GERMAN EMPIRE

VENETIAN REP. (Venice)

PAPAL STATES

Pisa

K. of ACRE

P. of TRIPOLI

MAMLUKE SULTANATE

Mediterranean Sea

HAFSID CALIPHATE

K. of SCOTLAND

K. of ENGLAND

P. of WALES

(Eng.)

KINGDOM of FRANCE

K. of NAVARRE

KINGDOM of ARAGON

K. of CASTILE

E. of GRANADA

PORTUGAL

MARINID SULTANATE

Western Christian   Islamic

Eastern Christian   Mongol

Mongol Campaigns (1237–1242)

ELEVEN

THE POLITICS OF HIGH-MEDIEVAL EUROPE

While the frontiers of Western Christendom were expanding, developments of the greatest historical significance were occurring in the Western European heartland. England and France evolved into centrally governed kingdoms on the road to nationhood. The papacy and the Holy Roman Empire, on the other hand, were locked in struggle. On the eve of their conflict, in 1050, Germany had the mightiest monarchy in Western Christendom, and the German king—or Holy Roman emperor—held the papacy in his palm. By 1300 the Holy Roman Empire was reduced to a specter of its former greatness, and the papacy, after 250 years of political prominence, was exhausted, battle-scarred, and on the brink of a prolonged decline.

The Papacy and the Holy Roman Emperors

The second half of the eleventh century was an epoch of religious awakening and reform. The Christianization of the European countryside had been proceeding steadily over the previous centuries, and a wave of religious enthusiasm was now sweeping through the new towns. Ever since the early tenth century, monastic reform had been surging through Europe, and a centralized network of reform monasteries known as the Congregation of Cluny had become, by the eleventh century, a potent agent of spiritual regeneration.

The Holy Roman Empire with orb and sceptre: manuscript illumination from the Gospel Book of Otto III, A.D. 1000.

224   The High Middle Ages: First Flowering of European Culture

Despite papal claims of the spiritual authority of churchmen over laymen and popes over bishops, the papacy had long been weak, and the church of the mid-eleventh century remained under the firm control of the lay* aristocracy. This arrangement had become traditional and unquestioningly accepted, but to the bearers of the soaring new piety, a captive church—well-fed, conservative, docile, and mildly corrupt—was unacceptable. Pious Christians such as the monks of Cluny protested against the widespread vices of clerical marriage and simony (the purchasing of church offices). And reformers of a still more radical stance, including many of the later-eleventh-century cardinals and popes, challenged the feudal and princely domination of the social order. They insisted that churchmen must not be appointed by laymen but must be elected by other churchmen in accordance with ecclesiastical law. The aristocracy, long accustomed to governing through loyal ecclesiastical subordinates, fought violently against the new reformers. But despite this lay hostility, the reformers gained control of the Roman Synod of 1059 and issued two ringing decrees that, ultimately, shifted the power structure of medieval Europe.

The Investiture Controversy

Striking out in behalf of ecclesiastical independence, the Synod of 1059 declared (1) that thenceforth the pope would not be appointed by emperors or Roman nobles but would be elected by the cardinals, and (2) that laymen would no longer invest new churchmen with the symbols of their offices. For when a layman invested a bishop-elect with the symbolic ring and pastoral staff, the implication was that the bishop owed his office to his lay patron. Henceforth, the church would be its own master.

For nearly 250 years thereafter a powerful, independent papacy strove with considerable success to rule a centralized, hierarchical church—to wrest ecclesiastical appointments from lay control to subordinate monarchs to its spiritual jurisdiction, and to build a vast Papal administration adequate to the needs of an international government. Throughout this era the papacy's chief antagonists were the Holy Roman emperors, who struggled to keep control of

*The term "lay" means anyone not in holy orders; its opposite is clerical.

the imperial church and to extend their political authority deep into Italy. Geographically, papacy and empire were cheek to jowl; ideologically, they were worlds apart.

During the long struggle, the empire employed military power against the papacy, and the papacy replied with potent spiritual sanctions against the emperors—excommunicating them, declaring them deposed, even ordering the suspension of church services (the *interdict*) throughout their domains. There were, oftentimes, imperially supported antipopes and papally supported anti-emperors. The papacy would counter imperial force with the military force of its own allies—the Sicilian Normans, the particularistic German princes, or the North Italian towns. And, at times, England and France were drawn into the conflict, always on opposite sides.

The first great papal-imperial crisis occurred during the pontificate of the fiery reformer Gregory VII (1073–1085). Pope Gregory reissued the lay-investiture ban and took steps to prevent imperial appointments to north-Italian bishoprics. He was immediately challenged by the young emperor Henry IV (1056–1106). The crisis deepened as Gregory excommunicated Henry IV's advisers, Henry declared Gregory deposed, and Gregory declared Henry deposed and excommunicated. At this point many restive German princes, irritated by the ever-tightening imperial centralization, rose against their excommunicated sovereign and threatened to choose another monarch unless Henry IV obtained Gregory's forgiveness. So it was that in 1077 Henry crossed the Alps and stood penitent and barefoot in the snow before Gregory at the Tuscan castle of Canossa. This ultimate act of royal humiliation was also an act of political expedience, for at Canossa Henry was forgiven and reinstated. He returned to Germany to rebuild his power, and once his throne was secure he resumed the struggle against papal reform. Amidst the thunder of armed clashes and renewed excommunications and depositions, Gregory VII died. But there were other popes who would fight, as Gregory had, for a papal monarchy over a free international church—for the supremacy of *ecclesia* over *imperium*. And there were other kings and emperors who, like Henry IV, would struggle grimly to retain their prerogatives over both laymen and churchmen within their dominions.

The Investiture Controversy itself was settled by compromise in 1122. The emperor yielded the right to invest churchmen, while retaining a real, if indirect, voice in their appointment. But the core of the church-state struggle remained untouched. The rival claims of monarchs who aspired to fuller sovereignty and of an international church that aspired to power and independence within each state could not be reconciled.

Frederick Barbarossa, Innocent III, Frederick II

The conflict broke out anew in the reign of the great German emperor, Frederick Barbarossa (1152–1190), who sought to establish firm imperial control in northern Italy and met the fierce opposition of the papacy and the Lombard League of North Italian city-states. The struggle continued during the pontificate of Innocent III (1198–1216), the most powerful of all popes, who directed his astute diplomatic skills not only against recalcitrant emperors but against the kings of England and France as well. He forced King Philip Augustus of France to return to an abandoned first wife; he forced King John of England to accept an archbishop that John had not wanted; and, maneuvering shrewdly through the quicksand of German politics, he enforced his will in a disputed imperial succession.

The final phase of the struggle commenced just after Innocent III's death, when his youthful handpicked emperor, Frederick II (1211–1250), defied the papacy and sought to bring all Italy under his rule. Frederick II matured into a brilliant anticlerical skeptic, known to his admirers as *stupor mundi*—the Wonder of the World —and suspected by his enemies of being the incarnate antichrist. He inherited the Norman Kingdom of Sicily from his mother and Germany from his father. And it took all the skill of the papacy and the unremitting efforts of the North Italian cities to defeat his armies and thwart his ambitions. Shortly after Frederick II's death, the imperial office fell vacant and remained unoccupied for 19 years (1254–1273). At length, it passed to Rudolph of Hapsburg, through election by the German princes and with papal approval.

Consequences of the Papal-Imperial Struggle

By now the imperial office had lost its power. Two centuries of conflict had transformed Germany from a strongly governed state into a chaos of independent magnates. The ambitious princes had usurped imperial lands, revenues, and rights, until, by the late thirteenth century, they had become powers unto themselves. The papal policy of promoting internal dissension and of encouraging rival emperors from competing houses had destroyed the hereditary principle in Germany. The emperors were now elected by the chief princes, and a son succeeded his father only if the powerful princely electors approved. Thus, the papal-imperial conflict doomed Germany to centuries of disunity and political impotence in the affairs of Europe.

Italy suffered, too, for it was the chief papal-imperial battleground. Yet the North Italian cities, encouraged and supported by the papacy, won their independence from imperial authority and emerged from the conflict as independent communes. Cities like Milan, Florence, and Siena—once under imperial jurisdiction—were now autonomous city-states in which, by the late thirteenth century, a rich urban culture was brewing.

The papacy emerged victorious over the empire, yet it, too, lost much in the struggle. Pope Gregory VII had ridden the wave of the new popular piety and, by and large, the townsmen and monastic reformers had been with him. Innocent III, on the contrary, was no man of the people but an aristocratic canon lawer who presided over an immense, complex papal administrative machine. He and his successors were highly skilled in the fields of law, diplomacy, and administration. They built a superb bureaucracy and they humbled monarchs. But gradually, almost imperceptibly, they lost touch with the religious aspirations of the common people. Basically, the power of the papacy rested on its spiritual prestige, and the flock of Christ would not always give its full allegiance to lawyers, tax-gatherers, and politicians. The high-medieval papacy was not a corrupt institution. Rather, it was the victim of its own impulse to enter dynamically into all human affairs. In the beginning it aspired to be a great spiritual force in the world; in the end it became worldly.

As the thirteenth century closed, the papacy was itself humbled, not by the weakened Holy Roman Empire but by the rising monarchies of England and France, whose kings taxed their churchmen against papal wishes and defied the fulminations of Rome. In 1303 French troops seized the proud, intransigent Pope Boniface VIII, and a few years later a French pope, Clement V, abandoned Rome and made his capital at Avignon, in the shadow of the French monarchy. The old medieval powers—papacy and empire—were, by the end of the High Middle Ages, giving way before the centralized kingdoms that would dominate early modern Europe.

Chronology of the Papal-Imperial Conflict

1056–1106:	Reign of Henry IV
1059:	Papal Election Decree
1073–1085:	Pontificate of Gregory VII
1075:	Gregory VII bans lay investiture.
1076:	Gregory VII excommunicates and deposes Henry IV.
1077:	Henry IV humbles himself at Canossa.
1122:	Concordat of Worms
1152–1190:	Reign of Frederick I, "Barbarossa"
1198–1216:	Pontificate of Innocent III
1211–1250:	Reign of Frederick II
1254–1273:	Interregnum
1273–1291:	Reign of Rudolph of Hapsburg
1294–1303:	Pontificate of Boniface VIII
1303:	Boniface VIII humiliated at Anagni.

England

England was already a unified monarchy by the mid-eleventh century. In the course of the High Middle Ages it became far more tightly unified, far more sophisticated in its laws and administration, and far richer and more populous. In 1066 William, Duke of Normandy, won a momentous victory at Hastings and established a new royal dynasty in England. William the Conqueror's new kingdom was unique in its lucrative royal land tax—the danegeld*—and in its well-functioning system of local courts. The Conqueror further centralized his power by adding significantly to the royal estates and by granting extensive lands as military fiefs to loyal Norman vassals who usually respected the royal authority. William I's great land survey of 1086, recorded in *Domesday Book*, illustrates both the administrative precocity of his government and its claim to ultimate jurisdiction over all of England's lands and people.

The process of political consolidation gathered momentum under William I's twelfth-century successors, particularly Henry I (1100–1135) and Henry II (1154–1189). Henry I, for example, developed a remarkable royal accounting bureau—the Exchequer—which processed the revenues collected by the royal representatives in the

---

*This tax had originated long before the Norman Conquest as a source of royal revenue for buying off the invading Danes. In time the Danish threat ceased, but the tax did not. Taxes seldom do.

shires—the sheriffs ("shire reeves"). And under Henry II, significant steps were taken toward the development of a common law, under the jurisdiction of royal courts, to supersede the various and complex jurisdictions of local and feudal courts. Generally speaking, legal actions relating to the all-important subject of land tenure passed under royal jurisdiction in Henry II's reign. The political unification of England by the Anglo-Saxon kings beginning in the late ninth century was now being paralleled by a legal unification under the expanding jurisdiction of the twelfth-century royal courts.

The era also witnessed the dynastic fusion of England with portions of northern France. The effect of William's conquest in 1066 was the formation of an Anglo-Norman state, and, as a result of successive royal marriages, Henry II ruled not only England and Normandy but Anjou, Aquitaine, and other French principalities as well. This immense constellation of territories—known as the "Angevin Empire"—remained intact for half a century (1154–1204), dwarfing the domains of the French crown. At length, King Philip Augustus of France seized the northern French districts of the Angevin Empire from the unlucky King John of England (1199–1216). Thenceforth, for more than a century, English royal jurisdiction was limited mainly to the British Isles. John made important advances in Ireland and, late in the thirteenth century, Edward I (1272–1307) conquered Wales. But not until the 1330s and 1340s, with the opening of the Hundred Years' War, did an English king once again lead his armies into northern France.

During the thirteenth century the English central administration continued to increase in refinement and scope. Royal authority over lands and law, which had been advanced so promisingly under Henry II, reached its climax in Edward I's reign. The central government was now issuing statutes binding on all Englishmen, and the common law was carried everywhere by a powerful system of fixed and itinerant royal courts. Full administrative records were being maintained, and the simple Exchequer of Henry I's day had evolved into a complex and highly efficient machine, drawing large revenues from the prosperous manors and bustling towns of thirteenth-century England.

The Rise of Parliament

But the steady growth of the thirteenth-century royal administration gave rise to a concurrent trend toward limiting the powers of the

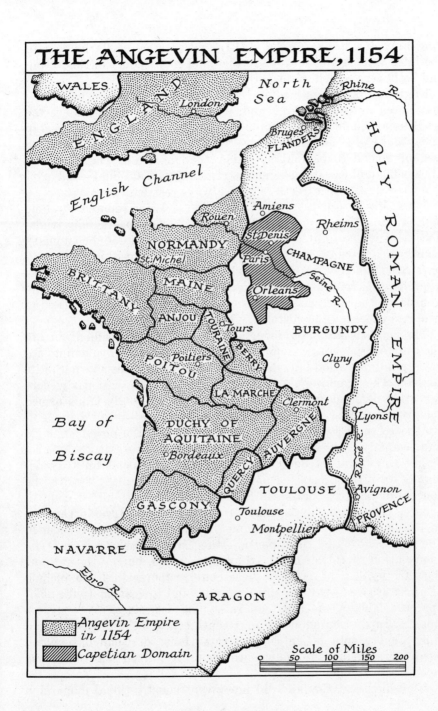

THE ANGEVIN EMPIRE, 1154

WALES

ENGLAND

London

North Sea

Rhine R.

English Channel

Bruges

FLANDERS

HOLY ROMAN EMPIRE

Rouen

Amiens

Rheims

St.Denis

NORMANDY

St.Michel

Paris

CHAMPAGNE

BRITTANY

MAINE

Seine R.

ANJOU

TOURAINE

Tours

BERRY

BURGUNDY

POITOU

Poitiers

Orleans

LA MARCHE

Clermont

Cluny

Bay of

Biscay

DUCHY OF
AQUITAINE

Bordeaux

AUVERGNE

Lyons

Rhone R.

QUERCY

GASCONY

TOULOUSE

Avignon

PROVENCE

Toulouse

Montpellier

NAVARRE

Ebro R.

ARAGON

Angevin Empire
in 1154

Capetian Domain

Scale of Miles
0   50   100   150   200

king himself: *Magna Carta* (1215) and the rise of Parliament in the later thirteenth century are the chief monuments in this trend, and both were rooted in the earlier feudal order.

England, like other medieval kingdoms, was a feudal monarchy dominated by the lord-king and his aristocratic vassals. Since the traditional feudal relationship of lord and vassal was a relationship of *mutual* rights and obligations, a monarchy arising out of such a system tended to be limited rather than absolute. The king was always bound by customs—feudal, regional, and national—and arbitrary royal taxes or directives were always resisted.

Thus, *Magna Carta* (or the Great Charter), the reputed keystone of England's "government under the law," was a profoundly feudal document which limited royal exploitation of feudal and customary rights in a variety of specific ways. It was, indeed, a product of baronial resistance to the centralizing policies of the monarchy—designed to strengthen and make more specific the traditional safeguards of the lord-vassal relationship against an ambitious king who had exceeded the customary limits of his lordship.

The English baronage undertook several major rebellions during the thirteenth century—not with the purpose of weakening the royal administration but, rather, with the purpose of sharing in its control. The monarchy, forced to recognize these essentially conservative demands of its feudal magnates, gradually transformed the great baronial royal council—the *curia regis*—into Parliament. By the reign of Edward I, late in the century, the power struggle had been largely resolved. When the king issued his statutes, or proclaimed new unprecedented taxes, or made unusual military demands on his subjects, he now did so "in parliament"—with the consent of the great barons of the realm sitting with him in council. Indeed, the soaring prosperity of town and countryside resulted in the inclusion in royal parliaments of representative townsmen and members of the rural gentry—the "knights of the shire." The composition of Edward I's parliaments varied, but by the close of the thirteenth century they were coming increasingly to include all three classes—barons, shire knights, and townsmen (with bishops and abbots meeting separately in ecclesiastical "convocations"). In the course of the fourteenth century the townsmen and shire gentry split off into a separate House of Commons, which gradually, during the fourteenth century, gained control of the royal purse strings.

High-medieval England did not invent constitutional monarchy.

Similar constitutional developments were occurring in France, the Spanish kingdoms, the German principalities, and elsewhere. And, as in England, they always evolved out of old Germanic and feudal notions that held custom superior to king and upheld the rights of vassals with respect to their lords. In England alone, however, do we find the evolution from feudalism to constitutionalism occurring as a continuous process down to modern times.

France

The French monarchy began the High Middle Ages far weaker than its English counterpart and ended far less restricted by national customs and national assemblies. The Capetian dynasty, which had gained the weak French throne in 987, remained, at the time of the Norman Conquest, limited to an uneasy jurisdiction over the dimunitive Ile de France around Paris and Orleans. To realize the immense potential of their royal title, the Capetians had three great tasks before them: (1) to master and pacify their turbulent barons in the Ile de France itself, (2) to expand their political and economic base by bringing additional territories under direct royal authority, and (3) to make their lordship over the feudal duchies and counties of France a reality rather than a mere formality.

During the twelfth and thirteenth centuries a series of remarkable Capetian kings pursued and achieved these goals. Their success was so complete that by the opening of the fourteenth century, the Capetians controlled all France, either directly or through obedient vassals. They had developed by this time a sophisticated royal bureaucracy almost as efficient as England's and far more single-mindedly devoted to the interests of the king. The Capetians followed no set formula. Instead, their success depended on a combination of luck and ingenuity—on their clever exploitation of the powers that, potentially, they had always possessed as kings and feudal overlords. They succeeded in avoiding the family squabbles that had, at times, divided Germany and England. Whereas Germany exhausted herself in struggles with the papacy, and even England was torn at times by church-state conflicts, the Capetians maintained relatively good relations with the church. They had the enormous good fortune of an unbroken sequence of direct male heirs from 987 to 1328. Above all, they seldom overreached themselves.

They avoided grandiose schemes, preferring to pursue modest, realistic goals. They extended their power gradually and cautiously by favorable marriages, by confiscating the fiefs of vassals who died without heirs, and by dispossessing vassals who violated their feudal obligations to the monarchy. Yet they had no desire to absorb all the territories of their vassals. Rather they sought to build a kingdom with a substantial core of royal domain lands surrounded by the fiefs of loyal, obedient magnates.

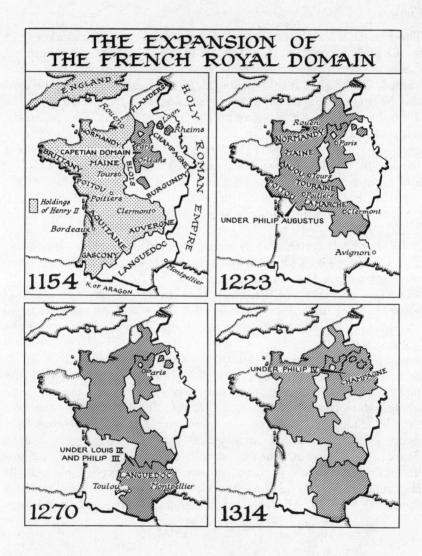

THE EXPANSION OF
THE FRENCH ROYAL DOMAIN

The Early Capetian Kings

In the period beginning about 1060 and lasting until about 1180, the Capetians succeeded in taming the Ile de France and in bringing some of their powerful vassals into a condition of increased dependency. The years between 1180 and 1314 were dominated by the rule of three great Capetian kings—Philip II "Augustus" (1180–1223), St. Louis IX (1226–1270), and Philip IV "the Fair" (1285–1314) —who built a powerful, encompassing monarchy on their ancestors' foundations. King Philip Augustus, whose Ile de France was dwarfed by the vast French dominions of the Angevin kings of England, worked shrewdly and tirelessly to shatter the Angevin Empire. His success came, at last, during King John's reign. Philip Augustus, utilizing his position as supreme feudal lord over John's French lands, summoned John to his feudal court in Paris to be tried for a relatively minor act of malfeasance. John refused to submit to the trial, and Philip, accordingly, declared John's French fiefs forfeited. In the role of the just lord, Philip sent armies against Normandy and Anjou. John fought ineffectively for a time, then fled to England, and his immense dominions in northern France passed into the French royal domain (1204). In one stroke, Philip Augustus had won the extensive territorial base essential for Capetian control over France.

St. Louis

The golden age of the Capetian monarchy occurred in the reign of Philip Augustus' grandson, Louis IX (1226–1270), later made a saint. Louis was a strong, pious king who ruled France wisely and firmly, winning invaluable prestige for the crown through his crusades and charities while his devoted royal officials worked unremittingly to extend the king's power. Capetian officials, unlike their English counterparts, were drawn largely from among ambitious townsmen and university graduates—men lacking strong local roots, utterly devoted to the royal interest. The fusion of local and royal interests, evident in the English administration in general, and the English Parliament in particular, failed to develop in France. Rebellion became the chief instrument of the French nobility for curbing royal power. Thus the potentialities for both royal absolutism and anarchy were present in thirteenth-century France, although neither threat materialized until after the close of the High Middle Ages.

Medieval culture reached its climax in St. Louis' France. Town life flourished, and in the towns superb Gothic cathedrals were being erected. This was the great age of the medieval universities, and the most distinguished university of the age, the University of Paris, enjoyed the favor and protection of the French crown. The universities produced brilliant and subtle theologians; they also produced learned, ambitious lawyers—men of a more secular cast who devoted their talents to the king and took over the royal bureaucracy. The Capetian government became steadily more complex, more efficient, and from the aristocracy's standpoint, more oppressive.

Philip IV, "the Fair"

These trends reached their culmination under St. Louis' ruthless grandson, Philip IV, "the Fair" or the "the Handsome" (1285–1314)—a mysterious, silent figure whose reign was marked by unceasing royal aggression against neighboring lands, against the papacy, and against the nobility. Philip the Fair sought to bypass the feudal hierarchy by demanding the direct allegiance of all Frenchmen. Royalist doctrine, anticipating the goal of later French monarchs, proclaimed the king supreme in France and France supreme in Europe. And in Philip the Fair's reign the doctrine came close to realization. The papacy was humbled. The wealthy crusading order of Knights Templars was looted and destroyed to fatten the royal purse. And France began to expand eastward at the expense of the weakened Holy Roman Empire. In 1302 the French Estates General was summoned for the first time, for reasons akin to those that prompted the development of the English Parliament. But, owing in part to the chasm between king and nobility, in part to the ingrained localism of rural France, the medieval Estates General lacked Parliament's potential for creative development as a vital organ of the central government. The Capetians had made the king supreme in France and, in so doing, had taken the initial steps along the road from feudal monarchy to absolutism.

**Chronology of the English and French Monarchies
in the High Middle Ages**

England		France	
1066:	Norman Conquest of England	987–1328:	Rule of the Capetian Dynasty
1066–1087:	Reign of William the Conqueror		
1100–1135:	Reign of Henry I		
1154–1189:	Reign of Henry II		
1189–1199:	Reign of Richard the Lion-Hearted	1180–1223:	Reign of Philip II, "Augustus"
1199–1216:	Reign of John		
1203–1204:	Loss of Normandy		
1215:	Magna Carta	1226–1270:	Reign of St. Louis IX
1216–1272:	Reign of Henry III		
1272–1307:	Reign of Edward I	1285–1314:	Reign of Philip IV, "the Fair"

TWELVE

NEW DIMENSIONS IN MEDIEVAL CHRISTIANITY

The Church in the High Middle Ages

Although the Middle Ages witnessed the beginnings of European nationhood, it was not until much later that nationalism began to play an important role in the European mind. In the twelfth and thirteenth centuries the majority of Europeans were still intensely local in their outlook, only vaguely aware of what was going on beyond their immediate surroundings. But alongside their localism was an element of cosmopolitanism—a consciousness of belonging to the great international commonwealth of Western Christendom, fragmented politically, but united culturally and spiritually by the Church. Paradoxically, high medieval Europe was at once more localized and more internationalized than the Europe of modern times.

The Church in the High Middle Ages was a powerful unifying influence. It had made notable progress since the half-heathen pre-Carolingian era. A flourishing parish system had by now spread across the European countryside to bring the sacraments and a modicum of Christian instruction to the peasantry. New bishoprics and archbishoprics were formed, and old ones were becoming steadily more active. The papacy never completely succeeded in breaking the control of kings and secular lords over their local bishops, but in the wake of the Investiture Controversy it exercised a very real control over the European episcopacy, and the growing efficiency of the papal bureaucracy evoked the envy and imitation of the rising royal governments.

The buoyancy of high medieval Europe is nowhere more evident than in the accelerating impact of Christian piety on European society. The sacraments of the Church introduced a significant religious dimension into the life of the typical European layman: His birth was sanctified by the sacrament of *baptism* in which he was cleansed of the taint of original sin and initiated into the Christian fellowship. At puberty he received the sacrament of *confirmation,* which reasserted his membership in the Church and gave him the additional grace to cope with the problems of adulthood. His wedding was dignified by the sacrament of *marriage.* If he chose the calling of the ministry, he was spiritually transformed into a priest by the sacrament of *holy orders.* At his death he received the sacrament of *extreme unction,* which prepared his soul for its journey into the next world. And throughout his life he could receive forgiveness from the damning consequences of mortal sin by repenting his past transgressions and humbly receiving the comforting sacrament of *penance.* Finally, he might partake regularly of the central sacrament of the Church—the *eucharist*—receiving the body of Christ into his own body by consuming the eucharistic bread.* Thus the Church, through its seven sacraments, brought God's grace to all Christians, great and humble, at every critical juncture of their lives. The sacramental system, which only assumed final form in the High Middle Ages, was a source of immense comfort and reassurance: it brought hope of salvation not simply to the saintly elite but to the sinful majority; it made communion with God not merely the elusive goal of a few

*Until the High Middle Ages, Christian laymen had traditionally received the body and blood of Christ by eating consecrated bread and by drinking consecrated wine from a common cup. In the course of the twelfth century, partly for hygienic reasons, the drinking of the eucharistic wine was limited to the officiating clergy.

mystics but the periodic experience of all believers. And, of course, it established the Church as the essential intermediary between God and man.

The ever-increasing scope of the Church, together with the rising vigor of the new age, resulted in a deepening of popular piety throughout Europe. The High Middle Ages witnessed a profound shift in religious attitude from the awe and mystery characteristic of earlier Christianity to a new emotionalism and dynamism. This shift is evident in ecclesiastical architecture, as the stolid, earthbound Romanesque style gave way in the later twelfth century to the tense, upward-reaching Gothic. A parallel change is evident in devotional practices as the divine Christ sitting in judgment gave way to the tragic figure of the human Christ suffering on the Cross for man's sins. And it was in the High Middle Ages that the Virgin Mary came into her own as the compassionate intercessor for hopelessly lost souls. No matter how sinful a person might be, he could be redeemed if only he won the sympathy of Mary, for what son could refuse the petition of his mother? Indeed, a legend of the age told of the devil complaining to God that the soft-hearted Queen of Heaven was cheating Hell of its most promising candidates. The God of Justice became the merciful, suffering God who died in agony to atone for the sins of men and to bring them to everlasting life.

Like all human institutions, the medieval Church fell far short of its ideals. Corrupt churchmen were in evidence throughout the age, and certain historians have delighted in cataloging instances of larcenous bishops, gluttonous priests, and licentious nuns. But cases such as these were exceptional. The great shortcoming of the medieval Church was not gross corruption but rather a creeping complacency which resulted sometimes in a shallow, mechanical attitude toward the Christian religious life. The medieval Church had more than its share of saints, but among the rank and file of the clergy the profundity of the Faith was often lost in the day-to-day affairs of the pastoral office and the management of far-flung estates.

The Crisis in Benedictinism

The drift toward complacency was a recurring problem in Christian monasticism—as in all human institutions. Again and again, the lofty idealism of a monastic reform movement was eroded and transformed by time and success until, at length, new reform movements arose in protest against the growing worldliness of the old ones. This cycle has been repeated countless times. Indeed, the sixth-century Benedictine movement was itself a protest against the excesses and inadequacies of earlier monasticism. St. Benedict had regarded his new order as a means of withdrawing from the world and devoting full time to communion with God. But Benedictinism, despite Benedict's ideal, quickly became involved in teaching, evangelism, and ecclesiastical reform, and by the tenth and eleventh centuries the whole Benedictine movement had become deeply involved in worldly affairs. Benedictine monasteries controlled vast estates, supplied contingents of knights in their service to feudal armies, and worked closely with secular princes in affairs of state. Early in the tenth century the Cluniac movement, which was itself Benedictine in spirit and rule, arose as a protest against the world-liness and complacency of contemporary Benedictine monasticism, but by the later eleventh century the Congregation of Cluny had come to terms with the secular establishment and was beginning to display traces of the very complacency against which it had originally rebelled. Prosperous, respected, and secure, Cluny was too content with its majestic abbeys and priories, its elaborate liturgical program, and its bounteous fields to throw its full support behind the radical transformation of Christian society for which Pope Gregory VII was struggling

The aims of Gregory VII were almost exactly the opposite of St. Benedict's, for whereas Benedict had sought to create monastic sanctuaries in which Christians might retire from the world, Gregory VII endeavored to sanctify society itself. His goal was not *withdrawal* but *conversion*. Rather than making Christians safe from the world, he would make the world safe for Christianity. During the Investiture Controversy and its aftermath, these two contrary tendencies—withdrawal and conversion—both had a profound impact on monastic reform.

In the opening decades of the High Middle Ages the Benedictine movement was showing signs of exhaustion. During the long, troubled centuries of the Early Middle Ages, Benedictine teachers and missionaries, scribes and political advisers, had provided indispensable services to society. Benedictine monasteries had served as the spiritual and cultural foci of Christendom. But in the eleventh and twelfth centuries, the Benedictines saw their pedagogical monopoly broken by the rising cathedral schools and universities of the new towns. These urban schools produced increasing numbers of well-trained scholars who gradually superseded the Benedictine monks as scribes and advisers to princes. In other words, the great urbanizing impulse of the High Middle Ages drastically diminished the traditional Benedictine contribution to the functioning of society.

Still, the Benedictines retained their great landed wealth. The Benedictine monastery was scarcely the sanctuary from worldly concerns that St. Benedict had planned. Nor was it any longer the vital force it had once been in Christianizing the world. Twelfth-century Benedictinism followed neither the path of withdrawal nor the path of conversion, and even in the arena of secular affairs it was losing its grip. The Benedictine life was beginning to appear tarnished and unappealing to sensitive religious spirits caught up in the soaring piety of the new page.

The New Monasticism

The monastic revolt against Benedictinism followed the two divergent roads of uncompromising withdrawal from society and ardent participation in the Christianization of society. The impulse toward withdrawal pervaded the Carthusian order which arose in eastern France in the later eleventh century and spread across Christendom in the twelfth. Isolated from the outside world, the Carthusians lived in small groups, worshiping together in communal chapels but otherwise living as hermits in individual cells. This austere order exists to this day and, unlike most monastic movements, its severe spirituality has seldom waned. Yet even in the spiritually charged atmosphere of the twelfth century it was a small movement, offering a way of life for only a minority of heroically holy men. Too ascetic for the average Christian, the Carthusian order was admired but seldom joined.

The greatest monastic movement of the twelfth century, the Cistercian order, managed for a time to be both austere and popular. The mother house of this order, Citeaux, was established in 1098 on a wild, remote site in eastern France. The Cistercian order grew very slowly at first, then gradually acquired momentum. In 1115 it had four daughter houses; by the end of the century it had five hundred.

The spectacular success of the Cistercians demonstrates the immense appeal of the idea of withdrawal to the Christians of the twelfth century. Like Citeaux, the daughter houses were deliberately built in remote wilderness areas. The abbeys themselves were stark and austere, in dramatic contrast to the elaborate Cluniac architecture and sculpture. Cistercian life was austere, too—less severe than that of the Carthusians but far more so than that of the Cluniacs. The Cistercians sought to resurrect the strict, simple life of primitive Benedictinism, but in fact they were stricter than Benedict himself. The lands surrounding their wilderness abbeys were cleared and tilled by Cistercian monks and lay brothers, rather than by the ordinary serfs who worked the Benedictine fields. The numerous Cistercian houses were bound together tightly, not by the authority of a central abbot as at Cluny but by an annual council of all Cistercian abbots meeting at Citeaux. Without such centralized control it is unlikely that the individual houses could have clung for long to the harsh, ascetic ideals on which the order was founded.

The key figure in twelfth-century Cistercianism was St. Bernard, who joined the community of Citeaux in 1112 and three years later became the founder and abbot of Clairvaux, one of Citeaux's earliest daughter houses. St. Bernard of Clairvaux was the leading Christian of his age—a profound mystic, a brilliant religious orator, and a crucial figure in the meteoric rise of the Cistercian order. His moral influence was so immense that he became Europe's leading arbiter of political and ecclesiastical disputes. He persuaded the king of France and the Holy Roman Emperor to participate in the Second Crusade. He persuaded Christendom to accept his candidate in a hotly disputed papal election in 1130. On one occasion he even succeeded in reconciling the two great warring families of Germany, the Welfs and Hohenstaufens. He rebuked the pope himself: "Remember, first of all, that the Holy Roman Church, over which you hold sway, is the mother of churches, not their sovereign mistress—that you yourself are not the lord of bishops but one among them. . . ." And he took an uncompromising stand against one of the rising movements of his day: the intoxicating dream of reconciling the Catholic Faith with human reason, which was spearheaded by the brilliant twelfth-century philosopher, Peter Abelard. In the long run Bernard failed to halt the reconciliation of faith with reason, but he succeeded in making life miserable for the unfortunate Abelard and in securing the official condemnation of certain of Abelard's teachings (see pp. 275–276).

Bernard's career demonstrates vividly the essential paradox of Cistercianism. For although the Cistercians strove to dissociate themselves from the world, Bernard was drawn inexorably into the vortex of secular affairs. Indeed, as the twelfth century progressed, the entire Cistercian movement became increasingly worldly. Like the later Puritans, the Cistercians discovered that their twin virtues of austere living and hard work resulted in an embarrassing accumulation of wealth and a concomitant corrosion of their spiritual simplicity. Their efforts to clear fields around their remote abbeys placed them in the vanguard of the internal frontier movement. They become pioneers in scientific farming and introduced notable improvements in the breeding of horses, cattle, and sheep. The English Cistercians became the great wool producers of the realm. Altogether the Cistercians exerted a powerful, progressive influence on European husbandry and came to play a prominent role in the European economy. Economic success brought ever-increasing wealth to the order. Cistercian abbey churches became steadily more elaborate and opulent, and the primitive austerity of Cistercian life was progressively relaxed. In later years there appeared new offshoots, such as the Trappists, which returned to the strict observance of original Cistercianism.

The Cistercians had endeavored to withdraw from the world, but despite their goal they became a powerful force in twelfth-century Europe. At roughly the same time, other orders were being established with the deliberate aim of participating actively in society and working toward its regeneration. The Augustinian Canons, for example, submitted to the rigor of a monastic rule, yet carried on normal ecclesiastical duties in the world, serving in parish churches and cathedrals and staffing the hospitals that were being built just then in great numbers all across Europe. The fusion of monastic discipline and worldly activity culminated in the twelfth-century Crusading orders—the Knights Templars, the Knights Hospitallers, the Teutonic Knights, and similar groups, whose ideal was a synthesis of the monastic and the military life for the purpose of expanding the political frontiers of Western Christendom. These and other efforts to direct the spiritual vigor of monastic life toward the Christianization of society typify the bold visions and lofty hopes of the new, emotionally charged religiosity that animated twelfth-century Europe.

Heresies and the Inquisition

The new surge of popular piety also raised serious problems for the Church and society, for it resulted in a flood of criticism against churchmen. It was not that churchmen had grown worse, but rather that laymen had begun to judge them by more rigorous standards. Popular dissatisfaction toward the work-a-day Church manifested itself in part in the rush toward the austere twelfth-century monastic orders. Yet the majority of Christians could not become monks, and for them, certain new heretical doctrines began to exert a powerful appeal.

The heresies of the High Middle Ages flourished particularly in the rising towns of southern Europe. The eleventh-century urban revolution had caught the Church unprepared; whereas the new towns were the real centers of the burgeoning lay piety, the Church, with its roots in the older agrarian feudal order, seemed unable to minister effectively to the vigorous and widely literate new burgher class. Too often the urban bishops appeared as political oppressors and enemies of burghal independence rather than inspiring spiritual directors. Too often the Church failed to understand the townsmen's problems and aspirations or to anticipate their growing suspicion of ecclesiastical wealth and power. Although the vast majority of townsmen remained loyal to the Church, a troublesome minority, particularly in the south, turned to new, anticlerical sects. In their denunciation of ecclesiastical wealth, these sects were doing nothing more than St. Bernard and the Cistercians had done. But many of the anticlerical sects crossed the boundary between orthodox reformism and heresy by preaching without episcopal or papal approval; far more important, they denied the exclusive right of the priesthood to perform sacraments.

One such sect, the Waldensians, was founded by a merchant of Lyons named Peter Waldo who c. 1173 gave all his possessions to the poor and took up a life of apostolic poverty. At first he and his followers worked within the bounds of orthodoxy, but gradually their flamboyant anticlericalism and their denial of special priestly powers earned them the condemnation of the Church. Similar groups, some orthodox, some heretical, arose in the communes of Lombardy and were known as the *Humiliati*. These groups proved exceedingly troublesome and embarrassing to the local ecclesiastical hierarchies, but generally they escaped downright condemnation unles they themselves took the step of denying the authority of the Church. Many did take that step, however, and by the thirteenth century heretical, anticlerical sects were spreading across northern Italy and southern France, and even into Spain and Germany.

The most popular and dangerous heresy in southern France was sponsored by a group known as the *Cathari* (the pure) or the

Albigensians, after the town of Albi, where they were particularly strong. The Albigensians represented a fusion of two traditions, (1) the anticlerical protest against ecclesiastical wealth and power and (2) an exotic theology derived originally from Persian dualism. The Albigensians recognized two gods—the god of good who reigned over the universe of the spirit and the god of evil who ruled the world of matter. The Old-Testament God, as creator of the material universe, was their god of evil; Christ, who was believed to have been a purely spiritual being with a phantom body, was the god of good. Albigensian morality stressed a rigorous rejection of all material things—of physical appetites, wealth, worldly vanities, and sexual intercourse—in the hope of one day escaping from the prison of the body and ascending to the realm of pure spirit. In reality this severe ethic was practiced only by a small elite; the rank and file ate well, begat children, and participated only vicariously in the rejection of the material world—by criticizing the affluence of the Church. Indeed, their opponents accused them of gross licentiousness, and it does seem to be true that certain Provençal noblemen were attracted to the new teaching by the opportunity of appropriating Church property in good conscience.

However this may be, Albigensianism was spreading rapidly as the thirteenth century dawned and was becoming an ominous threat to the unity of Christendom and the authority of the Church. Pope Innocent III, recognizing the gravity of the situation, tried with every means in his power to eradicate Albigensianism. At length, in 1208, he summoned a Crusade against the Albigensians —the first Crusade ever to be called against European Christians. The Albigensian Crusade was a ruthless, savage affair which succeeded in its purpose but only at the cost of ravaging the vibrant civilization of southern France. The French monarchy intervened in the Crusade's final stages and thereby extended its sway to the Mediterranean. The Albigensian Crusade was an important event in the development of French royal power, and it succeeded in reversing the trend toward heresy in southern Europe. It also disclosed the brutality of which the Church was capable when sufficiently threatened.

In the years of the Albigensian Crusade, there emerged an institution that will always stand as a grim symbol of the medieval Church at its worst—the Inquisition. The Christian persecution of heretics dates from the later fourth century, but it was not until the High Middle Ages that heterodox views presented a serious problem to European society. Traditionally, the problem of converting or punishing heretics was handled at the local level, but in 1223 the papacy established a permanent central tribunal for the purpose of standardizing procedures and increasing efficiency in the suppression of heresies. The methods of the Inquisition included the use of torture, secret testimony, conviction on the testimony of only two witnesses, the denial of legal counsel to the accused, and other procedures offensive to the Anglo-American legal tradition but not especially remarkable by standards of the times. Indeed, many of these procedures—including torture—were drawn from the customs of Roman Law. In defense of the Inquisition it might be said that convicted heretics might escape death by renouncing their "errors," and that far from establishing a reign of terror, the Inquisition often seems to have enjoyed popular support.

Some historians have adduced other arguments in an attempt to defend an indefensible institution. Let us say here merely that the Christian Faith was far more important to the people of medieval Europe than national allegiance—that the medieval Church, with its elaborate charitable activities, its hospitals and universities, and its other social services, performed many of the functions of the modern state, and that therefore medieval heresy is more or less analogous to modern treason. To the medieval Christian, heresy was a hateful, repugnant thing, an insult to Christ, and a source of contamination to others. Today, when political and economic doctrines are more important to most people than religious creeds, the closest parallel to medieval Waldensianism or Albigensianism is to be found in the Communist and Nazi parties in modern America. In examining popular opposition toward extremist groups such as these, perhaps we can gain an inkling of the state of mind that produced the medieval Inquisition.

Mendicantism

The thirteenth century found an answer to the heretical drift in urban piety which was far more compassionate and effective than the Inquisition. In the opening decades of the century two radically new orders emerged—the Dominican and the Franciscan—which were devoted to a life of poverty, preaching, and charitable deeds. Rejecting the life of the cloister, they dedicated themselves to religious work in the world, particularly in the towns. Benedictines and Cistercians had traditionally taken vows of personal poverty, but the monastic orders themselves could and did acquire great corporate wealth. The Dominicans and Franciscans, on the contrary, were pledged to both personal and corporate poverty and were therefore known as mendicants (beggars). Capturing the imagination of thirteenth-century Christendom, they drained urban heterodoxy of much of its former support by demonstrating to the townsmen of Europe that Christian orthodoxy could be both relevant and compelling.

St. Dominic (1170–1221), a Spaniard who had preached in southern France against the Albigensians, conceived the idea of an order of men trained as theologians and preachers, dedicated to poverty and the simple life, and to winning over heretics through argument, oratory, and example. Sanctioned by the papacy in 1216, the Dominicans expanded swiftly and, by midcentury, had spread across Christendom. The order produced some of the greatest philosophers and theologians of the age, including St. Thomas Aquinas. Dominicans also participated actively in the Inquisition, but their most effective work was done through persuasion rather than force. In time, the ideal of corporate poverty was dropped: the Dominicans came to recognize the great truth that full-time scholars and teachers could not beg or do odd jobs or be in doubt as to the source of their meal. But long after their original mendicant ideals were modified, the Dominicans remained faithful to their mission of championing orthodoxy by word and pen.

Dominic's remarkable achievement was overshadowed by that of his contemporary, St. Francis (c. 1182–1226), a warm and appealing man who is widely regarded as Christianity's greatest saint. Francis was a true product of the urban revolution. He was the son of a wealthy cloth merchant of Assisi, a northern Italian town with an influential Albigensian minority. After a boisterous but harmless adolescence, he underwent a profound conversion, lived in solitude for a brief time, and then returned to human society with a firm dedication to give up all worldly goods and to devote his life to the service of the poor and diseased. Francis was firm, but he was anything but grim. Indeed, it was his joyousness no less than his deep sanctity that captivated his age. As disciples flocked to his side, he wrote a simple rule for them based on the imitation of Christ through charitable activity in the world, total dedication to the work of God, and the absolute rejection of worldly goods. In 1210 he appealed to Pope Innocent III for approval of his rule, and that mightiest of all popes, with some misgivings, authorized the new order. In the years that followed, the Franciscan Order expanded phenomenally. The irresistibly attractive personality of Francis himself was doubtless a crucial factor in his order's popularity, but it also owed much to the fact that Franciscan ideals appealed with remarkable effectiveness to the highest religious aspirations of the age. Urban heresy lost its allure as the cheerful, devoted Franciscans began to pour into Europe's cities, preaching in the crowded streets and setting a living example of Christian sanctity.

Pious men of other times have fled the world; the Albigensians renounced it as the epitome of evil. But Francis embraced it joyfully as the handiwork of God. In his "Song of Brother Sun," he expressed poetically his holy commitment to the physical universe:

Praise to Thee, my Lord, for all Thy creatures,
Above all Brother Sun
Who brings us the day, and lends us his light;
Beautiful is he, radiant with great splendor,
And speaks to us of Thee, O most high.
Praise to Thee, my Lord, for Sister Moon and for the stars;
In heaven Thou hast set them, clear and precious and fair.
Praise to Thee, my Lord, for Brother Wind,
For air and clouds, for calm and all weather
By which Thou supportest life in all Thy creatures.
Praise to Thee, my Lord, for Sister Water
Which is so helpful and humble, precious and pure.
Praise to Thee, my Lord, for Brother Fire,
By whom Thou lightest up the night.
And fair is he, and gay and mighty and strong.
Praise to Thee, my Lord, for our sister, Mother Earth,
Who sustains and directs us.
And brings forth varied fruits, and plants and flowers bright....
Praise and bless my Lord, and give Him thanks.
And serve Him with great humility.

Early Franciscanism was too good to last. As the order expanded it outgrew its primitive ideals, and even before Francis' death in 1226, the papacy was obliged to authorize a more elaborate and practical rule for his order. In time Franciscan friars began devoting themselves to scholarship and took their places alongside the Dominicans in Europe's universities. Indeed, Franciscan scholars such as Roger Bacon in thirteenth-century England played a central role in the revival of scientific investigation, and the minister general of the Franciscan Order in the later thirteenth century, St. Bonaventure, was one of the most illustrious theologians of the age.

The very weight and complexity of the Franciscan organization forced it to compromise its original ideal of corporate poverty. Although it neither acquired nor sought the immense landed wealth of the Benedictines or Cistercians, it soon possessed sufficient means to sustain its members. In time, therefore, the Franciscans followed the course of earlier orders; their primitive simplicity and enthusiasm were exhausted by time and attenuated by popularity and success. A splinter group known as the "Spiritual Franciscans" sought to preserve the apostolic poverty and artless idealism of Francis himself, but the majority of Franciscans were willing to meet reality halfway. They continued to serve society, but by the end of the thirteenth century they had ceased to inspire it.

The pattern of religious reform in the High Middle Ages is one of rhythmic ebb and flow. A reform movement is launched with high enthusiasm and lofty purpose, it galvanizes society for a time, then succumbs gradually to complacency and gives way to a new and different wave of reform. But with the passing of the High Middle Ages one can detect a gradual waning of spiritual vigor. Until the Protestant Reformation, no new religious order attained the immense popularity and social impact of thirteenth-century Franciscanism. Popular piety remained strong, particularly in northern Europe, where succeeding centuries witnessed a significant surge of mysticism. But in the south a more secular attitude was slowly beginning to emerge. Young men no longer flocked into monastic orders; soldiers no longer rushed to Crusades; papal excommunications no longer wrought their former terror. The electrifying appeal of a St. Bernard, a St. Dominic, and a St. Francis was a phenomenon peculiar to their age. By the fourteenth century, their age was passing.

Chronology of High Medieval Monasticism and Heterodoxy

910:	Founding of Cluny
1084:	Establishment of Carthusian Order
1098:	Establishment of Citeaux
1112–1153:	Career of St. Bernard of Clairvaux as a Cistercian
1128:	Original rule of Knights Templars
1173:	Beginning of Waldensian sect
1208:	Innocent III calls Albigensian Crusade
1210:	Innocent III authorizes Franciscan Order
1216:	Dominican Rule sanctioned by papacy
1226:	Death of St. Francis
1233:	Inquisition established

THIRTEEN

THOUGHT, LETTERS, AND THE ARTS

The Dynamics of High Medieval Culture

Thirteenth-century Paris has been described as the Athens of medieval Europe. It is true, of course, that a vast cultural gulf separates the golden age of Periclean Athens from the golden age of thirteenth-century France, but it is also true that these two golden ages had something in common. Both developed within the framework of traditional beliefs and customs which had long existed but were being challenged and transformed by powerful new forces. The social-religious world of the Early Middle Ages, like the social-religious world of the early Greek polis, was parochial and rather tradition-bound. As the two cultures passed into their golden ages, the values of the past were being challenged by new intellectual currents, and the old economic patterns were breaking down before a sharp intensification of commercial activity. Yet, for a time, these dynamic new forces resulted in a heightened cultural expression of the old values. The Parthenon, dedicated to the venerable civic goddess Athena, and the awesome Gothic cathedral of Paris dedicated to Notre Dame (Our Lady) are both products of a new creativity harnessed to the service of an older ideology. In the long run, the new creative impulses would prove subversive to the old ideologies, but for a time, both ancient Greece and medieval Europe achieved an elusive equilibrium between old and new. The results, in both cases, were spectacular.

Thus twelfth- and thirteenth-century Europe succeeded, by and large, in keeping its vibrant and audacious culture within the bounds of traditional Catholic Christianity. And the Christian world view gave form and orientation to the new creativity. Despite the intense dynamism of the period, it can still be called, with some semblance of accuracy, an Age of Faith.

Europe in the High Middle Ages underwent a profound artistic and intellectual awakening which affected almost every imaginable form of expression. Significant creative work was done in literature, architecture, sculpture, law, philosophy, political theory, and even science. By the close of the period, the foundations of the Western cultural tradition were firmly established. The pages that follow will provide only a glimpse at a few of the remarkable cultural achievements of this fertile era.

Literature

The literature of the High Middle Ages was abundant and richly varied. Poetry was written both in the traditional Latin—the universal scholarly language of medieval Europe—and in the vernacular languages of ordinary speech that had long been evolving in the various districts of Christendom. Traditional Christian piety found expression in a series of somber and majestic Latin hymns, whose mood is illustrated (through the clouded glass of translation) by these excerpts from "Jerusalem the Golden":

> *The world is very evil, the times are waxing late.*
> *Be sober and keep vigil; the judge is at the gate....*
> *Brief life is here our portion; brief sorrow, short-lived care.*
> *The life that knows no ending, the tearless life, is there....*
> *Jerusalem the Golden, with milk and honey blessed,*
> *Beneath thy contemplation sink heart and voice oppressed.*

I know not, O I know not, what social joys are there,
What radiancy of glory, what light beyond compare.

At the opposite end of the spectrum of medieval Latin literature one encounters poetry of quite a different sort, composed by young, wandering scholars and aging perpetual-undergraduate types. The deliberate sensuality and blasphemy of their poems are expressions of student rebelliousness against the ascetic ideals of their elders.

For on this my heart is set, when the hour is nigh me,
Let me in the tavern die, with a tankard by me,
While the angels, looking down, joyously sing o'er me . . . etc.

One of these wandering-scholar poems is an elaborate and impudent expansion of the Apostles' Creed. The phrase from the Creed, "I believe in the Holy Ghost, the Holy [Catholic] Church . . ." is embroidered as follows:

I believe *in wine that's fair to see,*
And in the tavern of my host
More than in the Holy Ghost
The tavern will my sweetheart be,
And the Holy Church *is not for me.*

These sentiments should not be regarded as indicative of a sweeping trend toward agnosticism. Rather, they are distinctively medieval expressions of the irreverent student radicalism that most ages know.

For all its originality, the Latin poetry of the High Middle Ages was overshadowed both in quantity and in variety of expression by vernacular poetry. The drift toward emotionalism, which we have already noted in medieval piety, was closely paralleled by the evolution of vernacular literature from the martial epics of the eleventh century to the delicate and sensitive romances of the thirteenth. Influenced by the sophisticated romanticism of the southern troubadour tradition, the bellicose spirit of northern France gradually softened.

In the eleventh and early twelfth centuries, heroic epics known as *Chansons de Geste* (Songs of Great Deeds) were enormously popular among the feudal nobility of northern France. Many of these *Chansons* were exaggerated accounts of events surrounding the reign of Charlemagne. The most famous of all the *Chansons de Geste,* the *Song of Roland,* told of a heroic and bloody battle between a horde of Moslems and the detached rearguard of Charlemagne's army as it was withdrawing from Spain. Like old-fashioned

Westerns, the *Chansons de Geste* were packed with action, and their heroes tended to steer clear of sentimental entanglements with women. Warlike prowess, courage, and loyalty to one's lord and fellows-in-arms were the virtues stressed in these heroic epics. The battle descriptions were characterized by gory realism.

> *He sees his bowels gush forth out of his side*
> *And on his brow the brain laid bare to sight.*

In short, the *Chansons de Geste* were mirrors of the rough, warrior ethos of eleventh-century feudal knighthood.

During the middle and later twelfth century the martial spirit of northern French literature was gradually transformed by the influx of the romantic troubadour tradition of southern France. In Provence, Toulouse, and Aquitaine, a rich and colorful culture had been developing in the eleventh and twelfth centuries; out of this vivacious society came a lyric poetry of remarkable sensitivity and enduring value. The lyric poets of the south were known as *troubadours.* Most were court minstrels, but some, including a duke of Aquitaine himself, were members of the upper nobility. Their poems were far more intimate and personal than the *Chansons de Geste* and placed much greater emphasis on romantic love. The delicacy and romanticism of the troubadour lyrics betoken a more genteel and sophisticated nobility than that of the feudal north—a nobility that preferred songs of love to songs of war. Indeed, medieval southern France was the source of the entire romantic-love tradition of Western Civilization, with its idealization of women, its emphasis on male gallantry and courtesy, and its impulse to embroider relations between man and woman with potent emotional overtones of eternal oneness, undying devotion, idealization, agony, and ecstasy:

> *I die of wounds from blissful blows,*
> *And love's cruel stings dry out my flesh,*
> *My health is lost, my vigor goes,*
> *And nothing can my soul refresh.*
> *I never knew so sad a plight,*
> *It should not be, it is not right. . . .*
> *I'll never hold her near to me*
> *My ardent joy she'll ever spurn,*
> *In her good grace I cannot be,*
> *Nor even hope, but only yearn.*
> *She tells me nothing, false or true,*
> *And neither will she ever do.*

The author of these lines, Jaufré Rudel (mid-twelfth century), unhappily and hopelessly in love, finds consolation in his talent as a poet, of which he has an exceedingly high opinion. The song from which the lines above are taken concludes on an optimistic note:

> *Make no mistake, my song is fair,*
> *With fitting words and apt design.*
> *My messenger would never dare*
> *To cut it short or change a line. . . .*
> *My song is fair, my song is good,*
> *'Twill bring delight, as well it should.*

The Romance

Midway through the twelfth century, the southern tradition of courtly love began to spread to the courts of northern France and, soon after, into England and Germany. As its influence grew, the northern knights discovered that more was expected of them than loyalty to their lords and a life of carefree slaughter. They were now expected to be gentlemen as well—to be courtly in manner and urbane in speech, to exhibit delicate and refined behavior in feminine company, and to idolize some noble lady. Such, briefly, were the ideals of courtly love. Their impact on the actual behavior of knights was distinctly limited, but their effect on the literature of Northern Europe was revolutionary. Out of the convergence of vernacular epic and vernacular lyric there emerged a new poetic form known as the romance.

Like the *Chanson de Geste,* the romance was a long narrative poem, but like the southern lyric, it was sentimental and imaginative. It was commonly based on some theme from the remote past: the Trojan War, Alexander the Great, and, above all, King Arthur —the half-legendary sixth-century British king. Arthur was transformed from a misty figure of Welsh legend into an idealized twelfth-century monarch surrounded by charming ladies and chivalrous knights. His court at Camelot, as described by the great French poet, Chrétien de Troyes, was a center of romantic love and refined religious sensitivity where knights worshiped their ladies, went on daring quests, and played out their chivalrous roles in a world of magic and fantasy.

In the *Chanson de Geste* the great moral imperative was loyalty to one's lord, in the romance, as in the southern lyric, it was love for one's lady. From *The Song of Roland* came the words:

> *Men must face great privation for their lord,*
> *Must suffer cold for him, and searing heat,*
> *And must endure sharp wounds and loss of blood.*

But from the southern French lyric poetess Beatrz de Dia (*c.* 1160) came sentiments of a radically different sort:

> *My heart is filled with passion's fire.*
> *My well-loved knight, I grant thee grace,*
> *To hold me in my husband's place,*
> *And do the things I so desire.*

Several northern romances portray the old and new values in direct conflict. An important theme in both the Arthurian romances and the twelfth-century romance of Tristan and Iseult is a love affair between a vassal and his lord's wife. Love and feudal loyalty stand face to face, and love wins out. Tristan loves Iseult, the wife of his lord, King Mark of Cornwall. King Arthur's beloved knight Lancelot loves Arthur's wife, Guinevere. In both stories the lovers are ruined by their love, yet love they must—they have no choice—and although the conduct of Tristan and Lancelot would have been regarded by earlier feudal standards as nothing less than treason, both men are presented sympathetically in the romances. Love destroys the lovers in the end, yet their destruction is itself romantic—even glorious. Tristan and Iseult lay dead side by side, and in their very death their love achieved its deepest consummation.

Alongside the theme of love in the medieval romances, and standing in sharp contrast to it, is the theme of Christian purity and dedication. The rough-hewn knight of old, having been taught to be courteous and loving, was now taught to be holy. Lancelot was trapped in the meshes of a lawless love, but his son, Galahad, became the prototype of the Christian knight—pure, holy, and chaste. And Perceval, another knight of the Arthurian circle, quested not for a lost loved one but for the Holy Grail of Christ's Last Supper.

The romance flourished in twelfth- and thirteenth-century France and among the French-speaking nobility of England. It was also a crucial element in the evolution of German vernacular literature. The German poets—known as *minnesingers*—were influenced by the French lyric and romance but developed these literary forms along highly original lines. The *minnesingers* produced their own deeply sensitive and mystical versions of the Arthurian stories, which, in their exalted symbolism and profundity of emotion, surpass even the works of Chrétien de Troyes and his French contemporaries.

Vernacular poetry came late to Italy, but in the works of Dante (d. 1321) it achieved its loftiest expression. Dante's *Divine Comedy*, written in the Tuscan vernacular, is a magnificent synthesis of medieval literature and medieval thought. Rich in allegory and symbolism, it tells of Dante's own journey through hell, purgatory, and paradise to the very presence of God himself. This device allows Dante to make devastating comments on past and contemporary history by placing all those of whom he disapproved—from local politicians to popes—in various levels of hell. Virgil, the archetype of ancient rationalism, is Dante's guide through hell and purgatory; the lady Beatrice, a symbol of purified love, guides him through the celestial spheres of paradise; and St. Bernard, the epitome of medieval sanctity, leads him to the threshold of Almighty God. Having traversed the entire cosmos of medieval thought, Dante ends his journey and his poem, alone in the divine presence:

> *Eternal Light, thou in thyself alone*
> *Abidest, and alone thine essence knows,*
> *And loves, and smiles, self-knowing and self-known. . . .*
> *Here power failed to the high fantasy,*
> *But my desire and will were turned—as one—*
> *And as a wheel that turneth evenly,*
> *By Holy Love, that moves the stars and sun.*

Architecture: From Romanesque to Gothic

The High Middle Ages are one of the great epochs in the history of Western architecture. Stone churches, large and small, were built in prodigious numbers: In France alone, more stone was quarried during the High Middle Ages than by the pyramid and temple builders of ancient Egypt throughout its three-thousand-year history. Yet the real achievement of the medieval architects lay not in the immense scope of their activities but in the splendid originality of their aesthetic vision. Two great architectural styles dominated the age—the Romanesque style evolved in the eleventh century, rose to maturity in the early twelfth, and during the latter half of the twelfth century gave way gradually to the Gothic style. From about 1150 to 1300 the greatest of the medieval Gothic cathedrals were built. Thereafter the Gothic style became increasingly elaborate; basic structural innovation gave way to opulent decoration. But during the High Middle Ages it constituted one of humanity's most audacious and successful architectural experiments.

High medieval architecture was deeply affected by two of the basic cultural trends of the period. First of all, the great cathedrals were products of the urban revolution and the rise of intense urban piety. Second, the evolution from Romanesque to Gothic closely parallels the shift which we have already observed in literature and piety toward emotional sensitivity and romanticism. Romanesque architecture, although characterized by an exceeding diversity of expression, tended in general toward the solemnity of earlier Christian piety and the study power of the *chansons de Geste*. Gothic architecture, on the other hand, is dramatic, upward-reaching, and structurally sophisticated.

The development from Romanesque to Gothic can be understood as an evolution in the principles of structural engineering. The key architectural ingredient in the Romanseque churches was the round arch. Romanesque roof design was based on the various elaborations of the round arch, such as the barrel vault and the cross vault (See Figures (*a*) and (*b*)). These heavy stone roofs required thick supporting walls; windows were necessarily few and small. A church in the fully developed Romanesque style conveys a powerful feeling of unity and earthbound solidity. Its massive arches, vaults, and walls, and its somber, shadowy interior give the illusion of mystery and otherworldliness, yet suggest at the same time the steadfast might of the universal Church.

(*a*)

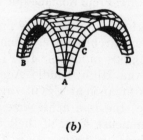
(*b*)

(*a*) Barrel Vault. (*b*) Cross Vault.

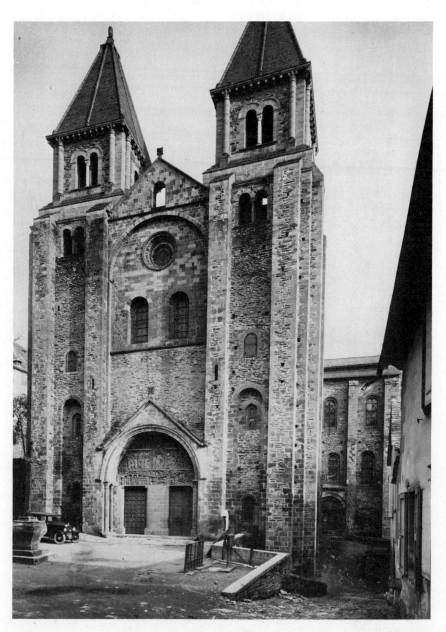

Romanesque exterior: Sainte-Foy in Conques (c. 1050-c. 1120).

Romanesque interior: Saint-Etienne in Nevers (c. 1083–1097).

During the first half of the twelfth century, new structural elements began to be employed in the building of Romanesque churches: first, ribs of stone that ran along the edges of the arched cross vaults and helped to support them; next, pointed arches that permitted greater flexibility and height in the vaulting. By mid-century these novel features—ribbed vault and pointed arch—were providing the basis for an entirely new style of architecture, no longer Romanesque but Gothic. They were employed with such effect by Abbot Suger in his new abbey church of Saint-Denis near Paris, around 1140, that Saint-Denis is often regarded as the first true Gothic church.

French Gothic churches of the late twelfth century—such as Notre Dame in Paris—disclose the development of ribbed vault and pointed arch into a powerful and coherent new style. But not until the thirteenth century were the full potentialities of Gothic architecture realized. The discovery of the ribbed vault and pointed arch, and of a third Gothic structural element—the flying buttress—made it possible to support weights and stresses in a totally new way. The traditional building, of roof supported by walls, was transformed into a radically new kind of building—a skeleton—in which the stone vault rested not on walls but on slender columns and graceful exterior supports. The wall became structurally superfluous, and the vast areas between the supporting columns could be filled with glass. Concurrent with this architectural revolution was the development, in twelfth and thirteenth century Europe, of the art of stained glass making. The colored windows created in these centuries, with episodes from the Bible and religious legend depicted in shimmering blues and glowing reds, have never been equalled.

During the first half of the thirteenth century all the structural possibilities of the Gothic skeleton design were fully exploited. In the towns of central and northern France there now rose churches of delicate, soaring stone, with walls of lustrous glass. Never before in history had windows been so immense or buildings so lofty; and never since has European architecture been at once so assured and so daringly original.

Gothic sculpture, like Romanesque, was intimately related to architecture, yet the two styles differed markedly. Romanesque fantasy, exuberance, and distortion gave way to a serene, self-confident naturalism. Human figures were no longer, as in the Romanesque churches, crowded together on the capitals of pillars. The Gothic sculptors created the first free-standing statues since

Gothic interior: Bourges Cathedral (1195).

The High Middle Ages: First Flowering of European Culture

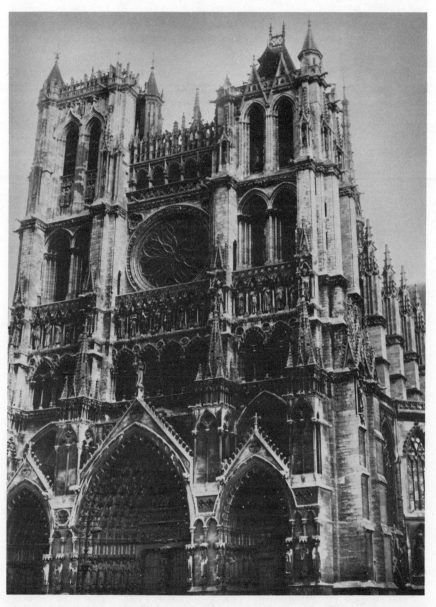

Gothic architecture: west facade of Amiens Cathedral, France, thirteenth century.

"Adoration of the Magi," Cloister capital, Moissac (1100).

Nave capital, Anzy-le-Duc (late eleventh century)

antiquity and arranged them in long rows across the cathedral exteriors. Saints, prophets, kings, angels, and Christ and the Virgin were depicted as tall, slender figures, calm yet warmly human —or as beautiful young women, placid and often smiling. The greatest Gothic churches of thirteenth century France—Bourges, Chartres, Amiens, Reims, Sainte-Chapelle—are superb syntheses of many separate arts. Their interiors convey a striking illusion of graceful stone vaulting springing up from walls of luminous colored glass. The pictures in the glass, the sculpture, and the architecture of the buildings themselves became a single, majestic setting for the greatest of all medieval dramas—the reenactment of Christ's redemption of mankind in the Mass. Here, all the arts of the Middle Ages were directed to a single end: the expression and illumination of a deep, vital faith.

The Rise of Universities

Like the Gothic cathedral, the university was a product of the medieval town. The urban revolution of the eleventh and twelfth centuries brought about the decline of the old monastic schools which had done so much to preserve culture over the previous centuries. They were superseded north of the Alps by cathedral schools located in the rising towns, and in Italy by semi-secular municipal schools. Both the cathedral schools and the municipal schools had long existed, but it was only in the eleventh century that they arose to great prominence. Many of these schools now became centers of higher learning of a sort that Europe had not known for centuries. Their enrollments increased steadily and their faculties grew until, in the twelfth century, some of them evolved into universities.

In the Middle Ages, *university* was an exceedingly vague term. A university was simply a group of persons associated for any purpose. The word was commonly applied to the merchant guilds and craft guilds of the rising towns. A guild or university of students and scholars engaged in the pursuit of higher learning was given the more specific name, *studium generale*. When we speak of the medieval university, therefore, we are referring to an institution that would have been called a *studium generale* by a man of the thirteenth century. It differed from lesser schools in three significant respects. (1) The *studium generale* was open to students from many lands, not simply those from the surrounding district; (2)

Gothic sculpture: (above) Apostle's head, from the Cathedral of Sens, France, c. 1190–1200.

the *studium generale* was a large school with a number of teachers rather than merely one omnicompetent master; (3) the *studium generale* offered both elementary and advanced curricula. It offered a basic program of instruction in the traditional "seven liberal arts"—astronomy, geometry, arithmetic, music, grammar, rhetoric, and dialectic—and also instruction in one or more of the "higher" disciplines—theology, law, and medicine. Upon the successful completion of his liberal arts curriculum, the student could apply for a license to teach, but he might also wish to continue his studies by specializing in medicine, theology, or—most popular of all—civil or cannon law. Legal training offered as its reward the promise of a lucrative administrative career in royal government or the Church.

Fundamentally, the medieval university was neither a campus nor a complex of buildings, but a *guild*—a privileged corporation of teachers, or sometimes of students. With its classes normally held in rented rooms, it was a highly mobile institution, and on more than one occasion when a university was dissatisfied with local conditions it won important concessions from the townsmen simply by threatening to move elsewhere.

In the thirteenth century, flourishing universities were to be found at Paris, Bologna, Naples, Montpelier, Oxford, Cambridge, and elsewhere. Paris, Oxford, and a number of others were dominated by guilds of instructors in the liberal arts. Bologna, on the other hand, was governed by a guild of students who managed to reduce the exorbitant local prices of food and lodgings by threatening to move collectively to another town. The student guild of Bologna established strict rules of conduct for the instructors. In this Golden Age of student government, professors were given such outrageous requirements as having to begin and end their classes on time and to cover the prescribed curriculum. It is important to point out, however, that Bologna specialized in legal studies and that its pupils were older professional students for the most part —men who had completed their liberal arts curriculum and were determined to secure sufficient training for successful careers in law.

The students of the medieval universities were, on the whole, rowdy and exuberant, imaginative in their pranks, and hostile toward the surrounding towns. Thus the history of the medieval universities is punctuated by frequent town-gown riots. New students were hazed unmercifully; unpopular professors were hissed, shouted down, and even pelted with stones. Most of the students were of relatively humble origin—from the towns or the ranks of the lesser nobility—but they were willing to spend their student days in abject poverty if necessary in order to acquire the new knowledge and prepare themselves for the rich social and economic rewards that awaited many graduates.

Despite the enormous difference between medieval and modern university life, it should be clear that the modern university is a direct outgrowth of the institution that came into being in high medieval Europe. We owe to the medieval university the concept of a formal teaching license, the custom—unknown to antiquity—of group instruction, the idea of academic degrees, the notion of a liberal arts curriculum, the tradition of professors and students dressing in clerical garb (caps and gowns) on commencement day, and numerous other customs of university life. Even the letters written by medieval students to their parents or guardians have a curiously modern ring:

This is to inform you that I am studying at Oxford with the greatest diligence, but the matter of money stands greatly in the way of my promotion, as it is now two months since I have spent the last of what you sent me. The city is expensive and makes demands; I have to rent lodgings, buy necessities, and provide for many other things which I cannot now specify. [A fuller elaboration here would have been illuminating.] Wherefore I respectfully beg your paternity that by the promptings of divine pity you may assist me, so that I can complete what I have well begun. For you must know that without Ceres and Bacchus, Apollo grows cold.

Medicine and Law

The chief medical school of medieval Europe was the University of Salerno in southern Italy. Here, in a land of vigorous cultural intermingling, scholars were able to draw from the medical heritage of Islam and Byzantium. In general, medieval medical scholarship was a bizarre medley of cautious observation, common sense, and gross superstition. In one instance we encounter the advice that a person should eat and drink in moderation, but we are also instructed that onions will cure baldness, that the urine of a dog is an admirable cure for warts, and that all one must do to prevent a woman from conceiving is to bind her head with a red ribbon. Yet in the midst of this nonsense, important progress was being made in medical science. The writings of the great second-century scientist Galen, which constituted a synthesis of classical medical knowledge, were studied and digested, as were the important works of Arab students of medicine. And to this invaluable body of knowledge European scholars were now making their own original contributions on such subjects as the curative properties of plants and the anatomy of the human body. It is probable that both animal and human dissections were performed by the scholars of twelfth-century Salerno. These doctors, their crude and primitive methods notwithstanding, were laying the foundations on which Western European medical science was to rise.

Medieval legal scholarship addressed itself to two distinct bodies of material—canon law and civil law. The study of canon law or Church law was enormously stimulated by the Investiture Controversy and subsequent Church-state struggles. Drawing their precedents from the Bible, from the writings of the Latin Church Fathers, and from papal and conciliar decrees, the canon lawyers of Bologna and elsewhere elaborated difficult points of law, struggled to reconcile discordant canons, and assembled a series of great canonical collections. Many canon lawyers were enthusiastic supporters of the papal cause and devoted their scholarship to the task of providing a powerful legal foundation for the sweeping claims of the twelfth- and thirteenth-century papacy. Indeed, as we have seen, many of the popes were themselves canon lawyers.

Civil lawyers, on the other hand, tended to exalt the emperor and the kings under whom so many of them served. The science of civil law was built on the framework of Justinian's *Corpus Juris Civilis* (see p. 163), which was first studied seriously in the West in late-eleventh-century Bologna. Roman law appealed to the legal scholars of the High Middle Ages as a uniquely comprehensive and rational body of jurisprudence. Although it contained a strong element of constitutionalism, it inherited from Justinian's age a tendency toward imperial absolutism which was put to effective use by the court lawyers of the rising monarchies. Roman law became the basis of most of the legal systems of continental Europe, where it served to make government at once more systematic and more autocratic. Thus the civil lawyers played a significant role in the evolution of France from the limited Germanic monarchy of the earlier Capetians toward the absolutism of later times. And the development and durability of a parliamentary regime in England owed much to the fact that a strong monarchy, based on the principles of Germanic law, was already well established before Europe felt the full impact of the Roman law revival.

It is only to be expected that an age that witnessed such sweeping economic and political developments and such vigorous creativity in religious and artistic expression would also achieve notable success in the realm of abstract thought. Medieval philosophy is exceedingly variegated and is marked by boundless curiosity and heated controversy. Among the diverse investigations and conflicting opinions of the medieval thinkers, three central issues deserve particular attention: (1) the degree of interrelationship between faith and reason, (2) the relative merits of the Platonic-Augustinian and the Aristotelian intellectual traditions, and (3) the reality of the Platonic archetypes or "universals."

The issue of faith versus reason was perhaps the most far-reaching of the three. Ever since Tertullian in the third century, there had been Christians who insisted that God so transcended reason that any attempt to approach Him through logic was not only useless but blasphemous. It was the mystic who knew God, not the theologian. Against this view, medieval philosophers such as Anselm and Thomas Aquinas maintained that faith and reason were dual avenues to truth, that they often led to the same conclusions, and that in no case were their conclusions contradictory.

The conflict between the systems of thought of Plato-Augustine and Aristotle did not emerge clearly until the thirteenth century when the full body of Aristotle's writings came into the West in Latin translations from Greek and Arabic. Until then most efforts at applying reason to faith were based on the Platonic tradition transmuted and transmitted by Augustine into the medieval West. Many philosophers of the more conservative type were deeply suspicious of the newly recovered Aristotelian writings, regarding them as pagan in viewpoint and dangerous to the Faith. Others, such as St. Thomas Aquinas, were much too devoted to the goal of reconciling faith and reason to ignore the works of a man whom they regarded as antiquity's greatest philosopher. St. Thomas sought to Christianize Aristotle as Augustine had Christianized Plato. In the middle decades of the thirteenth century, as high medieval philosophy was reaching its climax, the Platonic and Aristotelian traditions flourished side by side, and in the works of certain English thinkers of the age they achieved a singularly fruitful fusion.

The contest between medieval Platonism-Augustinianism and

medieval Aristotelianism carried the seeds of still another controversy: the problem of archetypes or universals. Plato had taught that terms such as "dog," "man," or "cat" not only described certain creatures but also had reality in themselves—that individual cats are imperfect reflections of a model cat, an archetypal or universal cat. Again, we call certain acts "good" because they partake of a universal good which exists in heaven. In short, these universals—cat, dog, beauty, goodness, etc.—exist apart from the multitude of individual cats, dogs, and beautiful and good things in this world. And the person who seeks knowledge ought to meditate on these universals rather than study the world of phenomena in which they are reflected only imperfectly. St. Augustine accepted Plato's theory of universals with one amendment: that the archetypes existed in the mind of God rather than in some abstract realm, and that God put a knowledge of universals directly into our minds by a process which Augustine called "divine illumination." Both Plato and Augustine agreed that the universal existed apart from the particular and, indeed, that the universal was *more real* than the particular. In the High Middle Ages those who followed the Platonic-Augustinian approach to the universals were known as *realists* —they believed that universals were *real*.

The Aristotelian tradition brought with it another viewpoint on universals: that they existed, to be sure, but only in the particular—only by studying particular things in the world of phenomena could men gain knowledge of universals. The universals were real, but in a sense less real than Plato and Augustine believed. Accordingly, medieval philosophers who inclined toward the Aristotelian position have been called *moderate realists*.

But medieval philosophers were by no means confined to a choice between these two positions. Several worked out subtle solutions of their own. As early as the eleventh century the philosopher Roscellinus declared that universals were not real at all. They were mere names that humans gave to arbitrary classes of individual things. Reality was not to be found in universals but rather in the multiplicity and variety of objects which we can see, touch, and smell in the world around us. Those who followed Roscellinus in this view were known as *nominalists*—for them, the universals were *nomina*, the Latin for "names." Nominalism lurked in the intellectual background during the twelfth and thirteenth centuries but was revived in the fourteenth. Many churchmen regarded it as a dangerous doctrine, for its emphasis on the particular over the general or universal seemed to suggest that the Catholic Church was not, as good churchmen believed, a single universal body but rather a vast accumulation of individual believers.

Having examined briefly three important issues of high medieval philosophy—reason versus revelation, Plato-Augustine versus Aristotle, and the problem of universals—we shall now see how these issues developed in the minds of individual philosophers between the eleventh and fourteenth centuries.

St. Anselm

The philosophers of this period were known as "scholastics" because nearly all of them were connected with schools—monastic schools, cathedral schools, or universities. They first appeared in the later eleventh century as a product of the reawakening that Europe was just then beginning to undergo. The first great figure in scholastic philosophy was St. Anselm, an Italian who taught for many years in the vigorous monastic school of Bec in Normandy. In time he was appointed abbot of Bec, and in the 1090s he became archbishop of Canterbury. As archbishop he struggled vigorously against the Norman kings of England over the issue of lay investiture, and shortly after agreeing to a compromise settlement of the controversy he died in 1109. During his eventful career he found time to think and write profoundly on such subjects as the atonement of mankind through Christ's crucifixion, the possibility of a rational proof of God, and the relationship between faith and reason. Anselm stood solidly in the Platonic-Augustinian tradition and was singularly important in the development of medieval thought because of his confidence that reason was not incompatible with faith. He taught that faith must precede reason but that reason could serve to illuminate faith. His emphasis on reason, employed within the framework of a firm Christian conviction, set the stage for the significant philosophical developments of the following generations, and his keen analytical mind made him the most notable Western philosopher since Augustine. With Anselm, Western Christendom regained at last the intellectual level of the fourth-century Latin Fathers.

Peter Abelard

The twelfth-century philosophers, intoxicated by the seemingly limitless possibilities of reason and logic, advanced boldly across new intellectual frontiers at the very time when their contemporaries were pushing forward the geographical frontiers of Europe. The most brilliant and audacious of these twelfth-century Christian rationalists was Peter Abelard (1079–1142), an immensely popular teacher, dazzling and egotistical, whose meteoric career ended in tragedy and defeat.

Abelard is perhaps best known for his love affair with the young Heloise, an affair that ended with Abelard's castration at the hands of thugs hired by Heloise's enraged uncle. The lovers were then separated permanently, both taking monastic vows, and in later years Abelard wrote regretfully of the affair in his autobiographical *History of My Calamities*. There followed a touching correspondence between the two lovers in which Heloise, now an abbess, confessed her enduring love and Abelard, writing almost as a father confessor, offered her spiritual consolation but nothing more. Abelard's autobiography and the correspondence with Heloise survive to this day, providing modern students with a singularly intimate and tender picture of romance and pathos in a society far removed from our own.*

Abelard was the supreme logician of the twelfth century. Writing several decades prior to the great influx of Aristotelian thought in Latin translation, he anticipated Aristotle's position on the question of universals by advocating a theory of moderate realism. Universals, Abelard believed, had no separate existence but were derived from particular things by a process of abstraction. In a famous work entitled *Sic et Non (Yes and No)*, Abelard collected opinions from the Bible, the Latin Fathers, the councils of the Church, and the decrees of the papacy on a great variety of theological issues, demonstrating that these hallowed authorities very often disagreed on important religious matters. Others before Abelard had collected authoritative opinions on various legal and theological issues but never so thoroughly or systematically. Abelard, in his *Sic et Non*, employed a method of inquiry that was developed and perfected by canon lawyers and philosophers over

---

*The entire correspondence has recently been branded as a forgery of the late twelfth and thirteenth centuries. Is nothing sacred to the modern revisionist historian?

the next several generations. But his successors sought to reconcile the contradictions and arrive at conclusions, whereas Abelard left many of the issues unresolved and thereby earned the enmity of his conservative contemporaries. Abelard was a devoted Christian, if something of an intellectual show-off, but many regarded him as a dangerous skeptic. Thus he left himself open to bitter attacks by men such as St. Bernard who were deeply hostile to his merger of faith and reason. The brilliant teacher was hounded from one place to another and finally condemned for heresy in 1141. He died at Cluny, on his way to Rome to appeal the condemnation.

The New Translations of Aristotle

But twelfth-century rationalism was far more than a one-man affair, and the persecution of Abelard failed to halt its growth. In the later twelfth and early thirteenth centuries the movement was powerfully reinforced by the arrival of vast quantities of Greek and Arabic writings in Latin translation. Significant portions of the philosophical and scientific legacy of ancient Greece now became available to European scholars. Above all, the full Aristotelian corpus now came into the West through the labors of translators in Spain and Sicily.

These translations were by no means fortuitous. They came in answer to a deep hunger on the part of Western thinkers for a fuller knowledge of the classical heritage in philosophy and science. Still, the introduction of certain new Aristotelian works created a profound intellectual crisis in Christendom, for they contained implications which seemed hostile to the Faith. The apparent incompatibility between these new Aristotelian writings and Christianity was heightened by the fact that they came into the West accompanied by the commentaries of a great heterodox Spanish Muslim philosopher, Averroes. This brilliant skeptic emphasized Aristotle's doctrine that the world had always existed and was therefore uncreated. He also interpreted Aristotle in such a way as to deny personal immortality. Averroes reconciled these views with orthodox Islam by a curious intellectual device known as the "doctrine of the twofold truth." He maintained that certain things could be true philosophically yet false from the standpoint of revealed religion. The importation of this twofold-truth doctrine into the West had two important consequences, (1) the development of a group of "Latin Averroists," who insisted on the philosophical validity of Aristotle's heterodox opinions yet defended the Christian Faith as ultimately true, even though at variance with reason, and (2) the condemnation of certain of Aristotle's writings by the Church.

Thomas Aquinas

Against this background there emerged in the mid-thirteenth century a bold group of men dedicated to the reconciliation of reason and faith and therefore to the fusion of Aristotle and Christianity. They sought to confound the Latin Averroists by demonstrating that reason and revelation pointed to one truth, not two. The greatest figures in this tradition were the German philosopher Albertus Magnus (Albert the Great) and his remarkable Norman-Italian pupil, Thomas Aquinas. Both men were Dominicans; both taught at the University of Paris, concurrently with the great Franciscan philosopher Bonaventure who was the thirteenth century's greatest exponent of the Platonic-Augustinian tradition. The confluence of men such as these made mid-thirteenth century Paris one of history's most notable intellectual centers.

St. Thomas Aquinas created medieval Europe's consummate synthesis of reason and revelation. In his immense *Summa Theologica*, St. Thomas explored all the great questions of philosophy and theology, political science and morality, using Aristotle's logical method and Aristotle's categories of thought but arriving at conclusions that were in complete harmony with the Christian faith. A moderate realist on the problem of universals, St. Thomas reasoned from sense experience rather than divine illumination. Like Abelard, he assembled every possible argument, pro and con, on every subject that he discussed, but unlike Abelard, he drew conclusions. Few philosophers before or since have been so generous in presenting and exploring opinions contrary to their own, and none has been so systematic and exhaustive. St. Thomas created a vast, unified intellectual system, ranging from God to the natural world, logically supported at every step. As the Gothic cathedral was the artistic embodiment of the high medieval world, so the philosophy of Aquinas was its supreme intellectual expression. It is not without reason that the *Summa Theologica* has been called a cathedral of thought.

To this day there are those who subscribe essentially to the philosophy of Aquinas. On the other hand, many of his own thirteenth-century contemporaries rejected it in whole or in part. Franciscan intellectuals such as Bonaventure were particularly suspicious of the *tour de force* of this gifted Dominican. In England, a profoundly un-Thomistic point of view was gradually emerging in the thirteenth century—a point of view that combined the mathematical tradition of Plato with the experimental tradition of Aristotle and directed them toward the investigation of the physical world.

Science

It was in thirteenth-century England that Western European science was born. The great English scholar Robert Grosseteste (d. 1253) was on intimate terms with neo-Platonic philosophy, Aristotelian physics, and the rich scientific legacy of Islam. He pioneered in the development of scientific method by outlining a procedure of observation, hypothesis, and experiment, and by urging the use of mathematical analysis whenever possible. Like other pioneers Grosseteste followed many false paths—his explanations of such phenomena as colors, heat, and rainbows were rejected in later centuries—but the experimental methods which he advocated were developed by his successors into a powerful intellectual tool. Grosseteste's disciple, the Franciscan Roger Bacon (*c.* 1214–1294), produced a fascinating body of scientific sense and nonsense. Roger was more an advocate of experimental science than a consistent practitioner of it, but at his best he was almost prophetic:

Experimental science controls the conclusions of all other sciences. It reveals truths which reasoning from general principles [the method of Abelard and St. Thomas] would never have discovered. Finally, it starts us on the way to marvelous inventions which will change the face of the world.

Hence the intense intellectual activity of the thirteenth century produced both the supreme synthesis of Christian rationalism and the genesis of a new method of scientific inquiry. In the realm of thought, as in so many other areas, the thirteenth century was both synthetic and creative. As the century drew to its close the intellectual synthesis of St. Thomas was being eroded by the doubts of his successors, who began to suspect that in seeking to reconcile reason and revelation he was attempting the impossible. Subsequent philosophers tended more and more to separate the two realms, some of them reverting to the Averroistic notion of the "twofold truth."

Universal systems such as that of St. Thomas have seldom been lasting, but for a few brief years Thomism represented, for many, the perfect merger of intellect and belief—of mind and soul. As such, it takes its place alongside the Gothic cathedral, the *Divine Comedy* of Dante, and the piety of St. Francis as a supreme and mature expression of the dynamic resurgence of high medieval Europe.

The world of the High Middle Ages is described in some outworn textbooks as stagnant, gloomy, and monolithic. At the other extreme, it has been portrayed as an ideally constituted society, free of modern fears and tensions, where men of all classes could live happily and creatively. In reality, it was an age of vitality, of striking contrasts, of dark fears and high hopes, of poverty that was often brutal yet gradually diminishing. Above all, it was an age in which Europeans awoke to the rich variety of possibilities that lay before them. A thirteenth-century poet, in his celebration of Springtime, captured perfectly the spirit of this reawakening:

> *The earth's ablaze again*
> *With lustrous flowers*
> *The fields are green again*
> *The shadows deep.*
> *Woods are in leaf again*
> *And all the world*
> *Is filled with joy again.*
> *This long-dead land*
> *Now flames with life again.*
> *The passions surge,*
> *Love is reborn,*
> *And beauty wakes from sleep.*

PART FIVE

THE LATE MIDDLE AGES: THE ORDEAL OF TRANSITION

FOURTEEN

CHURCH AND STATE IN THE FOURTEENTH CENTURY

The Decline of the High-Medieval Synthesis

Like most eras of transition, the fourteenth and fifteenth centuries were violent and unsettled, marked by a gradual ebbing of the self-confidence on which the high-medieval synthesis had rested. Prosperity gave way to sporadic depression, optimism to disillusionment, and the thirteenth-century dream of fusing the worlds of matter and spirit came to an end. Social behavior ran to extremes —to rebellion, sensualism, flagellation, cynicism, and witchcraft. Powerful creative forces were at work in these centuries, but they were less evident to most contemporary observers than the forces of disintegration and decay. The shrinking of Europe's economy, population, and territorial frontiers was accompanied by a mood of pessimism and claustrophobia, exploding periodically into frenzied enthusiasm or blind rage. The literature and art of the period express a preoccupation with fantasy, eccentricity, and death. England and France were torn by war, and both were ruled for a time by madmen. The Black Death struck Europe in the mid-fourteenth century and returned periodically to darken men's spirits and disrupt society.

These varied symptoms of social neurosis were associated with a gradual shift in Western Europe's political orientation—from a Christian commonwealth to a constellation of territorial states. The Roman Catholic Church fared badly during the Late Middle Ages. The western kingdoms were racked by civil and external war and, at times, by a near-breakdown of royal government. Yet during the final half-century of the period (c. 1450–1500) strong monarchies emerged in England, France, and Spain. These three states were destined to dominate Western European politics far into the future. By 1500 the monarchy was beginning to replace the Church as the object of men's highest allegiance. The pope had become mired in local Italian politics, and medieval Christian internationalism was breaking up into sovereign fragments.

Church and State in the Late Middle Ages

The late-medieval evolution from Christendom toward nationhood was not so much a transformation as a shift in balance. Even during the High Middle Ages the ideal of a Christian commonwealth, guided by pope and clergy, had never been fulfilled. At best, popes could win momentary political victories over kings and could achieve an uneasy equilibrium between royal and clerical authority within the European kingdoms. And by the end of the thirteenth century the balance was already tipping in favor of monarchs such as Edward I of England and Philip the Fair of France. Two centuries later, in 1500, the papacy was far weaker as an international force and the monarchies stronger, but "nationhood," by any strict definition, had not yet come. Still, papal authority over the churches within the various kingdoms, which had been a significant reality in the High Middle Ages, was becoming tenuous by 1500. The princely electors of Germany had long before denied the papacy any role in imperial elections or coronations, and papal influence in the appointment of French, English, and Spanish prelates had ebbed. More important still, the Late Middle Ages witnessed a collapse of papal spiritual prestige and a widening chasm between Christian piety and the organized church.

Christianity did not decline noticeably during this period; it merely became less ecclesiastical. The powerful movement of lay piety, which had been drifting away from papal leadership all through the High Middle Ages, now became increasingly hostile to ecclesiastical wealth and privilege, increasingly individualistic, and increasingly mystical. The wave of mysticism that swept across late-medieval Europe was not, for the most part, openly heretical. But by stressing the spiritual relationship between the individual and God the mystics tended to deemphasize the role of the ordained clergy and the sacraments as channels of divine grace. The mystic, although he believed in the efficacy of the Holy Eucharist, devoted himself chiefly to the direct mystical apprehension of God, for which no clerical hierarchy, no popes, and no sacraments were needed.

Mystics and Reformers

Mysticism had always been an element in Christian devotional life, and it was well known to the High Middle Ages. But with the breakdown of the high-medieval synthesis, and with the growth of complacency and corruption within the Church, mysticism became, for the first time, a large-scale movement among the laity. Early in the fourteenth century, the great Dominican mystic, Meister Eckhart (d. 1327), taught that man's true goal is utter separation from the world of the senses and absorption into the Divine Unknown. Eckhart had many followers, and as the century progressed, several large mystical brotherhoods took form. The greatest of them, the Brethren of the Common Life, was founded about 1375 by the Flemish lay preacher Gerard Groot, a student of one of Eckhart's disciples. The Brethren of the Common Life devoted themselves to simple lives of preaching, teaching, and charitable works. Their popularity in fifteenth-century Northern Europe approached that of the Franciscans two centuries before, but the Brethren, unlike the Franciscans, took no lifetime vows. Their schools were among the finest in Europe and produced some of the leading mystics, humanists, and reformers of the fifteenth and sixteenth centuries. Erasmus and Luther were both products of the Brethren's schools, as was Thomas à Kempis (d. 1471) whose *Imitation of Christ* stands as the supreme literary expression of late-medieval mysticism.* The *Imitation of Christ* typifies the mystical outlook in its emphasis on adoration over speculation, inner spiritual purity over external "good works," and direct experience of God over the sacramental avenues to divine grace. The *Imitation* remained well within the bounds of Catholic orthodoxy, yet it contained ideas that had great appeal to the sixteenth-century Protestant reformers. The emphasis on individual piety, common to all the mystics, tended to erode the medieval Christian commonwealth by transforming the Catholic Church into a multitude of individual souls, each groping his way toward salvation alone.

This element of Christian individualism was carried at times to the point of outright heresy. John Wycliffe (*d.* 1384), a professor at Oxford, anticipated the later Protestants by placing the authority of Scriptures over the pronouncements of popes and councils. Extending the implications of contemporary mysticism to their limit, Wycliffe stressed the individual's inner spiritual journey toward God, questioned the real presence of Christ in the Holy Eucharist, deemphasized the entire sacramental system, and spoke out strongly against ecclesiastical wealth. This last protest had been implicit in the thirteenth-century Franciscan movement, although St. Francis had shown his devotion to apostolic poverty by living it rather than forcing it on others. The compromises of later Franciscanism on the matter of property had given rise to a zealous splinter group —the "Spiritual Franciscans"—whose insistence on universal ecclesiastical poverty had made them anticlerical and antipapal. John XXII (1316–1334), the shrewd Avignonese "financier-pope," had been obliged in 1323 to denounce the doctrine of apostolic poverty as heretical. And Wycliffe, more than half a century later, was stripped of his professorship and convicted of heresy. Owing to his powerful friends at court, and to the unpopularity of the papacy in fourteenth-century England, he was permitted to die peacefully, but his followers, the Lollards, were hunted down. Their fate is suggested by the title of a parliamentary act of 1401: "The Statute on the Burning of Heretics."

English Lollardy represented an extreme expression of a growing discontent with the official Church. Wycliffe's doctrines spread to faraway Bohemia where they were taken up by the reformer John Hus. The Hussites used Wycliffe's anticlericalism as a weapon

* Although most scholars attribute *The Imitation of Christ* to Thomas à Kempis, the attribution is not certain.

in the struggle for Czech independence from German political and cultural influence. John Hus was burned at the stake at the Council of Constance in 1415, but his followers survived into the Reformation era as a dissident national group. Both Wycliffe and Hus represented, in their opposition to the organized international church, a reconciliation of personal religious faith with the idea of national sovereignty. If Christianity was to be an individual affair, then the political claims of popes and prelates were meritless, and secular rulers might govern without ecclesiastical interference. Thus the radical thrust of late-medieval Christianity, by its very anticlericalism, tended to support the growing concept of secular sovereignty. Ardent religious spirits such as John Hus—and Joan of Arc, burned as a heretic in 1431—could fuse Christian mysticism with the beginnings of patriotism

Crisis of the Papacy: The Schism and the Conciliar Movement

The mystics and reformers, implicitly or explicitly, rejected the pope as the mediator between God and the Christian community. Actually, the late-medieval papacy did little to merit the awesome responsibility of mediator. Under pressure from King Philip the Fair the papacy had moved to Avignon, on the Rhône River, officially outside the domains of France yet always in their shadow. There a series of French popes ruled from 1309 to 1376. The Avignon popes were subservient to the French crown only to a degree. They were capable of independent action, particularly when France had weak rulers, but their very location suggested to non-Frenchmen that they were no longer an impartial international force. Until 1376 attempts to return the papacy to Rome were foiled by the insecurity and violent factionalism of the holy city. Meanwhile the Avignon popes carried the thirteenth-century trend toward administrative and fiscal efficiency to its ultimate degree. Englishmen and Germans resented paying high taxes to an apparent tool of the French crown. And the immense bureaucracy of papal Avignon could hardly be expected to inspire mystics and reformers. As one contemporary observed, the pope's proper role was to shepherd Christ's flock, not to fleece it.

In 1376, Pope Gregory XI finally moved the Holy See from Avignon back to Rome. Chagrined by the turbulent conditions he encountered there, he made plans to return to France, but died in 1378 before he could carry them out. Urged on by a Roman mob,

the cardinals—most of whom were homesick Frenchmen—grudg-
ingly elected an Italian to the papal throne. The new pope, Urban
VI, had previously been a colorless functionary in the ecclesiastical
establishment. Now to everyone's surprise, he became a zealous
reformer and began taking steps to reduce the cardinals' revenues
and influence. The French cardinals fled Rome, canceled their
previous election on the grounds of mob intimidation, and elected
a French pope who returned with them to Avignon. Back in Rome,
Urban VI appointed new cardinals, and for the next 37 years the
Universal Church was torn by schism. When the rival popes died,
their cardinals elected rival successors. Excommunications were
hurled to-and-fro between Rome and Avignon, and the states of
Europe chose their sides according to their interests. France and
its allies supported Avignon, England and the Holy Roman Empire
backed Rome, and the Italian states shifted from one side to the
other as it suited their purposes. Papal prestige was falling in
ruin, yet in the face of agelong papal claims to absolute spiritual
authority, there seemed no power on earth that could claim to
arbitrate between two rival popes. The Church was at an impasse.

As the schism dragged on, increasing numbers of Christians
became convinced that the only solution was the convening of a
general church council. Both popes argued that councils were inferior to them and could not judge them, and Christians were per-
plexed as to who, if not the popes, had the authority to summon a
council. At length the cardinals themselves, in both camps, called
a council to meet in Pisa. There, in 1409, a group of 500 prelates
deposed both popes and elected a new one. Since neither pope
recognized the conciliar depositions, the effect of the Council of Pisa
was to transform a two-way schism into a three-way schism. The
situation was not only scandalous but ludicrous.

At length, the Holy Roman emperor, drawing on the ancient
precedent of the Emperor Constantine, summoned the prelates of
Europe to the Council of Constance (1415–1418). Here, at last,
the depositions of all three popes were voted and enforced, and
the schism was healed by the election of a conciliar pope, Martin V
(1417–1431).

To many thoughtful Christians the healing of the schism was not
enough. The papacy stood discredited, and it was argued that future popes should be guided by general councils meeting regularly
and automatically. The role of councils and assemblies was familiar
enough to contemporary secular governments. Why should not the
church, too, be governed "constitutionally"? Such views were being

urged by political philosophers such as Marsilius of Padua in the fourteenth century and Nicolas of Cusa in the fifteenth, and they were widely accepted among the prelates at Constance. That these delegates were essentially conservative is suggested by their decision to burn John Hus, who came to Constance with an imperial promise of safe conduct. Yet the Council of Constance made a genuine effort to reform the constitution of the church along conciliar lines. The delegates affirmed, against papal objection, the ultimate authority of councils in matters of doctrine and reform, and they decreed that thenceforth general councils would convene at regular intervals.

These broad principles, together with a number of specific reforms voted by the Council of Constance, met with firm opposition from Pope Martin V and his sucessors, who insisted on absolute papal supremacy. The popes reluctantly summoned a council in 1423 and another in 1431, but worked to make them ineffective. The last of the important medieval councils, the Council of Basel (1431–1449), drifted gradually into open schism with the recalcitrant papacy and petered out ingloriously in 1449. By then Europe's enthusiasm for conciliarism was waning; the conciliar movement died, and a single pope ruled unopposed once more in Rome.

The men who sat on the papal throne between the dissolution of Basel (1449) and the beginning of the Protestant Reformation (1517) were radically different from their high-medieval predecessors. Abandoning much of their former jurisdiction over the international Church, they devoted themselves to the beguiling culture and bitter local politics of Renaissance Italy. By now the popes were normally Italians, and so they would remain on into the future. Struggling to strengthen their hold on the Papal States, maneuvering through the shifting sands of Italian diplomacy, they conceded to northern monarchs an extensive degree of control over church and clergy in return for a formal recognition of papal authority and an agreed division of church revenues between pope and king.

Chronology of the Late-Medieval Church

1305–1378:	Avignon Papacy
1305–1314:	Pontificate of Clement V
1316–1334:	Pontificate of John XXII
1327:	Death of Master Eckhart
1370–1378:	Pontificate of Gregory XI; Return to Rome
1372:	Wycliffe Attacks Papal Domination of the Church

1378–1417: The Great Schism
1409:   Council of Pisa Fails to Heal Schism
1414–1449: Era of Conciliarism
1414–1418: Council of Constance Heals Schism, Burns John Hus
1417–1431: Pontificate of Martin V
1431–1449: Council of Basel

The Rise of the State

The shift in emphasis from international Catholicism toward secular sovereignty was ably and forcefully expressed in Marsilius of
Padua's important treatise, the *Defensor Pacis* (1324). Here the
dilemma of conflicting sovereign jurisdictions, secular and ecclesiastical, was resolved uncompromisingly in favor of the state. The
Church, Marsilius argued, should be stripped of political authority,
and the state should wield sovereign power over all its subjects, lay
and clerical alike. Thus the Church, united in faith, would be divided
politically into dozens of state churches obedient to their secular
rulers and not to the pope. In its glorification of the sovereign state,
the *Defensor Pacis* foreshadowed the evolution of late-medieval
and early-modern politics.

It was only after 1450, however, that the western monarchies
were able to assert their authority with any consistency over the
particularistic nobility. During the period from the early-fourteenth
to the mid-fifteenth century, the high-medieval trend toward royal
centralization seemed to have reversed itself. The major Iberian
powers—Aragon, Castile, and Portugal—were tormented by sporadic internal upheavals and made no progress toward reducing
Granada, the remaining Islamic enclave in the peninsula. For most
of the period, England and France were involved in the Hundred
Years' War (1337–1453), which drove England to the brink of
bankruptcy and ravaged the French countryside and population.

England: The Growth of Parliament and the Hundred Years' War

Nevertheless, the unwritten English "constitution" developed significantly during these years. In the course of the fourteenth century, Parliament changed from a body that met occasionally to a
permanent institution and split into Lords and Commons. The House
of Commons, consisting of representative townsmen and shire

knights, bargained with a monarchy hard pressed by the expenses of the Hundred Years' War. Commons traded its fiscal support for important political concessions, and by the century's end it had gained the privilege of approving or disapproving all taxation not sanctioned by custom. With control of the royal purse strings secured, Commons then won the power to legislate. Adopting the motto, "redress before supply," it refused to pass financial grants until the king had approved its petitions, and in the end, Commons petitions acquired the force of law.

Without belittling these constitutional advances, one must recognize that the late-medieval Commons was largely controlled by the force or manipulation of powerful aristocrats. Elections could be rigged; representatives could be bribed or overawed. And although Parliament deposed two English kings in the fourteenth century— Edward II in 1327 and Richard II in 1399—in both instances it was simply ratifying the results of aristocratic power struggles. It is significant that such parliamentary ratification should seem necessary to the nobility, but one must not conclude that Parliament had yet become an independent agent. Symbolically, it represented the will of the English community; actually it remained vulnerable to aristocratic force and tended to affirm decisions already made in castles or on battlefields.

The Hundred Years' War, which proved such a stimulus to the growth of parliamentary privileges, also constituted a serious drain on English wealth and lives. Beginning in 1337, the war dragged on fitfully for 116 years with periods of savage warfare alternating with prolonged periods of truce. Broadly speaking, the conflict was a continuation of the Anglo-French rivalry that dated from the Norman Conquest. Since 1066 England and France had battled on numerous occasions. In 1204 the Capetian crown had won the extensive northern French territories of the Angevin Empire. Normandy, Anjou, and surrounding lands had fallen more-or-less permanently into French royal hands, but the English kings retained a tenuous lordship over Gascony in the southwest. The English Gascon claim, cemented by a brisk commerce in Bordeaux wine and English cloth, gave rise to an expensive but inconclusive war (1294–1303) between Philip the Fair of France and Edward I of England. Competing English and French claims to jurisdiction in Gascony constituted one of several causes for the resumption of hostilities in 1337.

Another cause of the Hundred Years' War was the Anglo-French diplomatic struggle for control of Flanders, which France needed to round out its territories and which England needed to secure its profitable wool trade. Tension mounted in 1328 when, on the death of the last French Capetian, King Edward III of England (1327–1377) laid claim to the throne of France. Edward III's mother was a daughter of Philip the Fair, but the French nobility, refusing to be governed by an English monarch, revived the ancient custom that the succession could not pass through a female. Accordingly, they chose Philip VI (1328–1350), the first king of the long-lived Valois dynasty. Edward III accepted the decision at first, but in 1337, when other reasons prompted him to take up arms, he renewed his claim and titled himself king of France and England.

None of these causes can be considered decisive, and war might yet have been avoided had Edward III and Philip VI not been chivalric, high-spirited romantics longing for heroic clashes of arms. The same spirit infected the nobility on both sides, although the French knights lost their ardor when English longbowmen won smashing victories at Crecy (1346) and Poitiers (1356). The English revered Edward III so long as English arms were victorious, but they deposed his successor, Richard II (1377–1399), who showed no interest in fighting Frenchmen. Henry V (1413–1422) revived hostilities and gained the adulation of his subjects by winning a momentous victory over the French at Agincourt in 1415. But Henry V's early death, and the subsequent career of Joan of Arc (see p. 295), turned the tide of war against the English. By 1453, when the long struggle ended at last, England had lost all of France except the port of Calais. The centuries-long process of

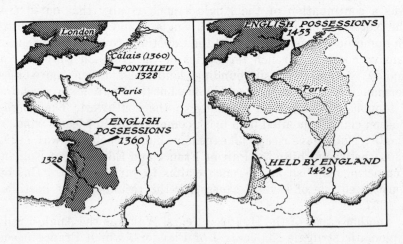

Anglo-French disentanglement was completed, and Joan of Arc's vision was realized: her Dauphin (crown prince) ruled France unopposed as King Charles VII.

The Hundred Years' War had been over for scarcely two years when England entered an era of civil strife between the rival houses of York and Lancaster, both claiming the throne. The Wars of the Roses, which raged off and on between the years 1455 and 1485, were the medieval English nobility's last orgy of violence. Weary of endless bloodshed, ordinary Englishmen longed for firm royal governance. They achieved it, to a degree, in the reign of the Yorkist Edward IV (1461–1483). And after a final burst of warfare, strong monarchy came permanently to England with the accession of the first Tudor king, that crafty, treacherous miser, Henry VII (1485–1509). Both Edward IV and Henry VII sought peace, a full treasury, and effective government, and by the late fifteenth century these goals were coming within reach. The economy was reviving, many of the more troublesome nobles had perished in the Wars of the Roses, and most Englishmen were willing to exchange violent independence for obedience and peace. All that was needed now was strong royal leadership, and that was supplied in full measure by the willful, determined Tudors.

France

The Hundred Years' War was a far greater trial to France than to England. All the fighting took place on French soil, and mercenary companies continually pillaged the French countryside. King John the Good (1350–1364)—a very bad king indeed—was powerless to cope with the English or bring order to a demoralized, plague-ridden land. In 1356, a decade after the French military debacle at Crecy and eight years after the onset of the Black Death (see p. 000), France was stunned by a crushing defeat at Poitiers. French nobles fell in great numbers, and King John himself was taken prisoner by the English.

The Estates General, meeting in Paris under the leadership of a dynamic Parisian cloth merchant, Etienne Marcel, momentarily assumed the reins of government. In 1357 they forced King John's son, the young Dauphin Charles, to issue a radical constitutional statute known as the "Great Ordinance." This statute embodied the demands of the bourgeois-dominated Estates General to join with the monarchy in the governance of France. The Estates

General were thenceforth to meet on regular occasions and to supervise the royal finances, courts, and administration through a small standing committee. The Dauphin Charles, deeply hostile to this infringement of royal authority, submitted for a time, then fled Paris to gather royalist support in the countryside.

By 1358 the horrors of plague, depression, and mercenary marauders had goaded the French peasantry into open revolt. The Jacquerie—as the rebellious peasants were called—lacked coherent goals and effective leaders, but they managed for a time to terrorize rural France. On one occasion they are reported to have forced an aristocratic wife to eat her roasted husband, after which they raped and murdered her. But within a few months the aristocracy and urban elites succeeded in crushing the Jacquerie with a savagery worthy of the rebels themselves. The peasants' rebellion of 1358 evoked a widespread longing for order and a return to the ways of old. This conservative backlash resulted in a surge of royalism which doomed Etienne Marcel's constitutional movement in Paris. Marcel himself was murdered in midsummer, 1358, and the Dauphin Charles returned to the city in triumph.

The Great Ordinance of 1357 became a dead letter after Marcel's fall, and in later centuries the Estates General met less and less frequently. The Dauphin Charles, who became the able King Charles V (1364–1380), instituted new tax measures that largely freed the monarchy from its financial dependence on assemblies and made it potentially the richest in Europe. The Estates General, unlike the English Parliament, failed to become an integral part of the government, and French kings reverted more and more to their high-medieval practice of dealing with their subjects through local assemblies. There were "Parlements" in France—outgrowths of the central and regional courts—but their functions remained largely judicial; they did not deliberate on the granting of taxes, and they did not legislate. French national cohesion continued to lag behind that of England primarily because France was much larger, more populous, and culturally diverse. During the Late Middle Ages its great dukes still ruled whole provinces with little interference from Paris. In the absence of an articulate national parliament the only voice that could claim to speak for all the French people was the voice of their king.

Charles V succeeded in turning the tide of war by avoiding pitched battles. His armies harassed the English unceasingly and forced them, little by little, to draw back. By Charles's death the French monarchy was recovering, and the English, reduced to small outposts around Bordeaux and Calais, virtually abandoned the war for a generation.

But Charles V was succeeded by the incompetent Charles VI (1380–1422)—"Charles the Mad"—who grew from a weak child into a periodically insane adult. His reign was marked by a bloody rivalry between the houses of Burgundy and Orleans. The Duke of Orleans was Charles the Mad's brother, the Duke of Burgundy his uncle. In Capetian times, such powerful fief-holding members of the royal family had usually cooperated with the king, but now, with a madman on the throne, Burgundy and Orleans struggled for control of the kingdom. In the course of the fifteenth century, the Orleanist faction became identified with the cause of the Valois monarchy, and Burgundy evolved into a powerful independent state between France and Germany. But at the time of Charles the Mad all was uncertain.

With France ravaged once again by murder and civil strife, King Henry V of England resumed the Hundred Years' War and, in 1415, won his overwhelming victory at Agincourt. The Burgundians then joined the English, and Charles the Mad was forced to make Henry V his heir. But both kings died in 1422, and while Charles the Mad's son, Charles VII (1422–1461), carried on a halfhearted resistance, the Burgundians and English divided northern France between them and prepared to crush the remaining power of the Valois monarchy.

At the nadir of his fortunes, Charles VII, as yet uncrowned, accepted in desperation the military services of the peasant visionary, Joan of Arc. Joan's victory at Orleans, her insistence on Charles' coronation in Rheims, and her capture and death at the stake in 1431 have become legendary. The spirit that she kindled raised French hopes, and in the two decades following her death Charles VII's armies went from victory to victory. The conquest of France had always been beyond English resources, and English successes in the Hundred Years' War had been mainly a product of wretched French leadership and paralyzing internal division. Now, as the war drew at last to a successful close, Charles VII could devote himself to the rebuilding of the royal government. He was supported in his task by secure tax revenues, a standing army, and the steady development of effective administrative institutions.

Centralization was carried still further by Louis XI (1461–1483), known as the "Spider King"—a name befitting both his appearance and his policies. Son and heir of Charles VII (whom he despised), Louis XI wove webs about his various rivals, removing them by murder, beheadings, and treachery. The Burgundian threat dissolved in 1477 when the last duke of Burgandy died fighting Louis' Swiss allies, and the Spider King swiftly confiscated the entire duchy. Plotting his way through a labyrinth of shifting alliances and loyalties, he advanced significantly toward the goals of French unification and Valois absolutism.

By 1500 the French monarchy was ruling through a central administration of middle-class professional bureaucrats. The nobility was pampered but apparently tamed, the towns were flourishing, and new royal armies were carrying the dynastic claims of the Valois kings into foreign lands.

Chronology of Late-Medieval England and France

England		France	
1307–1327:	Reign of Edward II	1328–1589:	Valois Dynasty
1327–1377:	Reign of Edward III	1328–1350:	Reign of Philip VI
1337–1453:	Hundred Years' War	1337–1453:	Hundred Years' War
1346:	Battle of Crecy	1346:	Battle of Crecy
1348–1349:	Black Death	1348–1349:	Black Death
		1350–1364:	Reign of John the Good
1356:	Battle of Poitiers	1356:	Battle of Poitiers
		1357:	The Great Ordinance
		1358:	Jacquerie Rebellion
1377–1399:	Reign of Richard II	1364–1380:	Reign of Charles V
1381:	Peasants' Revolt	1380–1422:	Reign of Charles VI "The Mad"
1413–1422:	Reign of Henry V		
1415:	Battle of Agincourt	1415:	Battle of Agincourt
		1422–1461:	Reign of Charles VII
		1429–1431:	Career of Joan of Arc
1455–1485:	Wars of the Roses		
1461–1483:	Reign of Edward IV	1461–1483:	Reign of Louis XI
1485–1509:	Reign of Henry VIII. Beginning of Tudor Dynasty		

Spain

The course of Spanish history in the Late Middle Ages runs parallel to that of England and France, with generations of internal turmoil giving way in the later fifteenth century to political coherence and ruthless royal consolidation. As the high-medieval *Reconquista* slowed to a halt around 1270, the Iberian Peninsula contained two strong Christian kingdoms—Castile and Aragon—the weaker Christian Kingdom of Portugal along the western coast, and Muslim Granada in the extreme south. Aragon, smaller than Castile, was more highly urbanized and far more imperialistic. During the thirteenth and fourteenth centuries its kings conquered the Islamic Mediterranean islands of Majorca, Minorca, Sardinia, and Sicily. The old Norman kingdom of Sicily (including southern Italy) had passed, after the death of Emperor Frederic II, to a junior member of the French Capetian house. The Sicilians, rebelling against French control in 1282, invited King Peter III of Aragon to be their monarch, and after a savage twenty-year struggle—the War of the Sicilian Vespers—the kingdom was divided in two. Aragon thenceforth ruled the island of Sicily while, on the Italian mainland, a "Kingdom of Naples" remained under the control of the French dynasty. The two kingdoms, Sicily and Naples, were reunited in 1435 under an Aragonese king, but for long years thereafter southern Italy and Sicily remained a source of antagonism between Spain and France.

Aragon and Castile were both plagued by civil turbulence during the Late Middle Ages. Aragonese kings strove with only limited success to placate the nobility and townsmen by granting significant concessions to the Cortes—the regional representative assemblies. A prolonged revolt by the mercantile class in the Aragonese province of Catalonia was put down in 1472 only with the greatest difficulty. Castile, in the meantime, was torn by constant aristocratic uprisings and disputed royal successions. Peace and strong government came within reach at last when Ferdinand of Aragon married Isabella of Castile in 1469. Isabella inherited her throne in 1474; Ferdinand inherited his in 1479. And thereafter, despite the continuation of regional Cortes, tribunals, and customs, an efficient central administration governed the two realms and eventually transformed them into the Kingdom of Spain.

In 1492 Columbus' voyage to America opened the great age of the Spanish global empire. And in the same year, Spain completed a long-delayed *Reconquista* by conquering Muslim Granada. Working grimly toward the enforcement of obedience, unity, and orthodoxy, the Spanish monarchy presented its Muslim and Jewish subjects with the choice of conversion or banishment, and the consequent Jewish exodus drained the kingdom of valuable mercantile and

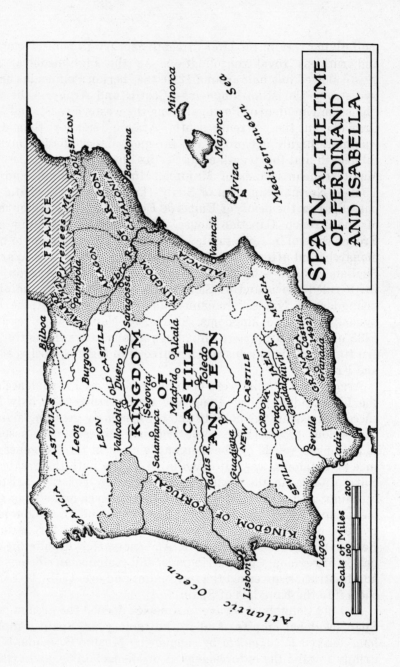

SPAIN AT THE TIME OF FERDINAND AND ISABELLA

FRANCE

Roussillon

Pyrenees Mts.

NAVARRE (to 1512)

Pampelona

ARAGON

Barcelona

CATALONIA

R. of

Saragossa

Ebro R.

ARAGON

KINGDOM

VALENCIA

Valencia

Minorca

Majorca

Iviza

Mediterranean Sea

Bilboa

Burgos

OLD CASTILE

Duero R.

Vallodolid

Segovia

KINGDOM

OF

Madrid

Alcalá

CASTILE

Toledo

AND LEON

MURCIA

GRANADA (to Castile 1492)

Granada

ASTURIAS

Leon

LEON

Salamanca

NEW CASTILE

Tagus R.

Guadiana R.

JAEN

CORDOVA

Cordova

Guadalquivir R.

SEVILLE

Seville

Cadiz

GALICIA

KINGDOM OF PORTUGAL

Lagos

Lisbon

Atlantic Ocean

Scale of Miles

0   100   200

intellectual talent. The Catholic Inquisition became a tool of the state and, as an instrument of both political and doctrinal conformity, it brought the crown not only religious unity but lucrative revenues as well. The nobility was persuaded that its best interests lay in supporting the monarchy rather than in opposing it, and regional separation was curbed. With unity established and with the immense wealth of the New World soon to be pouring in, Spain in 1500 was entering a period of rich cultural expression and international power.

The wealth of Spain and Portugal in the sixteenth century resulted from their strategic location at the extreme west of Europe, facing the Atlantic. Important advances in shipbuilding and navigation opened the way for long ocean voyages, and by 1500 European captains had traversed the Atlantic and Indian Oceans. The conquest of these seas brought Spain a New World empire and the wealth of the Incas and Aztecs. It brought Portugal a direct sea-route to India and a vast commercial empire in the Far East. The first Atlantic explorations, however, were pioneered by Italian seamen who could draw on their experience in Mediterranean commerce. In the early fourteenth century, Venetian galley fleets were making yearly expeditions through the Straits of Gibraltar to England and Flanders, and Genoese merchants were trading with the Canary Islands. By the mid-fifteenth century the Canaries, Madeiras, Azores, and Cape Verde Islands had all passed into Spanish or Portuguese hands, but the ships of the Iberian monarchies continued to depend often on the skill of Italian captains and crews. It was the Genoese captain, Christopher Columbus, who brought the Spanish monarchy its claim to the New World.

Missionary zeal, curiosity, and greed were the mixed motives of these explorations. In the long run, greed was the primary consideration of both the sponsoring monarchies and the captains and private merchants who stood to make their fortunes from successful voyages. But the great patron of Portuguese West-African exploration, Prince Henry the Navigator (1394–1460), seems to have been driven in large measure by the hope of Christian evangelism and the longing to discover unknown lands. From his court at Sagres, ships were sent westward to the Atlantic islands and southward down the African coast and, at Sagres itself, Prince Henry collected an invaluable store of geographical and navigational data for the instruction of his captains. The Portuguese West-African voyages continued intermittently after Prince Henry's death and reached their climax in 1497–1499, when Vasco da Gama rounded the Cape of Good Hope and reached India. The 6000 percent profit realized by da Gama's voyage demonstrated emphatically the commercial potentialities of this new, direct route to the Orient.

By 1500, therefore, the Spanish were beginning their settlement of America, and the Portuguese had initiated their great commerce with the Far East. Vasco da Gama and Christopher Columbus had changed the direction of history: the subsequent Spanish Golden Age would be financed by American silver, while the Portuguese trade route to the Orient, short-circuiting the traditional overland routes with their countless middlemen, would depress the once-flourishing commerce of the Ottoman Empire and Renaissance Italy, while enriching Portugal beyond all dreams. Europe's global career was underway, and Spain and Portugal, whose enterprise began it all, were its first beneficiaries.

Germany and Italy

Late medieval Germany and Italy suffered from much the same sort of regional particularism that afflicted England, France, and the Iberian Peninsula, but the late fifteenth century brought no corresponding trend toward centralization. Both lands passed into the modern era divided internally and incapable of competing with the western monarchies. The weak elective Holy Roman Empire that emerged in Germany from the papal-imperial struggles of the High Middle Ages was given formal sanction in the Golden Bull of 1356. The Bull excluded any papal role in the imperial appointment or coronation, leaving the choice of succession to the majority vote of seven great German princes. These "electors" included the arch-bishops of Mainz, Trier, and Cologne, the Count Palatine of the Rhine, the Duke of Saxony, the Margrave of Brandenburg, and the King of Bohemia. The electoral states themselves remained rela-tively stable, as did other large German principalities such as the Hapsburg duchy of Austria, but the empire itself became powerless. Germany in 1500 was a jigsaw puzzle of more than 100 principali-ties—fiefs, ecclesiastical city-states, free cities, counties, and duchies —their boundaries shifting periodically through war, marriage, and inheritance. Imperial authority in Italian politics was as dead as papal authority in imperial elections. Germany and Italy were disengaged at last, but both continued to suffer the political disin-tegration that resulted from their former entanglement.

The political crazy-quilt of late-medieval Italy evolved during the fifteenth century, through the domination of small states by larger ones, into a delicate power balance between five strong political units: the Kingdom of Naples, the Papal States, and the three northern city-states of Florence, Milan, and Venice. Naples was ruled by French or Aragonese dynasties. The Papal States were under tenuous papal control, compromised by the particularism of local aristocrats and the political turbulence of Rome itself. Milan, and later, Florence, ceased to be republics and fell under the rule of self-made despots. And Venice remained a republic dominated by a narrow commercial oligarchy.

The despots, ruling without the sanction of anointment or legitimate succession which a royal title confers, governed by their wits and by the realities of power, uninhibited by traditions or customs. They have often been regarded as symbols of the "new Renaissance man," but in fact their opportunism was a quality well known to the northern monarchs, and their ruthlessness would have surprised neither William the Conqueror nor Philip the Fair. Yet the very insecurity of their positions and the fragile equilibrium of the five major Italian powers gave rise to a considerable refinement of traditional diplomatic practices. Ambassadors, skilled at compliments and espionage, were exchanged on a regular basis, and emerging from the tendency of two or three weaker states to combine against a stronger one came the shifting alliances known as the "balance of power" principle.

The Italian power balance was upset in 1494 when a powerful French army invaded the peninsula. For generations thereafter Italy was a battleground for French-Spanish rivalries, and the techniques and concepts of Italian Renaissance diplomacy passed across the Alps to affect the relations of the northern kingdoms. The modern tendency to ignore moral limitations and ecclesiastical mediation—to base diplomacy on a calculated balance of force—was growing throughout late-medieval Europe, but it reached fruition first in Renaissance Italy.

Eastern Europe

Eastern Europe was, in general, no more successful than Germany and Italy in achieving political cohesion. Poland, Lithuania, and Hungary (as well as the Scandinavian states to the north) were all afflicted by aristocratic turbulence and dynastic quarrels. The Teutonic Knights were humbled by Slavic armies and internal rebellions, and the kingdoms of Serbia and Bulgaria were overwhelmed by the Ottoman Turks. Only the Russians and Ottomans were able to build strong states, and both, by 1500, were uncompromisingly autocratic.

Begining in 1386, Poland united for a time with rapidly expanding Lithuania, and the Polish-Lithuanian state became the largest political unit in Europe. It was also, very possibly, the worst governed. Under the Lithuanian warrior-prince Jagiello (1377–1434), who converted to Catholicism when he accepted the Polish crown, the dual state humbled the Teutonic Knights at the decisive battle of Tannenberg (1410). But even under Jagiello, Poland-Lithuania had no real central government; its nobles would cooperate with their ruler only against the hated Germans, and even then only momentarily. Stretching all the way from the Black Sea to the Baltic, incorporating many of the former lands of the Teutonic Order and most of the old state of Kievan Russia, Poland-Lithuania lacked the skilled administrators and political institutions necessary to govern its vast territories. Its nobles were virtually all-powerful, and its peasantry was slipping toward serfdom. Its political impotence guaranteed that no strong state would emerge between Germany and Russia during Europe's early modern centuries.

Modern Russia evolved gradually out of the Muscovite Principality that had managed to survive and expand during the centuries of Mongol domination. The Grand Princes of Moscow extended their influence in northern Russia by collaborating with their Mongol Khans and winning the support of the Orthodox Church. They were appointed sole collectors of the Mongol tribute, and on occasion they helped the Mongols crush the rebellions of other Russian princes. Moscow became the headquarters of Russian Orthodox Christianity, and when the Turks took Constantinople in 1453, Moscow, the "Third Rome," claimed spiritual sovereignty over the Orthodox Slavic world. At first the Muscovite princes strengthened their position with the full backing of the Mongol Khans, but toward the end of the fourteenth century Moscow began taking the lead in anti-Mongol resistance. At last, in 1480, Ivan III, the Great, Grand Prince of Moscow and Czar of the Russians, repudiated Mongol authority altogether and abolished the tribute.

The Muscovite princes enjoyed a certain measure of popular support in their struggle against the Mongols, but their rule was autocratic to a degree worthy of Genghis Khan himself. Nascent republicanism in city-states such as Novgorod was crushed with the expansion of Muscovite authority. The grand princes were despots, inspired politically by Central Asia rather than by the West. Their

Saint Basil's Cathedral, Moscow, sixteenth century.

state had no local or national assemblies and no articulate middle class. Russia was eventually to acquire the material and organizational attributes of a great power, but the centuries of its Mongol isolation from the rest of Europe left their imprint.

The great outside threat to Eastern Europe came from the southeast, where the Ottoman Turks pressed into the Balkans from Asia Minor. These Altaic tribesmen, driven from their Central Asian

homeland by the Mongols, came into Asia Minor first as mercenaries, then as conquerors. Adopting the Islamic faith, the Ottomans
subjected the greater part of Asia Minor to their rule and inter-
married with the local population. In 1354, bypassing the diminutive
Byzantine Empire, they invaded Europe. During the latter half of
the fourteenth century they crushed Serbia and Bulgaria and
extended their dominion over most of the Balkan Peninsula.

At the decisive battle of Varna (1444), the Ottomans decimated
a Christian crusading army and consolidated their hold on southeastern Europe. After the great Ottoman victory at Varna, the
storming of Constantinople in 1453 was little more than a postscript. Yet all Europe recognized that the Sultan Mohammed II,
in conquering the unconquerable city, had ended an era.

The Ottoman Empire continued to threaten Europe for another
two hundred years. It endured until the twentieth century; as the
Republic of Turkey it endures still. Like the Muscovite princes,
the Ottoman sultans were autocrats. Slaves served in their administration and fought in their armies alongside mounted noblemen of
the Ottoman landed aristocracy. While the sultans were living in
splendor in the former capital of Byzantium, their government was
insulating southeastern Europe from the civilization of the West.
And western Europe, with its eastern trade routes blocked by the
Turks, set out into the Atlantic.

Chronology of Late-Medieval Central and Eastern Europe

1237–1242:	Mongols Invade Eastern Europe
1340:	Mongols Control Russia
1354–1400:	Ottoman Turks Conquer Balkans
1356:	Golden Bull Increase Powers of the Seven Imperial Electors
1377–1434:	Jagiello Rules Lithuania, Unites it with Poland (1386)
1453:	Contantinople Falls to the Turks
1462–1505:	Reign of Ivan III "The Great" who Ends Russian Tribute to Mongols (1480)

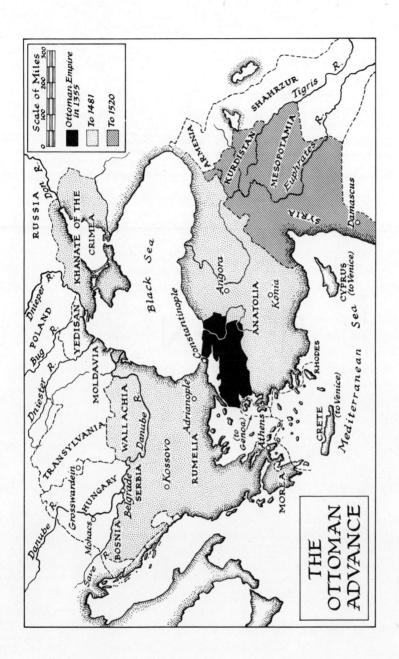

FIFTEEN

ECONOMIC AND CULTURAL CHANGE

The shift from boom to depression came gradually and unevenly to Western Europe in the years around 1300. From the early fourteenth century through much of the fifteenth, a number of related trends—shrinking population, contracting markets, an end to the long process of land reclamation, and a creeping mood of pessimism and retrenchment—resulted in a general economic slump and a deepening of social antagonisms. These trends were far from universal. They tended to be less marked in northern Italy than elsewhere, and various localities north of the Alps, by profiting from favorable commercial situations or technological advances, became more prosperous than before. At a time when many English towns were declining, Coventry and certain others grew wealthy from the rise of woolen-cloth production. The Flemish town of Bruges remained throughout most of the Late Middle Ages a bustling center of commerce on the northern seas. Florence, with its large textile industry and its international banking, became the focal point of Italian Renaissance culture. In Florence and elsewhere, enterprising individuals, and families grew wealthy from the profits of international commerce and banking. The Bardi, Peruzzi, and Medici were the great Florentine banking families, and they had their counterparts north of the Alps in such figures as Jacques Coeur of Bourges—financier of the fifteenth-century French monarchy—and the Fuggers of Augsburg, bankers of the Holy Roman Emperors. But such great financiers as these were exceedingly insecure in the turbulent years of the Late Middle Ages. The Bardi and Peruzzi houses collapsed in the mid-fourteenth century, and Jacques Coeur was ruined by his royal debtor, King Charles VII. Even though some fortunes continued to grow, the total assets of late-medieval bankers fell considerably below those of their thirteenth-century predecessors. The success of families such as the Medicis and Fuggars illustrates the late-medieval tendency toward an increasingly unequal distribution of wealth. The other side of the picture is to be seen in intensified urban strife and peasants' rebellions.

The Black Death

The late-medieval depression began well before the coming of the Black Death (1348–1349). The fundamental trends of demographic and economic decline were not initiated by the plague, but they were enormously aggravated by it. Carried by fleas that infested black rats, the bubonic plague entered Europe along the trade routes from the East and spread with frightening speed. The death toll cannot be determined with any precision. The best estimate would probably be one-fourth to one-third of Europe's population. It seems likely that in many crowded towns more than half the inhabitants died, whereas isolated rural areas tended to be spared. Consequently, the most progressive, most enterprising, and best-trained Europeans were hit hardest. Few urban families can have been spared altogether. Survivors of the terrible years 1348 to 1349 were subjected to periodic recurrences of the plague, which returned to Europe repeatedly over the next three centuries. Fourteenth-century medical science was at a loss to explain the process of infection, while lack of sanitation in the towns encouraged its spread. Some fled their cities in panic, some gave way to religious frenzy or debauchery, and some remained faithfully at their posts, hoping for divine protection against the pestilence. But none emerged unaffected from this monstrous eruption of suffering, grief, and death—this unspeakable catastrophe.

Town and Country

The towns of late-medieval Europe, confronted with shrinking markets and decreasing opportunities, lost their earlier social mobility and buoyancy. Privileged classes closed their ranks, the guilds guarded their monopolies, and heredity became the chief avenue to the status of guild master. In their grim efforts to retain their share of declining markets, guilds struggled with one another, with the district nobility, and with the increasingly desperate urban proletariat, its class consciousness growing as its upward mobility was choked off. Few towns of late-medieval Europe escaped being torn by class violence. In 1378 Florence experienced the most severe workers' rebellion of the period.

The rich businessmen of European towns usually managed to retain their privileged economic status in the face of lower-class pressure. They did so by allying with great magnates or kings or, in Italy, by abdicating their political power to despots. The wealthy merchants and bankers were generally able, through political control or manipulation, to keep down wages despite the plague-induced labor shortage and to smash the resulting lower-class uprisings.

The rural nobility of Western Europe, like the urban upper class, managed to survive the turbulent socio-economic changes of the Late Middle Ages. Faced with a gradual shift from a barter to a money economy, the nobles were able, with some exceptions, to hold their extensive lands and preserve much of their wealth. They responded to the decline in grain prices by accelerating the high-medieval processes of leasing their own lands to peasants and commuting customary peasant services to fixed money payments. In this way, aristocratic incomes were protected against deflation so long as peasants could manage the agreed payments. And consequently, the peasants continued to rise in legal status from land-bound serfs to free tenant farmers until, by 1500, serfdom had almost disappeared from Western Europe. But the passing of serfdom was by no means accompanied by increased peasant prosperity. On the contrary, the declining population and the contracting grain market resulted in abandoned fields and a growing class of landless paupers. Some rural noblemen retained direct control of their land, hiring workers to farm it or converting it from grain crops to the more profitable wool growing.

In general, then, the peasant passed from his former manorial status (of customary payments in goods and labor services) to a new status based on cash; by 1500 he tended to be either a rent-paying tenant or a landless wage earner. And the nobleman dealt in receipts and expenditures rather than in the exploitation of customary services. These changes had begun in the High Middle Ages and were largely completed by 1500. At times of drastic population decline, as in the decades following the Black Death, the resulting labor shortage tended to force up wages, and the nobility fought this tendency either through collective conspiracy or through legislation. In England, for example, the Statutes of Laborers of 1351 and thereafter were aimed at freezing wages in the wake of the plague. They succeeded only to a point, and at a price of creating a deep sense of grievance among the peasantry, a feeling that contributed to the abortive English Peasants' Revolt of 1381. This confused and bloody uprising was merely one of a considerable number that terrorized late-medieval Europe. Like the Jacquerie rebellion in France, and like many similar peasant insurrections of the period, it bore witness to an unbalanced society in which classes struggled bitterly for their share of a declining wealth.

In Eastern Europe the peasant's lot was even worse than in the west, for the eastern nobility was reducing its peasantry to serfdom at the very time that western peasants were achieving legal freedom. The late-medieval landed nobility of both Eastern and Western Europe jealously guarded its privileges against peasantry and monarchy, and for a time, in both east and west, this nobility seemed to be reversing the high medieval trend toward stronger royal government. With the exception of Russia, eastern monarchies made no real progress against their nobles, but by the later fifteenth century, western monarchies were beginning to curb the fractious independence of the landed aristocracy. The new Tudor monarchy in England tended to favor the mercantile class, but in Spain and France the nobility was rewarded for its political submissiveness by economic favoritism and privileged positions in the royal administration, the army, and the Church.

Thus, the western nobles evolved, during the High and Late Middle Ages, from robber barons into silk-clad courtiers. The traditional role of mounted knight in the feudal host was a thing of the past, for monarchs were now fighting with mercenaries, and foot-soldiers were winning most of the major battles. Moreover, the increasing use of gunpowder was making knightly armor and knightly castles highly vulnerable. But while the feudal knight was vanishing from European armies, he was becoming ever more prominent in art, literature, and court ceremonial. The fifteenth century was an age of elaborate shining armor, fairy-tale castles, coats of arms, and extravagant tournaments. Knighthood, driven from the battle-field, took refuge in fantasy, and an age of ruthless political cynicism saw the full flowering of a romantic code of chivalric ethics. Behind this fanciful façade, the landed aristocracy retained its privileged position atop the social order.

The consolidation of royal authority in late-fifteenth-century Western Europe coincided with a general economic surge following a long recession. Europe's population in 1500 may well have been lower than in 1300, but it was increasing again. Commerce was quickening and towns were growing. Technological progress had never ceased, and now water-driven fulling mills were increasing wool production, while water-driven pumps were draining mines. With advances in mining technology, Europe was increasing its supply of silver and the various metals essential to its rising industries: iron, copper, alum, and tin. The development of artillery and movable-type printing depended not merely on the inventive idea but also on many generations of progress in the metallurgical arts. Furthermore, advances in ship design and navigation lay behind the Atlantic voyages that would soon bring a torrent of wealth into Western Europe. By 1500 the long economic crisis had passed; Europe had entered on an era of economic growth and world expansion that would far outstrip her earlier surge in the High Middle Ages.

Intellectual and Cultural Evolution

Printing and gunpowder were the two most spectacular technological innovations of the Late Middle Ages. Gunpowder came first, and by the fifteenth century cannons were being used with some effect in the Hundred Years' War, the Turkish conquests and, indeed, most of the military engagements of Europe. Printing from movable type was developed midway through the fifteenth century, and although its effect on European culture was immense, the full impact was not felt until after 1500. Even among the "new men" of the Italian Renaissance, printed books were regarded as vulgar imitations of handwritten originals. This fact should warn us against viewing late-medieval Europe—and even Renaissance Italy —exclusively in terms of new beginnings. There was, to be sure, a strong sense of the new and "modern" among many creative Europeans of the period, but there was also a perpetuation of medieval ways, styles, and habits of thought. Often one encounters a sense of loss over the fading of medieval ideals and institutions, a conviction that civilization was declining. Some Renaissance writers were optimistic about the human condition, but others were not. The Italian humanist Aeneas Sylvius—later Pope Pius II (*d*. 1464)— could look at the Turkish threat and the strife among Christian states and conclude that there was nothing good in prospect. The generation living after 1500, aware of the voyages of exploration and of the growing prosperity and political consolidation, might well be hopeful of the future, but between 1300 and 1500 a gloom hung over much of Europe. The rise of modern civilization was less apparent than the decay of the Middle Ages.

Beneath the gloom one finds a sense of nervous unrest, a violent emotionalism that gives dramatic intensity to late-medieval works of art but robs them of the balanced serenity characteristic of the best thirteenth-century creations. Society was in a state of crisis. The practice of self-flagellation acquired wide popularity, and the Dance of Death became a favorite artistic theme. In an era of depression, plague, and disorder, the high-medieval synthesis could no longer hold together. Unity was giving way to diversity.

Philosophy

The breakdown of hierarchy and order expressed itself in a hundred ways—in the intensifying conflict between class and class, in the architectural shift from organic unity to flamboyant decoration, in the divorce between knightly function and chivalric fantasy, in the evolution from Christian commonwealth to territorial states, and in the disintegration of St. Thomas Aquinas' fusion of faith and reason. The medieval dream of a City of God on earth had achieved its supreme intellectual embodiment in Aquinas's hierarchical ordering and reconciliation of matter and spirit, body and soul, logic and revelation. The fading of that dream is nowhere more evident than in the attacks of fourteenth-century philosophers on the Thomist system.

St. Thomas' *Summa Theologica*, like the cathedral of Chartres, unifies religious aspiration and logical order on the basis of an omnipotent God who is both loving and rational. The fourteenth-century attack on this reconciliation was founded on two related propositions. (1) To ascribe rationality to God is to limit his omnipotence by the finite rules of human logic. Thus, the Thomist God of reason gave way to a God of will, and the high-medieval notion of a logical divine order was eroded. (2) Human reason, therefore, can tell us nothing of God; logic and Christian belief inhabit two separate, sealed worlds.

The first steps toward this concept of a willful, incomprehensible God were taken by the Oxford Franciscan, Duns Scotus (*d.* 1308), who produced a detailed critique of St. Thomas's theory of knowledge. Duns Scotus did not reject the possibility of elucidating revealed truth through reason, but he was more cautious in his use of logic than Aquinas had been. Whereas St. Thomas is called "The Angelic Doctor," Duns Scotus is called "The Subtle Doctor," and the extreme complexity of his thought prompted men in subsequent generations to describe anyone who bothered to follow Duns' arguments as a "dunce." The sobriquet is unfair, for Duns Scotus is an important and original figure in the development of late scholasticism. Yet one is tempted to draw a parallel between the intricacies of his intellectual system and the decorative elaborations of late-Gothic churches. A Christian rationalist of the most subtle kind, he nevertheless made the first move toward dismantling the Thomist synthesis and withdrawing reason from the realm of theology.

William of Ockham

Another Oxford Franciscan, William of Ockham (*d.* 1349), attacked the Thomist synthesis on all fronts. Ockham was a nominalist; he argued that the Platonic archetypes were not realities but merely names. Thus he saw the world as a countless multitude of individual concrete things, lumped together by the fallible human intellect into classes and categories of our own making. Ockham argued, further, that God and Christian doctrine, utterly undemonstrable, must be accepted on faith alone, and that human reason must be limited to the realm of observable phenomena. In this unpredictable world of an unpredictable Creator, one can reason only about things that one can see or directly experience. With this radical empiricism Ockham ruled out all metaphysical speculations, all rational arguments from an observable diversity of things to an underlying unity of things. And out of this great separation of reason and faith came two characteristic expressions of late-medieval thought: the scientific manipulation of material facts, and pietistic mysticism untouched by logic. In Ockham and many of his followers, one finds empiricism and mysticism side by side. For since the two worlds never touched, they were in no way contradictory. An intelligent Christian could keep one foot in each of them.

The Ockhamist philosophy served as an appropriate foundation for both late-medieval mysticism and later-medieval science. Some mystics, indeed, regarded themselves as empiricists. For the empiricist is a person who accepts only those things that he experiences, and the mystic, abandoning the effort to *understand* God, strove to *experience* him. Science, on the other hand, was now freed of its theological underpinnings and could proceed on its own. Nicholas Oresme, a teacher at the University of Paris in the fourteenth-century, attacked the Aristotelian theory of motion and proposed a rotating earth as a possible explanation for the apparent daily movement of the sun and stars across the sky. Oresme's theories probably owed more to thirteenth-century scientists such as Robert Grosseteste than to Ockham, but his willingness to tinker with the traditional explanations of the physical structure of God's universe is characteristic of an age in which scientific speculation was being severed from revealed truth.

Many late-medieval philosophers rejected Ockham's criticism and remained Thomists, but owing to the very comprehensiveness of Aquinas achievement, his successors were reduced to detailed elaboration or minor repair work. Faced with a choice between the tedious niggling of late Thomism and the drastic limitations imposed by Ockham on the scope of philosophical inquiry, many of Europe's finest minds shunned the great philosophical issues altogether for the more promising fields of science, mathematics, and classical learning. When the philosopher John Gerson (*d.* 1429), chancellor of the University of Paris, spoke out in his lectures against "vain curiosity in the matter of faith," the collapse of the faith-reason synthesis was all but complete.

Arts and Letters

The change from high-medieval synthesis to late-medieval diversity is clearly evident in the field of art. The high-Gothic balance between upward aspiration and harmonic proportion—between the vertical and the horizontal—was shifting in the cathedrals of the later thirteenth century toward an ever-greater emphasis on verticality. Formerly, elaborate capitals and horizontal string courses had balanced the soaring piers and pointed arches of the Gothic cathedrals, creating a sense of tense equilibrium between heaven and earth. But during the Late Middle Ages, capitals disappeared and stringcourses became discontinuous, leaving little to relieve the dramatic upward thrust from floor to vaulting. Late-medieval churches achieved a fluid, uncompromising verticality—a sense of heavenly aspiration that bordered on the mystical.

By about the mid-thirteenth century, the basic structural potentialities of the Gothic style had been fully exploited. Windows were as large as they could possibly be, vaultings could be raised no higher without structural disaster, and flying buttresses were used with maximum efficiency. The fundamental Gothic idea of a skeletal stone framework with walls of colored glass had been embodied in cathedrals of incomparable nobility and beauty. During the Late Middle Ages, cathedrals changed in appearance as tastes changed, but the originality of post-thirteenth-century Gothic architects was inhibited by their devotion to a style that had already achieved complete structural development. Accordingly, the evolution of late-Gothic architecture consisted chiefly in new and more elaborate decoration, with the result that many late-medieval churches are, to some modern tastes, overdecorated sculptural jungles. (To others, they are the most beautiful Gothic churches of all.) Unrestrained verticality and unrestrained decorative elaboration were the architectural hallmarks of the age, and both reflected a decline of rational unity and balance. Like Ockham's universe, the fourteenth- and fifteenth-century church became a fascinating miscellany of separate elements. Thus, the "flamboyant Gothic" style emerged in late-medieval France, while English churches were evolving from the "decorated Gothic" of the fourteenth century to the "perpendicular Gothic" of the fifteenth and sixteenth centuries, with its lace-like fan vaulting, its sculptural profusion, and its sweeping vertical lines. In the course of the sixteenth century, Gothic architecture, having reached its decorative as well as its structural limits, gave

Nave of Amiens Cathedral, begun 1220, showing the capitals and decorated stringcourse.

Choir of Saint-Etienne at Beauvais, 1506–c. 1550, showing the absence of capitals, inconspicuous and intrrupted stringcourse, and elaborate vaulting.

Tomb of Margaret of Austria with the choir stalls in the background in the church at Brou, 1516–1532.

An example of fan vaulting from "The New Building," Peterborough Cathedral, England: fifteenth century.

High Gothic sculpture: Le beau dieu, west portral of Amiens Cathedral: thirteenth century.

Three Mourners from the tomb of Philip the Bold of Burgandy, by Claus Sluter and Claus de Werve: fifteen century.

way throughout Northern Europe to the classical Greco-Roman style which had been revived and developed in fifteen-century Italy and flowed north with the spread of Renaissance humanism.

Sculpture and painting, like architecture and thought, evolved during the Late Middle Ages toward multiformity. The serene, idealized humanism of thirteenth-century sculpture gave way to heightened emotionalism and an emphasis on individual peculiarities. Painting north of the Alps reached its apogee in the mirror-like realism of the Flemish school. Painters such as Jan van Eyck (*d.* 1440), pioneering in the use of oil paints, excelled in reproducing the natural world with a devotion to detail that was all but photographic. Critics of the style have observed that detail seems to compromise the unity of the total composition, but in a world viewed through Ockham's eyes, such is to be expected. It was Italy, again, that developed a new style of painting and sculpture, based on the classical canon of realism subordinated to a unifying idea. And the Italian Renaissance style of painting, like Renaissance architecture,

The Madonna of the Chancellor Rolin, by Jan van Eyck.

streamed northward in the sixteenth century to bring a new vision to transalpine artists.

The decay of high-medieval forms of expression is vividly demonstrated in the late-medieval romance, which had once served as a vital literary form but now became a sentimentalized, formalized bore. Much of the popular literature of late-medieval Europe is beyond redemption, and writers could achieve vitality only by turning from warmed-over chivalry to graphic realism. Geoffrey Chaucer (*d.* 1400), in his *Canterbury Tales,* combines rare psychological insight with a descriptive skill worthy of the Flemish painters or the late-Gothic stone carvers. Chaucer describes one of his Canterbury pilgrims, a corrupt friar, in these words:

Highly beloved and intimate was he
With country folk wherever he might be,
And worthy city women with possessions;
For he was qualified to hear confessions,
Or so he said, with more than priestly scope;
He had a special license from the pope.
Sweetly he heard his penitents at shrift
With pleasant absolution, for a gift.

And François Villon (*d.* 1463), a brawling Parisian vagabond, expressed in his poems an anguished, sometimes brutal realism that captures the late-medieval mood of insecurity and plague:

Death makes one shudder and turn pale,
Pinches his nose, distends his veins,
Swells out his throat, his members fail,
Tendons and nerves grow hard with strains.

To Villon, writing in a society of sharp class distinctions, death was the great democrat:

I know this well, that rich and poor,
Fools, sages, laymen, friars in cowl,
Large-hearted lords and each mean boor,
Little and great and fair and foul,
Ladies in lace, who smile or scowl,
From whatsoever stock they stem,
Hatted or hooded, prone to prowl,
Death seizes every one of them.

Italian Renaissance Classicism

These northern moods and movements stood in sharp contrast to the growing, self-confident classicism of Renaissance Italy. Here, the late-medieval economic depression was less severe and less prolonged, and although endemic interurban warfare made conditions just as insecure as in the North, the civic spirit of the independent north-Italian communes encouraged innovation and novel forms of expression. Italy had never been entirely at ease with Gothic architecture, and the triumphs of high-medieval culture were more characteristically French than Italian. England and France had enjoyed relative peace during much of the thirteenth century, whereas Italy had been battered by papal-imperial wars. Italy, in short, harbored no fond memories of the High Middle Ages, and the coming of the Renaissance was not so much the advent of a new epoch in European history as a reassertion of Italian culture over French.

In an age of French arms and French culture, such as the thirteenth century had been, Italians could return in memory to the days when Rome ruled the world. Roman monuments and Roman sculpture were all around them, and when, in the fourteenth and fifteenth centuries, they abandoned the Gothic style and the intellectual habits of Paris theologians, it was to their indigenous classical heritage that they turned for inspiration. In sculpture, the calm spiritual nobility of stone saints gave way to a classical emphasis on the human body. The slender young Virgins of the High Middle Ages suddenly turned voluptuous. Architects, abandoning the Gothic spire and pointed arch, created buildings with domes and round arches and elegant classical façades. Scholars abandoned the logic of Aristotle and St. Thomas for the delights of Greco-Roman belles lettres. And painters, with few actual classical models to follow, pioneered in techniques of linear and atmospheric perspective and

Interior of S. Andrea at Matua, by Alberti.

The Golden Virgin, from the south portal of the Amiens Cathedral, High Middle Ages.

Venus, by Titian, Late Renaissance.

imposed a classical unity upon their likelike figures and land-
scapes.

The Italian Renaissance, while rebelling against the Middle Ages,
retained much that was medieval. In 1492, while a worldly Borgia
was acceding to the papacy and Columbus was discovering America, high-Renaissance Florence was passing under the influence
of the austere Christian revivalist, Savonarola. Renaissance humanism was always an élitist phenomenon, restricted to urban nobilities
and favored artists and leaving the Italian masses unchanged. Yet
for all that, the Renaissance style represents a profound shift from
the forms and assumptions of the Middle Ages. St. Thomas and his
contemporaries had studied the Greek philosophers, but men of the
Renaissance looked back on classical antiquity with a fresh perspective, seeing not a collection of ideas that might be used but a total
culture that deserved to be revered and revived. It was this vision
that underlay the new art and the new classical learning of early
modern Europe.

Sistine Madonna, by Raphael.

David, by Michelangelo, High Renaissance.

The Genesis of Modern Europe

Historians of the past have probably overemphasized the impact of the Renaissance on the development of modern civilization. The Renaissance contributed much to art and classical studies, and to habits of intellectual precision which had been cultivated by Italian literary scholars. It contributed to the evolution of diplomatic techniques, but scarcely at all to constitutional development. Renaissance humanists were essentially scholars of the "humanities" and were no more interested in science than, say, a modern professor of English literature or Latin. Modern science grew out of the medieval universities. And modern legislatures—even if they meet in domed, round-arched buildings—are outgrowths of medieval representative assemblies.

In the Europe of 1500, Italian Renaissance ideas were beginning to move across the Alps. But the promise of the future did not depend on the Renaissance alone. All across Europe commerce was thriving again and the population was growing. New non-

Renaissance inventions—gunpowder, the three-masted caravel, the windmill, the water pump, and the printing press—were changing the ways people lived. The papacy had degenerated into a local principality, but England, France, and Spain had achieved stable, centralized governments and were on the road toward nationhood. European ships had reached America and India, and the first cargo direct from the Orient had arrived in Portugal. The gloom was lifting and the world lay open.

Today, after half a millennium of European expansion, societies everywhere have been reshaped by traditions that extend back to the Middle Ages—to the parliamentary experiments of thirteenth-century England, the growth of rationalism and science in medieval universities, the evolution of governmental institutions in medieval royal households, the commercial revolution in medieval towns, the Gregorian dream of creating a justly-ordered society, and the experience of an expanding technology that by 1500 had produced the cannon and the printing press. In our own time European political dominion is ebbing, but European ideas and institutions, for better or worse, have spread across the globe and transformed it.

SUGGESTIONS
FOR FURTHER
READING

The asterisk indicates a paperback edition.

Prologue: The Legacy Of The Ancient Near East

*Chester G. Starr, *Early Man: Prehistory and the Civilizations of the Ancient Near East* (New York, 1973).
*V. Gordon Childe, *What Happened in History* (Baltimore, 1964).
*Sabatino Moscati, *The Face of the Ancient Orient* (New York, 1962).
*John A. Wilson, *The Culture of Egypt* (Chicago, 1959).
Robert C. Zaehner, *The Dawn and Twilight of Zoroastrianism* (New York, 1961).
*H. M. Orlinsky, *Ancient Israel* (Ithaca, N.Y., 1954).
*T. J. Meek, *Hebrew Origins* (New York, 1960).

Part I: Greece

*Leonard Cottrell, *The Bull of Minos* (New York, 1958).
*H. J. Rose, *Handbook of Greek Mythology* (New York, 1958).
J. B. Bury, *A History of Greece* (New York, 3rd ed., 1951).
*M. I. Finley, *The Ancient Greeks* (New York, 1963).
*M. I. Finley, ed. and trans., *Greek Historians* (New York, 1959).
*H. D. F. Kitto, *The Greeks* (Baltimore, 1957).
*Chester G. Starr, *The Ancient Greeks* (New York, 1971).
*Frank J. Frost, *Democracy and the Athenians* (New York, 1969).
*Thucydides, *The History of the Peloponnesian War*, trans. by Richard Crawley (New York, 1961).
The Portable Greek Reader, ed. W. H. Auden (New York, 1948).
*F. M. Cornford, *From Religion to Philosophy* (New York, 1957).
*G. M. Richter, *Handbook of Greek Art* (New York, 1960).
*H. J. Rose, *Handbook of Greek Literature* (New York, 1964).
*Bruno Snell, *The Discovery of the Mind* (New York, 1953).

*Benjamin Farrington, *Greek Science* (Baltimore, 1961).
*W. W. Tarn, *Hellenistic Civilization* (Cleveland, rev. ed., 1952),
John W. Snyder, *Alexander the Great* (New York, 1966).

Part II: Rome

*Michael Grant, *The World of Rome* (New York, 1960).
*Chester G. Starr, *The Ancient Romans* (New York, 1971).
*M. Rostovtzeff, *Rome* (New York, 1928).
*Thomas W. Africa, *Rome of the Caesars* (New York, 1965).
*H. H. Scullard, *From the Gracchi to Nero* (New York, 1959).
*Ronald Sime, *The Roman Revolution* (New York, 1959).
*R. Bultmann, *Primitive Christianity in its Contemporary Setting*
   (New York, 1956).
*C. N. Cochrane, *Christianity and Classical Culture* (New York,
   1944).
*Michael Gough, *The Early Christians* (New York, 1961).
*H. O. Taylor, *The Emergence of Christian Culture in the West*
   (New York, reprint, 1958).
*J. B. Bury, *History of the Later Roman Empire* (2 vols., New
   York, 1928).
The Portable Roman Reader, ed. B. Davenport (New York, 1951).
*Edward Gibbon, *The Triumph of Christendom in the Roman Empire* (New York, reprint, 1932).
A. H. M. Jones, *The Later Roman Empire* (3 vols., Oxford, 1964).
*Ferdinand Lot, *The End of the Ancient World and the Beginnings
   of the Middle Ages* (New York, 1931).
*Peter Brown, *Augustine of Hippo: A Biography* (Berkeley, 1969).

Part III: The Early Middle Ages

*Christopher Dawson, *The Making of Europe* (New York, 1946).
*M. L. W. Laistner, *Thought and Letters in Western Europe: A.D.
   500–900* (Ithaca, N.Y., reprint, 1957).
*Robert S. Lopez, *The Birth of Europe* (New York, 1967).
*J. M. Wallace-Hadrill, *The Barbarian West: 400–1000* (New York,
   1962).
*Jeffrey B. Russell, *A History of Medieval Christianity* (New York,
   1968).
*Peter Brown, *The World of Late Antiquity: 150–705* (New York,
   1971).

George Ostrogorsky, *History of the Byzantine State* (New Brunswick, N.J., rev. ed., 1969).

*Speros Vryonis, *Byzantium and Europe* (New York, 1967).

*G. E. von Grunebaum, *Medieval Islam* (Chicago, 2nd ed., 1963).

P. K. Hitti, *History of the Arabs* (New York, 6th ed., 1958).

*Bryce Lyon, *The Origins of the Middle Ages: Pirenne's Challenge to Gibbon* (New York, 1972).

*J. M. Wallace-Hadrill, *Early Germanic Kingship in England and on the Continent* (Oxford, 1971).

*Marc Bloch, *Feudal Society* (2 vols., Chicago, 1961).

*Marc Bloch, *French Rural History* (Berkeley, 1966).

*Jacques Boussard, *The Civilization of Charlemagne* (New York, 1968).

*F. L. Ganshof, *Frankish Institutions under Charlemagne* (Providence, 1968).

*Lynn White, Jr., *Medieval Technology and Social Change* (New York, 1962).

*Bede, *A History of the English Church and People* (Baltimore, 1955).

*Einhard, *Life of Charlemagne* (Ann Arbor, Mich., 1960).

*Gregory of Tours, *History of the Franks* (New York, 1969).

*Carolly Erickson, ed., *The Records of Medieval Europe* (Garden City, N.Y., 1971).

Part IV: The High Middle Ages

*John W. Baldwin, *The Scholastic Culture of the Middle Ages: 1000–1300* (Lexington, Mass., 1971).

*Christopher Brooke, *The Structure of Medieval Society* (New York, 1971).

*R. W. Southern, *The Making of the Middle Ages* (New Haven, 1953).

*Robert-Henri Bautier, *The Economic Development of Medieval Europe* (New York, 1971).

*David Douglas, *The Norman Achievement* (Berkeley, 1969).

*Robert S. Lopez, *The Commercial Revolution of the Middle Ages: 950–1350* (Englewood Cliffs, N.J., 1971).

*Steven Runciman, *A History of the Crusades* (3 vols., New York, 1964–1967).

David Knowles, *From Pachomius to Ignatius* (on monastic organization) (Oxford, 1966).

*Jean Leclerc, *The Love of Learning and the Desire for God* (a short history of monasticism) (New York, 1961).
*R. W. Southern, *Western Society and the Church in the Middle Ages* (Baltimore, 1970).
*Geoffrey Barraclough, *The Medieval Papacy* (New York, 1968).
*Friedrich Heer, *The Holy Roman Empire* (New York, 1968).
*C. Warren Hollister, *The Making of England: 55 B.C. to 1399,* (Lexington, Mass., 2nd ed., 1971).
*Robert Fawtier, *The Capetian Kings of France* (New York, 1960).
*James C. Holt, ed., *Magna Carta and the Idea of Liberty* (New York, 1972).
*Bertie Wilkinson, *The Creation of Medieval Parliaments* (New York, 1972).
*Christopher Brooke, *The Twelfth-Century Renaissance* (New York, 1969).
*C. Warren Hollister, ed., *The Twelfth-Century Renaissance* (New York, 1969).
*C. H. Haskins, *The Rise of the Universities* (Ithaca, N.Y., reprint, 1957).
*David Knowles, *The Evolution of Medieval Thought* (New York, 1964).
*John C. Moore, *Love in Twelfth-Century France* (Philadelphia, 1972).
*R. W. Southern, *Medieval Humanism and Other Studies* (Oxford, 1970).
*Walter Ullmann, *A History of Political Thought: The Middle Ages* (Baltimore, 1965).
*Dante Alighieri, *The Divine Comedy* (many translations).
Angel Flores, trans., *An Anthology of Medieval Lyrics* (New York, 1962).
Anton C. Pegis, trans., *Introduction to St. Thomas Aquinas* (New York, 1948).
The Song of Roland, trans. D. L. Sayers (Baltimore, 1957).
*Villehardouin and de Joinville, *Memoirs of the Crusades,* trans. F. Marzials (New York, 1908).

Part V: The Late Middle Ages

*Denys Hay, *Europe in the Fourteenth and Fifteenth Centuries* (New York, 1966).
*Robert E. Lerner, *The Age of Adversity: The Fourteenth Century* (Ithaca, N.Y., 1968).

*Jerah Johnson and William Percy, *The Age of Recovery: The Fifteenth Century* (Ithaca, N.Y., 1970).

*Norman Cohn, *The Pursuit of the Millennium* (on radical heresy) (New York, 1957).

*George Holmes, *The Later Middle Ages: 1272–1485* (on England) (New York, 1966).

P. S. Lewis, *Later Medieval France: The Polity* (New York, 1968).

*Edouard Perroy, *The Hundred Years War* (New York, 1965).

*Daniel Waley, *The Italian City Republics* (New York, 1969).

*Henri Pirenne, *Early Democracies in the Low Countries* (New York, 1963).

*Wallace K. Ferguson, *The Renaissance in Historical Thought* (New York, 1948).

*Johan Huizinga, *The Waning of the Middle Ages* (Garden City, N.Y., 1954).

*P. O. Kristeller, *Renaissance Thought* (New York, 1955).

*Gordon Leff, *Medieval Thought: St. Augustine to Ockham* (Baltimore, 1958).

*J. H. Plumb, ed., *Renaissance Profiles* (New York, 1965).

Meister Eckhart: A Modern Translation, trans. R. B. Blakney (New York, 1941).

*Jean Froissart, *Chronicles* (several editions).

*Thomas à Kempis, *The Imitation of Christ* (many editions).

The Portable Chaucer, ed. T. Morrison (New York, 1949).

The Portable Renaissance Reader, ed. J. B. Ross and M. M. McLaughlin (New York, 1953).

CREDIT LIST

Page 38: British Museum. Page 51: Staatliche Museen, Berlin. Page
61: Alinari/Art Reference Bureau. Page 62: Alinari/Art Reference
Bureau. Page 63: Marburg/Art Reference Bureau. Page 64: Ali-
nari/Art Reference Bureau. Page 69: Marburg/Art Reference
Bureau. Page 73: The Metropolitan Museum of Art, Rogers Fund,
1909. Page 87: Alinari/Art Reference Bureau. Page 93: Alinari/
Art Reference Bureau. Page 96: Alinari/Art Reference Bureau. Page
101: Anderson/Art Reference Bureau. Page 105: Alinari/Art
Reference Bureau. Page 107: Alinari/Art Reference Bureau. Page
109: Anderson/Art Reference Bureau. Page 120: Alinari/Art Ref-
erence Bureau. Page 134: Alinari/Art Reference Bureau. Page 167:
Roger Viollet. Page 173: British Museum. Page 180: Bibliotheque
Nationale, Paris. Page 182: Marburg/Art Reference Bureau. Page
183: Alinari/Art Reference Bureau. Page 203: Kunsthistorische
Museum. Page 224: Clm 4453, fol. 24 r, Staatsbibliothek, Munich.
Page 261: Marburg/Art Reference Bureau. Page 262: Marburg/
Art Reference Bureau. Page 264: Marburg/Art Reference Bureau.
Page 265: French Embassy Press and Information Division. Page
266: top, Marburg/Art Reference Bureau. Page 266: bottom, Mar-
burg/Art Reference Bureau. Page 268: Palais Synodale. Page 303:
Sovfoto. Page 316: Courtesy of Professor Whitney S. Stoddard—
Photography by Sandak, Inc., New York. Page 317: Courtesy of
Professor Whitney S. Stoddard—Photography by Sandak, Inc.,

New York. Page 318: Courtesy of Professor Whitney S. Stoddard—Photography by Sandak, Inc., New York. Page 319: Marburg/Art Reference Bureau. Page 320: Marburg/Art Reference Bureau. Page 321: 40.128 Purchase from the J. H. Wade Fund, 58.66-67 Bequest of Leonard C. Hanna, Jr., The Cleveland Museum of Art. Page 322: Cliché des Musées Nationaux, Louvre. Page 327: The Dresden Museum. Page 325: Marburg/Art Reference Bureau. Page 328: Alinari/Art Reference Bureau (Accademia, Florence). Page 326: Alinari/Art Reference Bureau (Uffizi). Page 324: Alinari/Art Reference Bureau.

INDEX

Abelard, Peter, 275-276
Abraham, 5-6
Aeschylus, 59-60
Albigensian Crusade, 247
Albigensians, 246-247
Alexander the Great, 67-68, 70, 80
Alfred the Great, 192-194
Ambrose, St., 137-138
Anselm, St., 274
Architecture, 61, 65, 315-321
 Gothic, 259-267
Arians, 135-136
Aristotle, 55-56, 68, 272, 273, 276
Assyrians, 8
Athens, 29-42, 56-57
 Delian League, 35-36
 drama, 57
 Empire of, 35, 36
 in fourth century, 40-41
 Golden Age, 36-37
 Peloponnesian War, 37-40
Augustine of Canterbury, St., 171
Augustine of Hippo, 138-140
Augustus, 99, 103-104, 106-107, 108
Aquinas, St. Thomas, 277, 278, 279, 312-313

Babylonian Captivity, 9-10

Barbarian invasions, 149-152
Bede the Venerable, St., 172-173
Benedictine monasticism, 169-170, 171-172, 241-242, 243, 244
Benedict of Nursia, St., 169, 242, 244
Bernard of Clairvaux, St., 244, 275, 276
Black Death, 308
Byzantine culture, 157, 161-163, 164, 167, 213, 215, 218
 legacy of, 163-164

Caesar, Julius, 99-100, 102-103
Caesaropapism, 137
Charlemagne, 179-180, 182, 184, 185, 186
Christianity, 120-127, 174, 213-214, 239
Canaanites, 4, 7
Capetians, 233-235
Carolingian, 177-186, 196
 Renaissance, 185
 technology, 185
Carthage, 92
Carthusians, 243
Cicero, 98-99, 100
Cistercians, 243-245
Civilization, 2
 birth of, 2-5

Egyptian, 2, 3, 4, 5
Etruscan, 2
Grecian, 4, 5, 15
Mesopotamian, 2, 3, 5
Minoan, 2, 15-16
Cleisthenes, 30-31, 32
 constitution of, 30-32
Columbus, 299-300
Constantine, 133-134, 135
Crusades, 216-218

Darius, 33
David, 8, 11
Democritus, 49
Diocletian, 130-132, 135
Dominic, St., 249
Dominicans, 248-249, 278, 285

Etruscans, 87-88, 90-91
Euripides, 59-60

Feudalism, 194-200
Francis, St., 249-250
Franciscans, Order of Friars
 Minor, 249-251, 285
Frederick II, Emperor, 227
Frederick Barbarossa, Emperor,
 227

Germanic peoples, 146-152, 168
Gods, 19-20
Greece, 15
 Colonization, 23-24
 Classical, 18-65
 Pre-classical, 15-18
 and Rome
 Social orders, 22
Greek, culture, 45-46
 dark age, 17-18
 Minoans, 16
 polis, 20-22
 tyrants, 24-26
Gregory I the Great, Pope,
 170-171
Gregory VII, Pope, 272

Hebrews, 6, 7, 8, 11-12
Hellenistic, 67, 68, 70, 72, 74,

92, 95
 culture, 74
 legacy of, 80
 religion and ethics, 75-78
 science, 78
Hesiod, 23
Homer, 15-16, 18, 19
Homeric Gods, 19-20
Hundred Years' War, 291-293

Innocent III, Pope, 227, 228,
 249
Inquisition, 245-246, 247, 248,
 299
Investiture controversy, 225-
 226, 240, 287, 288
Ionia, 32, 36, 46, 47, 48
 poets, 46-47
 philosophers, 47-48
Islam, 164-166, 167, 213, 215
Israelites, 6, 7, 8, 10, 11
 Yahweh, 10-11

Jerome, St., 138

Literature, High Middle Ages,
 255-258, 321-323
Louis, St., King, 235
Lycurgus, 27
 constitution of, 27-28

Magna Carta, 231-232
Magyars, 187
Medicine, 270-271
Mendicantism, 248
Merovingians, 177-178
Mohammed, 164-165
Monasticism, 169-172, 243
Moses, 7
Myceneans, 16
Mysticism, 285

Normans, 214-215

Otto I the Great, 200, 202
Ottomans, 301-304

Papacy, 223-225, 226-227, 228,

240, 284-285, 287
Parliament, 290-291
Peloponnesian War, 37-38, 40
Pepin the Short, 178
Periclean Culture, 56-57
Pericles, 32, 36-38, 58, 63
Persia, 32-33, 68, 70
 Persian Wars, 33
Philip IV the Fair, King of
 France, 237, 287
Philosophy, 273, 274, 275,
 312-314
Pisistratus, 29-30, 32
Plato, 52-54, 272, 273
Poland, 301-302
Polis, 20-22, 57
 decline of, 41-42
Prophets, 10
Pythagorean School, 48-49

Religion, 5
 Christianity, 120-127
 Egyptian, 5, 6
 Greek, 19-20
 Hebrew, 6-12
 Islam, 164-166
 Roman, 118-120, 121-127
Renaissance, 329
Rome, 85-153
 conquest, 91-92
 decline of, 128-130, 143-152
 Dominate, 131
 Golden Age, 103-104, 106-107,
 108
 Law, 117-118
 Principate, 112-114
 Republican, 85, 97, 98
 rise of, 85-86, 87
 Silver Age, 114
Russia, 301-303

Saul, 8
Saracens, 187
Science, 278
Slavery, 4-5
Socrates, 51-52
Solon, 29-30, 32
Sophists, 50-51, 60

Sophocles, 59-60
Sparta, 26-28, 35, 37-38, 40,
 57
 Constitution of, 27-28
 Peloponnesian War, 37-38, 40
Spartans, 33
Spain, 213-214

Towns, 308
Tyrants, 24-26

Universities,
 rise of, 267-270

Vikings, 187, 189, 191

William the Conqueror, 229,
 230
William of Ockham, 313-315
Wycliffe, John, 286

Xerxes, 33, 34, 61

Zoroastrianism, 6, 75, 161